THE ULTIMATE
BAR/BAT
MITZVAH
CELEBRATION
BOOK

מזל טוב

THE ULTIMATE
BAR/BAT
MITZVAH
CELEBRATION
BOOK

A Guide to
Inspiring Ceremonies and
Joyous Festivities

Jayne Cohen and Lori Weinrott

CLARKSON POTTER/PUBLISHERS
NEW YORK

Published by Clarkson Potter/Publishers, New York, New York.
Member of the Crown Publishing Group, a division of Random House, Inc.

www.crownpublishing.com

CLARKSON N. POTTER is a trademark and POTTER and colophon are registered trademarks of Random House, Inc.

Printed in the United States of America

Design by Maggie Hinders

Library of Congress Cataloging-in-Publication Data
Cohen, Jayne.
        The ultimate bar/bat mitzvah celebration book : a guide to inspiring ceremonies and joyous festivities / Jayne Cohen and Lori Weinrott.—1st ed.
Includes bibliographical references.
(pbk.)
        1. Bar mitzvah—Handbooks, manuals, etc. 2. Bat mitzvah—Handbooks, manuals, etc. I. Weinrott, Lori. II. Title.
        BM707.2.C63 2004
    296.4'424—dc22   2003017463

ISBN 0-609-80992-X

10 9 8 7 6 5 4 3 2 1

First Edition

ACKNOWLEDGMENTS

Our book, like the bar and bat mitzvah celebrations that are at its heart, has been a long, challenging, and inspiring journey for us, and we are enormously grateful to the many people who helped us along the road.

We thank Elise and Arnold Goodman, our agents. From the beginning, when they introduced us to each other, to their nurturing and unwavering faith in us, their guidance and good sense always helping us to stay the course, so much of the credit for this project truly belongs to them.

Pam Krauss, editorial director at Clarkson Potter, enthusiastically believed in the manuscript and allowed it to grow into the book it was meant to be. Adina Steiman, our insightful editor, shared our vision and our passion—even spending her vacation in Poland searching for the perfect paper-cut for the book's cover. Maggie Hinders's beautiful, elegant design has made our information-packed book remarkably clear and reader-friendly. We are also indebted to copyeditor Jim Gullickson, Cindy Berman, senior production editor, and Linnea Knollmueller, production manager, for their scrupulous attention to detail. Leigh Ann Ambrosi and Sarah Chance have worked so hard to get the word out.

But we could never have written this book were it not for the generosity of those who allowed us to be a part of their families as they shared their dreams and their simchas with us. We thank especially these families: Barbash-Riley, Berenholz, Beresin, Bricklin-Shultz, Cline-Campbell, Dichter-Schapiro, Dornstreich, Ellner-Theobald, Fertman, Finkel-Braemer, Fox-Edwards, Frank-Mermelstein, Fuchs-Kreimer, Goldwyn-Towarnicky, Handler, Katz, Kaye, Kind-Rubin, Irgang-Laden, Klebanoff-Smith, Lax, Lebowitz, Leebron-Tutelman, Loeb-Crimm, Margolis-Rupp, Mathisen-Aronowitz, Mervis, Munick-DiSabatino, Norry, Pasek, Post-Jacobs, Power-Hedley, Pulde, Quigley-Weinman, Resnick-Jones, Row, Sabra-Meier, Scearce-Horwitz, Schewel, Schindelheim, Seitchik, Shure-Kaufman, Shusterman, Simon, Steiker-Epstein, Stolper, Sunshine-Kagan, Swartz, Teutsch, Tillman-Wolk, Weinberg, Weinrott, Zibalese-Crawford, and Zimmerman-Katz.

Special mention must be made of those who took time out to tell us their personal stories and ideas, graciously answer our questions, and provide us with memories, mementos, and more: Irene Beer, Chana Crawford, Rosa Esquenazi, Martha Fertman, Amy Finkel, Belinda Glijansky, Elissa Goldberg, Kathy Hirsh-Pasek, Edward Kabak, Ben Laden, Brigitte Levy, Rod MacNeil, Magda and Tibor Mermelstein, Ivor Perl, Laura Pritchard,

Milo Pulde, Jodi Sabra, Ellen Golder Saft, Jane Shure, Betsy Platkin Teutsch, Cathi Tillman, Lesley Seitchik, Michael Stolper, Cy Swartz, and Hy Zelkowitz.

The talent and imagination of many creative people enriched these pages. We are grateful for the expertise of Anna Beresin, Andrew Bleckner, Margo Bloom, Lynn Brownstein, Jane Carroll, Jeffrey Cooper, Vincent Smith Durham, Wendy Epstein, Cynthia Flaxman, Cindy Goldstein, Lisa Goodgame and the Shoah Foundation, Brian Kappra, Mary Koneval, Susan Leviton, Susan Dwyer Metzger, Susan Moses, Joey Roberts, Don Sapatkin, Howie Shapiro, Christina Sidoti, Karen Tosto, Robert Woodward, Ken Ulansey, Pam Yowler, and Suzan Zoukis.

We are immensely appreciative of all of the staff at Peachtree & Ward for their input and hard work: Rena Coyle, who planted the seed, and especially Rachel Brill, Kelly Cook, Robert Kohlbrenner, and Lori's husband and partner, Jon Weinrott. Thanks also to Rita, Derek, Jackie, Sara, Linda, Gary, Ken, Mo, and Amanda.

We are deeply grateful to the learned rabbis who helped us: Rabbi Nancy Fuchs-Kreimer, Rabbi Don Goor, Rabbi Joel Goor, Rabbi Erin Hirsh, and Rabbi Joshua Toledano, and to Rabbi Yael Levy and Rabbi Brian Walt and their Congregation Mishkan Shalom.

Each of us is especially grateful to our respective families.

For Jayne: Warmest thanks to Lori, who first conceived this book so long ago, for her inspiration, creativity, and unerring eye; brother Steven Cohen for his support, and to the Schindelheim family for the boundless enthusiasm and invaluable advice of sister Sami, the organizational and research skills of niece Arielle, and the assistance of extraordinarily knowledgeable nephew Jake, who always made himself available to answer our questions. Daughter Alex, so gifted at editing, typing, or testing a recipe, and even more at talking things through late into the night. But as always, I thank my husband, Howard Spiegler, most of all, whose wise counsel, patience, good humor, and love kept me going every step of the way.

For Lori: Thanks and love to cousins Elise and Arnold, for encouraging me to pursue my idea and opening a door to a new world. To Jayne, for her incredible tenacity, hard work ethic, and fine sensibilities. She's a true spinner of words. To Yael, Brian, and Wendy, for their love and spiritual support. To Sam, for being "just Sam," and guiding us to Mishkan. To beautiful Sophie Seraphina, the next in line. And especially to Jon, for his love and for his wonderful spirit, be it at Peachtree, at Mishkan, or at home. He has stood beside me all along the way, knowing how much this project has meant to me, and how can you ask for more?

May this book be a blessing from generation to generation.

Contents

CONTENTS

INTRODUCTION

HER EASTERN EUROPEAN PARENTS *named the daughter born in Mexico City Rosa, but her grandmother called her Reizl, a "Little Rose" in Yiddish. Raised Orthodox, Rosa became bat mitzvah in a collective ceremony with her confirmation class. They came from diverse economic backgrounds, but all the girls wore identical dresses, so all would feel equal. A thousand guests gathered to celebrate with the girls in the large social hall the community had added onto the beautiful old Mexican synagogue. They feasted on buffets of ripe tropical fruits, chilaquiles, tortillas in green salsa, and gefilte fish with cumin-scented tomato sauce.*

. . . . .

When his son Marc told him to put a little "ruach" (spirit!) into his skating, Milo decided it was time to put some into planning the avid ice hockey player's upcoming bar mitzvah as well. Most of Milo's small family lived in Florida or New York City, and many had become estranged for a variety of reasons. He hadn't seen any of them for twenty or thirty years, and none had met Marc. So Milo called to invite them all, and offered to pay for the room and airfare for those who couldn't afford the trip to Boston. That brisk Shabbat, when they gathered at the country club after services, Uncle Nathan chanted the Kiddush blessing over the wine in his familiar baritone. "We took a sip from our glasses," Milo said, "and it was like we were at seder back in Rego Park, New

York, when my mom was alive. We're older, but we haven't changed all that much. Uncle Nat promised to reprise the blessing next year, when Sasha becomes a bat mitzvah."

. . . . .

At Branch Creek Farm in Perkasie, Pennsylvania, Mark and Judy reclaimed the traditional fruit and vegetable varieties of the area and raised the finest heirloom produce. Preserving their family heritage was even more important to them and their five children, and Judy, who prepared local kids for their bar and bat mitzvahs, tutored her oldest daughter in her Torah portion as she approached her thirteenth birthday. To celebrate her bat mitzvah, they erected a tent alongside the neat rows of French butter radishes and golden beets. Chefs who had been loyal customers for years came early to chop, slice, and dice the armfuls of produce freshly harvested that morning, and neighbors and friends brought potluck offerings tasting of fall. The makeshift ark was a rough-hewn table. There were moments when the squeaking sound of the porch rocking horse eclipsed the chanting of the Torah portion, but nothing could overshadow the image of three generations of Jewish women—grandmother, mother, and daughter—their faces caressed by the late-morning sun. Later, as Shabbat drew to a close, friends gathered around the kitchen table to serve themselves yet another slice of pumpkinseed bread spread with sweet butter and local honey while the kids played upstairs.

. . . . .

The Birmingham Temple in Michigan was packed on September 14, 2001. It was the first Friday night following the terrorist attacks on September 11, and many who had come seeking comfort were surprised to find that a bar mitzvah was scheduled for that evening.

Plaintive music opened the service, and the congregation mourned the victims, including the son of a temple member who had been on the ninety-fourth floor of the World Trade Center. But unspeakable acts of terror, from pogroms to recent appalling events, the rabbi said, set the stage for life-affirming acts, for heroism. And at this congregation of Humanistic Judaism, twelve-year-olds spend a year researching a Jewish hero or heroine, then share what they've learned with the congregation at their bar/bat mitzvah.

That night Jackson Klein told the story of Solly Ganor, a child his own age in Nazi-

occupied Lithuania. The courageous Solly suffered through incredible horrors to keep himself and his father fed, clothed—and alive—in the Kovne ghetto and later in Dachau. After reading Solly's book, Light One Candle, young Jackson had somehow found him, now a seventy-three-year-old in Israel, and the two had been corresponding by e-mail for the past year.

At the close of his moving presentation, when the thunderous applause finally receded, Jackson told the congregation that because all the airports had been shut down that week, none of his out-of-town guests had arrived for his bar mitzvah, except one. That person? Solly Ganor! Visiting San Diego at the time, he waited for hours at the airport until he got a flight to Detroit. "Since Mr. Ganor was not able to celebrate his bar mitzvah when he was thirteen, I would like him to join me now."

The gray-haired Ganor walked slowly up to the bimah and stood next to Jackson. He was crying, and it took several minutes for him to collect himself. Then the two read together in Hebrew and in English.

The service finished, the congregation sang as one the uplifting lyrics of Rabbi Sherwin Wine's "Ayfo Oree," whose words translate: "Where is my light? My light is in me./Where is my hope? My hope is in me./Where is my strength? My strength is in me./And in you."

W hen they become bar/bat mitzvah, children begin writing their own chapters in the Jewish story. It is a time to share in one of the most important days in the family's life, a time for the community to celebrate, welcoming new members and reaffirming centuries-old traditions. We invite you to join us on this beautiful coming-of-age journey, from the inspiring ceremony to a joyous party within the embrace of the rich Judaic heritage.

Families today want a memorable bar/bat mitzvah, imaginative yet meaningfully linked to their culture and values as well. Those who came of age during a period of intense assimilation are longing to come home. They have watched as Bob Dylan's son celebrated his bar mitzvah publicly in a spiritual ceremony at the Western Wall, and non-Jewish pop icons, like Mick Jagger and Madonna, studied the Kabbalah, the Jewish mystical canon. Celebrants now include Jews by choice, and nontraditional, nonobservant, and interfaith families as well. And of growing significance is the number of adult Jews becoming bar/bat mitzvah—those reaffirming their faith, as well as women, converts, and others who never celebrated their bar/bat mitzvah as youths. Enlarging the spiritual tent has created a new vitality in the community, and contemporary Jews are seeking a vision that will make sense in their lives.

As the Torah is passed from generation to generation—grandparents handing it to parents who place it in the hands of the child—we are filled with the awesomeness and responsibility of the moment. Because this rite of passage celebrates the bar/bat mitzvah child's new maturity, it is important to involve the child as much as possible in making decisions. The challenge is to celebrate this young individual, but within the context of the tradition and the community. The ritual reflects history and custom, yet it is intensely personal as well, and isn't this what adolescent coming of age is all about: finding your own voice and expressing it while at the same time taking your place in the larger world?

Here we come to the sensitive issue of what is appropriate for your celebration. It should be joyful and magical, but you do not need a vast budget or elaborate planning to create an event to remember. Little touches can make a big difference: a Warhol-inspired still life of soup cans and red roses for a mitzvah table centerpiece (later donated to a food bank) or changing lightbulbs for a soft candle-glow effect. Or you might serve an onion-crusted challah for the Motzi and continue the festivities with a *hora medora* (dance of the campfire) under an enchanted bower of quince and dogwood branches. We recognize that this is a matter of personal taste, and what feels comfortable to one family might seem excessive to another. Some might prefer a homemade Kiddush for the congregation. For others, a weekend-long bar/bat mitzvah offers a wonderful way to bring a far-flung extended family together.

The goal of the bar and bat mitzvah is to enter the larger community, while at the same time recognizing one's own unique individual spiritual and social circumstances. Making it personal, but within the tradition—this is the essence of Judaism. For unless we reinvent the customs so that they are meaningful to us, the ritual becomes stale and hollow.

PART ONE

THE
CEREMONY

WHAT IS A BAR/BAT MITZVAH?

The bar/bat mitzvah (plural: *bnai* mitzvah) celebrates a child's entry into the adult Jewish community, and by extension, the world community. Becoming an adult means taking on adult obligations, being socially responsible, and the bar/bat mitzvah marks the beginning of this process of taking responsibility for oneself and the rest of the world. It is a milestone on a lifetime journey.

The word *mitzvah* (plural: *mitzvot*) has two meanings. First, it translates as "a commandment of Jewish life." *Bar* means "son of" in Aramaic, and *bat* means "daughter" in Hebrew, so the bar or bat mitzvah is now "son or daughter of the commandment": He or she becomes responsible for fulfilling religious and social obligations. The child must now observe the fast days, and can be counted in a minyan (the group of ten adults required for Jewish communal worship), among other duties.

Becoming part of a minyan is a metaphor for joining the community: The child now assumes responsibility for thinking about others. Here we come to the second meaning of *mitzvah*: a kind, ethical deed. Judaism teaches that God created the world, but left it not quite finished, so that we could become God's partners in the creative process by completing the work. This creative process is called *tikkun olam* (literally, "the repair of the world"), and it is by performing mitzvot that we seek to restore what is damaged, to better what is imperfect in life.

According to the Talmud, "If a person resides in a town for 30 days, he becomes responsible for contributions to the soup kitchen," and the longer we live in a town, the greater is our responsibility for all of its citizens. The tradition of choosing a special mitzvah, or good deed, to perform as part of the bar/bat mitzvah is relatively new. According to some authorities, it is a recent effort to make the ritual more meaningful and relevant today. While not all children will mark their coming-of-age with a special mitzvah project, it has become increasingly popular to do so, and many synagogues, in fact, now require it as part of the process. Mitzvah projects are an integral part of all the bar/bat mitzvahs in this book. They are explained in more detail in chapter 3, "The Community: Widening the Circle," and examples of mitzvah projects are scattered throughout the text, especially in the sidebars titled "Make It a Mitzvah."

THE RITUAL

The ritual consists of a religious service and a festive meal, the *seudat mitzvah*, celebrating the completion of this mitzvah.

But actually, no formal ceremony is required at all. Jews are recognized as adult members of the community and become obligated to fulfill the commandments when they reach bar/bat mitzvah age, whether or not they have had a religious service.

THE HISTORY OF THE BAR MITZVAH

There is no mention of the bar/bat mitzvah in the Bible. We trace its origins to a reference made centuries later in the Babylonian Talmud: "At thirteen, a boy becomes responsible for fulfilling the commandments" (Pirkei Avot 5:21). There was no ceremony to mark the event: On the day of his thirteenth birthday, a boy automatically became a bar mitzvah; that is, he was subject to the law, and his father was no longer responsible for him.

The custom of acknowledging this transition to adulthood in a formal way evolved over time, and by the thirteenth or fourteenth century, the bar mitzvah ritual included the same elements as today's ceremony: The boy read from the Torah (the sacred parchment scroll containing the Five Books of Moses, beginning with Creation and ending with the death of Moses), the Haftarah (additional readings from the Prophets and historical texts like Joshua, Judges, Kings, and others that correspond, by date, to Torah portions and to special holidays), and the father recited a blessing releasing himself from responsibility for his son. Just as today, the boy's duties varied from community to community, from reading just a part of the Torah portion to conducting most of the Saturday morning service.

Following the ceremony, the family served a celebratory meal, during which the boy delivered a short sermon, exemplifying his Jewish learning. By 1595, what had begun as a modest festive meal had become so sumptuous that a communal tax was placed on the celebration to stop such excesses. And throughout the centuries, just as today, opinion has continued to seesaw as to what that meal should be. Rabbi Yisrael HaKohen (1838–1933) wrote in the *Mishnah Berurah*: "It is a mitzvah to make a meal on the day one's son becomes a bar mitzvah, just like the day of his wedding." In the twentieth century, the *seudat mitzvah* ran the gamut from a bit of cake, a sip of schnapps, and perhaps a piece of herring to the vast extravaganzas immortalized in Herman Wouk's *Marjorie Morningstar* and Mordecai Richler's *The Apprenticeship of Duddy Kravitz*.

THE HISTORY OF THE BAT MITZVAH

Beginning around the second or third centuries, as recorded in the Talmud, girls were considered responsible for fulfilling the commandments at twelve, the age that coincided with puberty for most. But many of those responsibilities centered around the family, like lighting candles on Shabbat. Women were exempted from the majority of religious obligations men were expected to perform.

The day a girl turned twelve has been acknowledged as a special occasion for generations in many different ways. In some communities, a father was called up for an *aliyah* on his daughter's twelfth birthday. In the seventeenth century, Rabbi Mussafya noted that the day a girl turned twelve called for a celebration and *seudat mitzvah*. Religious ceremonies that involved the bat mitzvah girl herself took place in France and Italy at least as far back as the mid-nineteenth century: In Marseille, girls took part in a collective bat mitzvah service; in northern Italy, the girl and her family were blessed in front of the ark on a weekday.

But the first bat mitzvah service that included reading from the Torah, as well as the Haftarah, that is, that marked the entrance of a girl into the community in the same way that a boy is welcomed, did not take place until 1922, when Mordecai Kaplan, founder of Reconstructive Judaism, "reconstructed" the ceremony for his daughter, Judith. Since that time, all but the most orthodox congregations have embraced some form of the bat mitzvah ritual.

Orthodox girls become bat mitzvah at twelve; depending on their congregation, they may acknowledge the occasion with celebrations ranging from a secular party for family and friends to reading from the Torah. Today in Conservative, Reform, and Reconstructionist congregations, as well as other smaller liberal denominations, girls participate in the identical ceremony boys do, usually at age thirteen.

WHY THIRTEEN?

To the ancients, thirteen was the age a boy begins the journey of self-discovery. According to Midrashic tradition, Abraham was thirteen when he rejected his father's idols, the first step on his path to discovering God; and the twin brothers Jacob and Esau were thirteen when they parted ways, embarking on their separate journeys. This was the age, scholars believed, that a child fought with the Evil Impulse and developed a conscience. And thirteen was the average age for the onset of puberty for boys, as twelve was for girls—that is, the age when they were physically capable of performing the first mitzvah: Be fruitful and multiply, bringing a child into the community.

Many Jews have questioned, however, whether this is the appropriate time for a coming-of-age ceremony in our modern world. Reform congregations even abandoned the bar mitzvah for many years, replacing it for a time with a confirmation ceremony at age sixteen or seventeen. Seventh and eighth graders, often confused and rebellious, certainly seem unprepared for starting their journeys today.

But as Rabbi Joel Goor of the Metropolitan Synagogue of New York explains, thirteen is the right year precisely because it is the most difficult age. At the brink of adolescence, a child begins to question everything: sexuality, food choices (this is a time many decide to try vegetarianism), friendships, parents, even religion itself. It is an age of transition and turbulence, as they push for independence while struggling with self-esteem.

He points out that when a child takes the bar/bat mitzvah journey seriously, he or she experiences a tremendous sense of accomplishment, "walking through the door to self-esteem. We live up to the expectations society places on us." And performing a meaningful mitzvah project as part of the process is immensely empowering for a child, reinforcing that feeling of achievement.

To illustrate his point, the rabbi talks about a boy he worked with many years ago in his former congregation in San Diego. Twelve-year-old Gary was so disruptive in class that his Hebrew school teacher expelled him. Angry and depressed, he was seeing a therapist and acting out at home and at school. The rabbi arranged for him to split his time at Hebrew school between private tutoring and working in the resource center, where technical equipment—lighting boards, visual aids like slide projectors, sound systems, and so on—for all the synagogue events were kept. The temple had an active social and community calendar, and Gary, who had exhibited real talent and creativity with the audiovisual equipment, was kept busy.

For the first time in three years, Gary began taking pride in his Hebrew studies. By the time his bar mitzvah came around, he was visibly more self-confident and relaxed. He chanted his Torah portion beautifully, and in his *dvar Torah* speech, he said that for him becoming a man was about fighting his demons. Smiling, he thanked the congregation for giving him the chance to win.

2

A FAMILY CELEBRATION

EMIL'S GRANDPARENTS, *Holocaust survivors, were in their eighties when he, the oldest of the grandchildren, turned thirteen. Because it was unlikely that they would live to see all the grandchildren become bar mitzvah—much less dance at their weddings—his bar mitzvah took on a special significance for the family. Like a reenactment of the ancient gathering of the clans, distant relatives from all over the world came to celebrate.*

The bar/bat mitzvah is a *family* event: a deeply affecting experience for grandparents, siblings, and extended relations, too, and an opportunity to strengthen family ties. This is a perfect time to begin or cement household traditions, like a special Friday night dinner or a long family walk on Saturday afternoon, or to reestablish a link to a past tradition.

Sometimes it seems to us as if the entire family becomes bnai mitzvah. Parents shopping for their child's tallit decide to purchase a custom-woven one for themselves; a younger child who was never given a Hebrew name suddenly chooses her own; the family begins hosting the seders at their home. For some, the decision to have their child become bar or bat mitzvah kindles or renews a passionate interest in Judaism, and elicits more active participation in their synagogue community. For others, it may inaugurate a return to a synagogue or other Jewish worship community after an absence of many years.

MAKING THE CELEBRATION A FAMILY EVENT

And he will turn the hearts of parents to their children,
and the hearts of children to their parents.
—MALACHI 4:5

The family should begin the initial discussions about the bar/bat mitzvah exploring the type of service, mitzvah project, and celebration each family member desires. Look for areas of common ground and ways to support one another during the process, and keep the lines of communication open. Talk about not only what you can afford, but how much you feel is appropriate to spend and how you want to spend your money. For example, a parent committed to supporting the synagogue may feel strongly that the reception be held there, instead of at a popular catering hall.

Parental guidance is essential here as Rabbi Joshua Toledano of Congregation Mekor Baruch in Merion, Pennsylvania, points out, "The bar mitzvah is a charge for parents: you are creating a memory." This is the event your child will be looking back to one day, when he or she is raising a family.

But it would be disingenuous of us to disregard the social pressures exerted on both parents and child to conform to the overblown "bar mitzvah du jour" syndrome. One way we have found to mitigate the effects of social pressure on your child is to start talking about the bar/bat mitzvah celebration early on, so you can instill a vision of the magical coming-of-age tradition it is meant to be before your child is unduly influenced by ideas you consider inappropriate from his or her peers. Participating as a family in some of the Judaic activities we describe below, as well as taking an active interest in your child's religious education, will go a long way toward creating a foundation for that vision.

Here are some suggestions for family activities during the bar/bat mitzvah year:

- Bake challah weekly or once a month. Check out our recipe, if you don't have your own family version.
- Find a Jewish-themed story or poem to read every week at Shabbat dinner. You'll find a wealth of Jewish folktales and other literature that will engage the whole family.
- Create a mitzvah adventure challenge. Make up a list of thirteen mitzvah projects that you can do together.
- Learn ten different Shabbat songs from different cultures.
- Find a Jewish family from another country about to become bar/bat mitzvah, and have a family pen pal or e-mail correspondence.
- Explore different Jewish arts: dancing, cooking, music, art history (studying Ben Shahn, Marc Chagall, Leonard Baskin, etc.), Jewish theater, and paper-cutting. Get experts from your synagogue or consult your library for information.
- Finally, instead of saving up your parental blessings in a long speech for the bar/bat mitzvah day, bless your child every week. Start by blessing the child in your own words at your Friday night dinner during the bar/bat mitzvah year. You'll be surprised at how the blessing will change from week to week, and ultimately serve as a rich basis for your blessing on the big day.

You will also find, no doubt, that many other parents are looking for ways to avoid falling into the peer pressure trap. Get together as soon as possible with the parents of your child's bnai mitzvah class to discuss the issue and support each other—unity will give you strength. Look for unique solutions, like sharing the festivities with a friend or cousin, or choosing a location that is off the beaten path.

We've also known families who have sidestepped the issue by celebrating the bar or bat mitzvah in Israel, some holding a service at their own synagogue and hosting a Kiddush for the congregation, family, and friends who were unable to celebrate with them in Israel. And others decide on a "kids-only" party, a thirteenth birthday party, completely separate from the bar/bat mitzvah celebration. (For more on kids-only parties, please see page 61.)

FROM GENERATION TO GENERATION

"Ten years ago, when my mother died, I developed an urgent desire to learn Yiddish," Ellen Cassedy wrote in the spring 2000 issue of *Bridges*. "I couldn't save my mother from cancer, but maybe I could help to save this other precious Jewish thing."

Cassedy described how, little by little, Yiddish took root in her life and bloomed in her house. She suggested to her daughter Meg that she study the language in preparation for her bat mitzvah. At her service, Meg not only read from the Torah in Hebrew, but delivered her *dvar* interspersed with Yiddish readings, songs, poems, and blessings. Meg noted, "I'm glad I connected myself with both the religious Jewish language and the more everyday one," linking her not only to her grandmother, but to all the generations before her.

Through potent rituals and traditions, we express our Jewish beliefs about the world, and transmit this identity and experience "from generation to generation." This concept, *l'dor v'dor* in Hebrew, is a recurrent theme throughout this book. Look for ideas and stories like Meg's in the sidebars called "From Generation to Generation."

A FAMILY IS A FAMILY IS A FAMILY

Of course, every family is unique, and our idea of family today also includes single and same-sex parents; blended families with prefixes like half-, step-, and ex-; long-lost relatives; families tenuously related to each other by blood, or not at all; friends who have taken the place of grandparents, parent, aunt, or brother. During the bar/bat mitzvah year, you will want to reach out to your family, however you define the term. Those less familiar with Jewish traditions and rituals and single parents in particular might find a mentor—a family member, close friend, or member of the synagogue community—especially helpful at this time.

Interfaith and Adoptive Families

The tent of Judaism today is very wide: It covers not only descendants of Jewish families from all over the globe, but also the newly Jewish, the offspring of interfaith marriages, and, increasingly in America, adopted children of African American, Asian, and

Latin American backgrounds. These contemporary multicultural Jewish families encourage their children to feel a sense of pride in their complex identities because they recognize that denying any part of a child's heritage sends the message that there is a part of this child that doesn't matter or isn't worth knowing, according to Shelly Kapnek Rosenberg, author of *Adoption and the Jewish Family*. They introduce their children to the culture of a birth mother, a non-Jewish parent or grandparent, while at the same time continuing to develop and strengthen the children's identity as members of the Jewish community. These families often choose to incorporate some aspect of this diverse background in the bar/bat mitzvah service or celebration, creating new traditions that reflect the unique Jewish family they are.

For example, as Helen Mintz Belitsky reported in InterfaithFamily.com, Dev Talvadkar's coming-of-age journey entwined the cultures of his Jewish American mother and Indian-born father. Like the bar mitzvah, the Hindu Thread Ceremony takes place when a boy turns thirteen; the name derives from the circular thread the child is given as he is told, "Now you are a man."

Dev flew to Bombay with his family, where, reenacting the ancient Hindu custom, he changed from beautiful silk clothes to simple cotton ones, and walked around his guests, asking for their blessings and collecting food and money for his spiritual journey. After his mother fed him sweets, he left the celebration space, symbolically departing from his childhood home to seek his *guru*, spiritual adviser. When he came back into the room, dressed again in silk, the guests lit a fire to welcome him and celebrated with a feast of delicious Indian foods.

Four days later, Dev kissed the mezuzah at Magen Hassidim, a one-hundred-year-old synagogue of India's Bene Israel community, as he entered to celebrate his bar mitzvah there. He lit the ancient oil lamps, then, surrounded on the bimah by his family, including his Indian grandparents, he performed the rituals, readings, and blessings he had learned back home in Chevy Chase, Maryland. His Torah portion was read in both Hebrew and Marathi.

Dev wore a tallit made of Indian raw silk and *tzitzit* (fringes) imported from Israel; its four corners featured the four initials of his given name, his father's Hindu name, and his father's and mother's family names. He walked around the room with the Torah, and as he held out his tzitzit for the congregants to kiss, this age-old ritual suddenly became a transcendent metaphor for embracing a new mosaic family.

Special Needs Families

"I wanted a chance to declare Joel's value and dignity before G-d, my family and friends, and the people who had helped Joel fight his way out of the solitude of autism," Becca Hornstein, executive director of the Council for Jews with Special Needs, wrote about her son in the magazine *Disability Solutions*. With the help of "a remarkable rabbi and congregation," Joel became bar mitzvah, following in the steps of all the generations before him, reciting the blessings and Torah portions in Hebrew and English in front of two hundred people, although he had only begun speaking a couple of years before.

As Hornstein points out, there are many ways a bar/bat mitzvah service can be modified to accommodate a child with even severe developmental and other disabilities, but you will need a rabbi, religious educators, and a community that are flexible and creative enough to meet the challenge. However, she adds, "Every parent who has experienced this event has reported feeling reconnected to their Judaism with an even greater depth of appreciation." And "being the 'bar mitzvah boy (or girl)' means being *special* . . . not special as in 'special needs,' . . . *special* as in being the center of attention . . . And *every* child deserves that."

For more information, contact Hornstein's organization, located in Scottsdale, Arizona (www.cjsn.org).

FAMILY ISSUES

Just prior to his bar mitzvah, Scott was diagnosed with juvenile diabetes. Robbie's grandmother passed away two weeks before he was called up to the Torah. Zoe's Torah portion was about the face-to-face meeting between Jacob and Esau, yet on the bimah, her parents, locked in a bitter divorce, couldn't bear to look at one another.

Life happens during the bar/bat mitzvah year. You may be faced with outside challenges: both new ones and those you have been dealing with for years. Sometimes we are fortunate enough to derive strength from them: Susannah, who knew her father, a rabbi, would not live to see her daughter called to the Torah, asked him to comment on his grandchild's portion; she included his words in her talk before the congregation. Years after a horrible divorce, one dad stood before the synagogue and blessed his ex-wife for raising their daughter into the wonderful young woman she had become.

But mostly we try to get by. During difficult times, you may want to consult with your rabbi about what is happening in your world. Plans can be changed: If necessary, the bar or bat mitzvah can be modified or postponed. Matt's dad was in the hospital on the spring day that was to have been his bar mitzvah, so Matt approached the bimah not with joy, but profound sadness, to recite the *misheberach* blessing to heal his ill father. But as Yom Kippur passed and the family realized they would all be inscribed in the Book of Life for another year, they set a new date. And what a celebration it was—not only of Matt's achievements that day, but also of the links connecting the family to the congregation that had helped them through those bleak days.

THE COMMUNITY:

WIDENING THE CIRCLE

For nearly all families, the bar/bat mitzvah journey will take place within the embrace of a worship community. Jewish practice ranges from the four major organized branches—Orthodox, Conservative, Reform, and Reconstructionist—to less formal groups, like the *havurah*, Humanistic Judaism, and Jewish Renewal groups. If you are still unaffiliated with a worship group, and wish to explore the differences in depth, it is best to visit local synagogues and talk to the rabbis there in person, because each synagogue has its own culture and personality, and every rabbi has his or her own way of leading the congregation.

In this chapter, we explore not only synagogue policies and procedures, but also how your congregation—and the wider community—can be a resource center and source of support during the journey.

STARTING THE SYNAGOGUE JOURNEY

While synagogue policies vary considerably, the child will usually meet with the rabbi, cantor, or other synagogue representative within two to three years of the bar/bat mitzvah year to discuss procedures and guidelines. In some congregations, the rabbi will call the entire bar/bat mitzvah class together for this initial meeting; in others, the family sets up an appointment to sit down face-to-face with the rabbi or cantor to get to know each other better, and to discuss the bar/bat mitzvah process, the service, and the celebration. In either case, you'll find it helpful to have a contact person at the synagogue you can count on as issues arise. He or she will talk to you about setting your child on a path appropriate to his or her abilities and interests, and when to start tutoring. Come prepared with a list of questions. This is the time to bring up special family concerns: dealing with a difficult ex-spouse, parents who don't know Hebrew, or learning problems and other special needs your child may have.

Inquire about special resources or committees within the synagogue. A little networking may unearth vast treasure chests of talent and expertise in diverse subjects: Molly interviewed ninety-two-year-old Pearl for her research project, "The Streets Were Paved with Cement," about Jewish immigration to New York's Lower East Side. Another child worked alongside the chairperson of the *tikkun olam* committee on various service projects. Some parents, especially single ones, may wish to enlist the help of the rabbi or the synagogue in setting up a mentoring program for their child: David, for example, was able to schedule monthly Torah study sessions with a retired university professor.

SETTING THE DATE

Although the child does become responsible for carrying out the commandments on his or her thirteenth birthday (twelfth for Orthodox girls), there is no "law" that says the bar/bat mitzvah event must be on the Sabbath nearest the birthday of the child. Traditional bnai mitzvah *must* be after the child's birthday on a day the Torah is read (Monday, Thursday, Saturday, and Rosh Hodesh, the day of the new moon). For Sabbath-observant Jews, holding the bar/bat mitzvah on a Monday, Thursday, or Rosh Hodesh, or on holidays like Purim, enables the celebrants to have music, photography, transportation to and from the event, and other elements prohibited on the Sabbath. A reception on a Monday holiday or even on Thanksgiving may also be less expensive than a weekend celebration. You might also want to consider choosing a day other than Shabbat if your child will be sharing a bar or bat mitzvah date with another classmate; it will obviate fears that all their mutual friends will decide to go to the other bar or bat mitzvah. Another option is to have the service on Saturday, and the reception on Sunday.

Some synagogues will permit you to schedule a bar or bat mitzvah at a late afternoon service (instead of the morning one), concluding with Havdalah, a hauntingly beautiful ceremony at dusk on Saturday night, followed by a nighttime reception. This was a perfect solution for the Kaye family, who were set on an evening reception so they could enjoy music at their synagogue party space. The numerous out-of-town guests they had invited would either have had to travel back and forth for the service and evening reception or endure a long wait in town between them. Because of the deep rift between her divorced parents, Linda actually celebrated her bat mitzvah twice, each at a different service. Since Torah readings are arranged so that the subsequent week's Torah portion is read at the *Mincha/Ma'ariv* service at the close of Shabbat (a sort of preview for the week to come), Linda chanted her portion at her father's synagogue at that service, followed by Havdalah and an *oneg* reception there with her father's family and friends. A week later, she chanted the same portion on Shabbat morning at her regular synagogue, and celebrated that evening with her mother's friends. Do keep in mind that if you choose a service other than the Shabbat morning one, regular attendees in the synagogue community may not attend.

While some synagogues assign the date and time of the ceremony years in advance, if your rabbi (or the bnai mitzvah coordinator) concurs, you may schedule a date later to accommodate special family needs. Or, depending on synagogue policy, you may be permitted to choose a special date if there is one that is particularly meaningful to the child or the family. Examples include a time when a favorite Torah portion is read (e.g., *Bereishit* [Creation]), a season or holiday particularly beloved (Sukkot in autumn; Tu B'Shevat [New Year for the Trees] for the environmentally concerned), or the birthday or *Yahrzeit* of someone important in the child's or family's life. Jewish feminists have started special feminist celebrations of Rosh Hodesh, and this might be a special time for a bat mitzvah.

For more on scheduling both the service and festivities, please see "When the Service Takes Place" (page 36) and "What Kind of Party Are You Hosting?" (page 190).

SYNAGOGUE BAR AND BAT MITZVAH PROCEDURES

Find out what your synagogue's policies are—most have written information and some even post their policies on a website. Though each differs in what they require, typically they will include details on:

- Hebrew school curriculum, including what the child is expected to learn and attendance requirements
- What the child will be required to do at the bar/bat mitzvah service and preparation timelines
- Mitzvah projects
- Tutoring information
- Information about special honors (such as aliyot), with forms to fill out
- How to create a program book
- Fees and tzedakah
- Policies on photography, videography, and music during the service
- Policies regarding the refreshments offered after the service (Kiddush) (see Chapter 13, "Celebration Food and Drink: Planning the Menu")
- Family attendance at Friday night and/or Shabbat services (always the best way to become familiar with bar/bat mitzvah procedures)
- Decorum in the sanctuary

YOUR CHILD'S SYNAGOGUE CLASS

As a bar/bat mitzvah family, you are not making this journey alone. Along the way, you'll enjoy the support not only of the synagogue, but of the Hebrew school community as well—especially the class of prospective bar and bat mitzvah children and their families from your child's year. In many synagogues, this group, which we refer to as the "bnai mitzvah class," finds ways to work together both formally and informally, by sponsoring teaching symposiums and meetings with the rabbi, family get-togethers, and group projects. During the bar/bat mitzvah year, the bnai mitzvah class may form co-ops to assist the "bar/bat mitzvah family of the week" with tasks like setting up the Kiddush, ushering, attending the parking lot, and even baking challahs.

Lori's synagogue hosts a Friday night service and potluck dinner every fall for the ten-year-olds, honoring those children starting off on their bar/bat mitzvah journeys. The children and their families light candles, sing songs, recite the Friday night Kiddush, and parents give a special blessing and a gift to their child as a way of saying *lech le-cha,* or go forth on your journey, as Abraham and Sarah did. The gift might be a keepsake necklace, a special book, a Jewish ritual item like a shofar, or a carved wooden box made by a great-grandfather long ago. With three years of study and hard work in Hebrew school ahead of them, this congenial gathering helps both parents and kids connect with one another, and share an inspiring moment or two together, a harbinger of so much more to come.

Developing strong ties with the other parents in the bnai mitzvah class will serve you well: You'll find they are an excellent source of information and support during the process.

MAKE IT A MITZVAH *Form a mitzvah collective: a fund supported by all the bnai mitzvah families, who will choose together which charitable project to underwrite. Encourage children in the bnai mitzvah class to participate in a mitzvah project together. One class helped reclaim a local nature sanctuary, restoring native plants and removing invasive vines. Another cleaned up an old cemetery, trimming the overgrown grass and removing graffiti from the headstones.*

SYNAGOGUE EXPENSES

Familiarize yourself with the costs related to the service: working with a tutor, rabbi, and cantor; gifts and special purchases, if any (for example, a prayer shawl for the child, or a kippot for the congregation—these will be discussed in more detail in chapter 4); and the expectations of the synagogue for charitable donations. Include the anticipated costs of the mitzvah project and other family charitable donations when writing your budget.

A DIFFERENT PATH . . .

The Nontraditional Bar/Bat Mitzvah

Some parents, disaffected by the synagogues of their youth and estranged from conventional temples today, are reexploring Jewish practice in different ways. A bar/bat mitzvah that is meaningful and personal can speak profoundly to less traditional families; being intimately involved in creating the event ensures that the experience will feel authentic and contemporary.

When Gabrielle and her family visited the local synagogues around their affluent community, they were turned off by the social scenes there, the bored and rather spoiled kids in the Hebrew schools preparing for over-the-top bar and bat mitzvahs. Determined to introduce his daughter to a more meaningful Judaism, Gabrielle's father enrolled her in Hebrew classes at the local Jewish Community Center. She was a little behind, but with private tutoring she caught up quickly. The rabbi the family found through the JCC lists made Gaby's bat mitzvah a rich, spiritual experience: In the Hillel sanctuary they rented at the University of Pennsylvania, she read the beautiful Shavuot Torah portion before close family and friends.

Some parents decide to join an *havurah*, a small, closely knit worship community. Highly participatory and egalitarian, *havurot* rely on members for everything from conducting most of the services (rabbis, when present, help guide and mentor the congregation instead of leading it) to educating the bnai mitzvah through tutoring and mentoring programs. At Lev Shalom in Atlanta, traditionally observant Jews, and those for whom old patterns and rituals no longer serve, celebrate their Judaism together, forming study groups and doing *tikkun olam*. Reflecting on the many mentors, ranging in age from twenty to ninety-one, who had helped him prepare for his bar mitzvah there, Daniel felt he was chanting his portion "in front of my family." For more information, contact the National Havurah Directory at www.havurah.org.

Other parents have forged a meaningful connection to their faith through Jewish feminist groups and Secular Humanist synagogues. At the latter, bnai mitzvah education stresses Jewish values, social responsibility and action projects, and immersion in the magnificent Jewish heritage, all within the framework of secular beliefs. In a profound and deeply personal journey, children work with an adult mentor on their chosen topic of inquiry.

And we have even met families that planned their own service for their community of friends and family—sometimes without benefit of a rabbi, as Ben did.

Ben, who played accordion sidekick to his puppeteer friend Mark, presenting shows to Lubavitcher communities and Hebrew day schools in the Philadelphia area, had home-schooled his children, Shia and Anastasia, in Hebrew. After a family discussion, brother and sister, just a year apart, decided to celebrate their bnai mitzvah together, and the family rented a local shul on Labor Day when the sanctuary was not in use. The kids conducted the entire service in front of their small community of friends, scripting every-thing from the opening klezmer melodies to the closing *Adon Olam*, with help from their dad, other community members, and Mark's life-size rabbi puppet, who ad-libbed, "Man oh Manischewitz . . . what are we doing here?" Shia and Asia translated some of the prayers into their own words: "Mah Tovu" became "Wow, Jacob, your tents are good!" "Rebecca, your tents are awesome!" At the close of the service, their mom's Rosh Hodesh group encircled the children for a simple loving blessing.

If you go this very challenging route, bear in mind that you can rent or borrow a Torah and an ark—as long as they are adequately insured.

The Adult Bar/Bat Mitzvah

Of increasing importance in contemporary Judaism is the bar and bat mitzvah of adults. Although technically they became bar or bat mitzvah when they reached age thirteen—whether they had a religious ceremony or not—many adults want to mark their com-mitment to Jewish life in a public way at a later point in life.

For some Jews, celebrating their spiritual coming-of-age at thirteen would have been impossible. The bat mitzvah, for example, has been a slowly evolving tradition through-out the twentieth century, and women's religious education was often ignored, even among practicing Jewish families. Today, many of the women who watched as their brothers stepped onto the bimah and into the spotlight are taking their turn. In one con-gregation, a woman who had been reading and praying in Hebrew for years felt there was "something missing" in her spiritual life until she became bat mitzvah at age ninety.

Other adults came of age at a time when their parents were gravely ill or dying, or they themselves were going through difficult times, or lived in a place where bnai mitzvah were not permitted, like Nazi Europe or countries in the former Soviet Union. Chris, raised as an Anglican by a parent who hid his identity during World War II and never returned to the Jewish faith, learned about his ancestry when he was twelve. His wife and son supported him during his spiritual journey from brit to bar mitzvah. His father also came to the synagogue for the adult bar mitzvah; when the service concluded, the rabbi called him up to the bimah, and, gently placing his hands on the shoulders of the two men, delivered the ancient blessing over both father and son.

The desire for Jewish renewal has also inspired many people to celebrate their bnai mitzvah as adults. For some, raised in assimilated families, the ceremony is an affirmation of their return to the Jewish community; for others, it is a reconsecration of the spiritual traditions that have nourished them throughout their lives.

TAKING ON THE COMMANDMENTS: TZEDAKAH AND THE MITZVAH PROJECT

From the earliest age, our children watch adults as they organize coat drives, make sandwiches in a local soup kitchen, write checks for *tikkun olam*. We try to teach them to put some of their own money in tzedakah boxes, and encourage them to collect from others for UNICEF if they go trick-or-treating. But when they become bnai mitzvah, the focus of their tzedakah effort changes as they undertake their own special mitzvah project. It is no longer Mommy, Daddy, their synagogue, or their school that initiates the mitzvah and takes responsibility for following through, but the children themselves.

A mitzvah has been called "a spiritual 'action-directive' " (Marcia Prager, *The Path of Blessing*). More than simply giving charity, the mitzvah project requires a real investment of time and should engage the child directly. Whether the idea for the project evolves from a special interest or from the Torah portion, the choice should be meaningful to the child.

Founder of the Ziv Tzedakah Fund, Danny Siegel's books and lectures have inspired bnai mitzvah around the country to come up with creative mitzvah projects that have proven kids really can make a difference. How does a child find the right mitzvah project? Siegel responds with the Four Questions you need to ask—not the "Mah Nishtanah" of the Passover seder, but these: "What am I good at? What do I like to do? What bothers me so much about what is wrong with the world that I get very angry and want to do whatever I can to change it? Whom do I know who could help me?"

Siegel offers many suggestions for projects to repair the world at his website (www.ziv.org) and in his books (see the bibliography). His practical, doable ideas range from seeking out local caterers, schools, and other institutions and convincing them to donate their leftover food to food pantries like City Harvest, to asking computer whiz kids to offer to computerize lists of volunteers, time schedules, places, and other details for charitable groups.

Many kids come up with their own ideas. On a visit to the United States Holocaust Memorial Museum, Rabbi Nancy Fuchs Kreimer and her twelve-year-old daughter Frances read about Righteous Gentiles, including the Danes who helped so many Jews escape the Nazis. When they got home, there was a request from one of the service organizations the family supported: $2,000 was urgently needed for a Bosnian refugee mission. It was shortly before Rosh Hashanah, so Frances decided to raise money for the project by picking apples with her friends at a local orchard, then combining them with jars of honey to make special New Year's baskets she could sell through the synagogue newsletter. Some of Frances's relatives contributed money, but told her they didn't need the baskets, so Frances brought these baskets to a senior center to be distributed to low-income Jews—a mega-mitzvah. The following year, after considerable research, Frances chose Haitian orphans as her recipients: Every $100 she earned through her Rosh Hashanah baskets would send a child to school for an entire year. She continued making the baskets and creating sweet new years for many autumns well beyond her thirteenth year.

Whenever possible, encourage your children to "put a face to the project" by making the donation in person. If they have collected sports equipment, have them accompany you when you drop it off. Seeing what they have accomplished by their own efforts can be a life-changing experience.

If the mitzvah project entails donating goods or services, your child should get in touch with the organization first, to inquire about any special guidelines or needs they can tell you about. Many organizations list specific requirements on their websites for the donations they will accept, and your child should check that your family's donation will meet those criteria before purchasing it. For example, if you want to donate baby clothes, and incorporate the new layettes you are buying in your centerpiece (see page

124, "Planning Your Flowers Around a Mitzvah"), you may be told that what they really need are clothes for toddlers, like T-shirts and overalls. Or you may be told that your book drive would work beautifully in conjunction with an after-school tutoring program. Plan ahead to find out where and how to transport everything; you don't want to buy or collect a lot of wonderful things and have no way to get them there. Older siblings, or even members of the congregation, with drivers' licenses might help out with the postparty work.

If your child is amenable, you might make the project a family endeavor: The child can select and initiate the project, and the family can join in later. (For example, the child begins volunteering in a soup kitchen; a few weeks later, the family starts working at the kitchen once a month.)

"When I marched in Selma," the eminent theologian Abraham Joshua Heschel said, "my feet were praying." Judaism teaches us to pray not only with our lips, but with our hands, by doing, and with our whole bodies, by taking social action.

THE WORLD WIDE WEB

The World Wide Web is a valuable tool in planning a bar/bat mitzvah; using the keywords "bar mitzvah" on a search engine, you will find hundreds of bar/bat mitzvah resources on the Internet. Many families also use the Web as a research tool to gather information and answer questions about the service. In addition to www.ziv.org, mentioned above, many other sites offer information on mitzvah projects, the Torah portions, and the celebration.

And some families start a website for their child's bar/bat mitzvah. These sites not only include pertinent information about the service and event (sometimes even permitting guests to RSVP online), but also enable a child to receive and exchange greetings and bar/bat mitzvah stories with adults and children worldwide.

In 1996, Jason Miller began a fabulous e-mail project as a bar mitzvah gift for his younger brother, Jacob. Jason sent an e-mail message to more than eighty listservs, Jewish organizations, celebrities, and individuals, noting that his brother's bar mitzvah was coming up, and requesting that people send him "good wishes, words of wisdom or advice, or just say, 'Mazel tov.'" By his bar mitzvah, Jacob had received more than five hundred responses from well-wishers like President Clinton and the actor Ed Asner.

Some, including several Holocaust survivors, sent stories and poems, or told of their own bar and bat mitzvah celebrations.

CELEBRATING WITH THE COMMUNITY

The budget, the guest list, finding a place, invitations, what's to eat—*oy vey!!!!* The budget and guest list will play a significant role in determining the kind of festive celebration you choose. Because the simcha is a major focus of the book, we will address all these aspects and more in Part Two, The Festivities.

4

THE SERVICE

The rabbi removes the Torah, the living, breathing body of Jewish law,
caressed like a loved one, whirled as a partner in dance during shtetl
weddings, buried and mourned if desecrated or burned. He hands the
scrolls covered with gold-stitched silk to Seymour, who ceremoniously
receives them, light as a child, heavy as history. The Torah is un-
dressed, unrolled and the silver pointer placed in Seymour's hand.
Well-schooled, he begins reading this day's portion . . .
—JOANN ROSE LEONARD, THE SOUP HAS MANY EYES

When your family is starting off on the journey, it is

sometimes hard to imagine that your child will arrive at the moment when he

or she is standing on the bimah in a grown-up suit or new dress, ready to re-

ceive the blessing of Torah in front of a crowd of well-wishers. The celebrant

must not only be well schooled in the bar/bat mitzvah ceremony, but well

versed in the rhythms of the regular worship service as well. A long road lies

ahead before you walk into the synagogue that day. In this chapter, we address

all the preparations to be made, from learning the Torah portion to writing a

parental blessing, and everything in between.

ELEMENTS OF THE BAR/BAT MITZVAH SERVICE

A child's responsibilities in the bar/bat mitzvah service will vary from congregation to congregation and from one branch of Judaism to another. Some read the words and some chant *(leyn)* them; some speak primarily in Hebrew, others in English. One child may recite more Haftarah, another more Torah. One may share the bar/bat mitzvah duties with another child; others may lead most of the regular Shabbat worship service themselves.

Most bar/bat mitzvah services generally include at least the following elements.

Torah

The Torah is much more than the Five Books of the Hebrew Bible it contains: Metaphorically, it is all of Jewish teaching. It is so sacred to Jewish life that a *parshah*, or portion of it, is read aloud in the synagogue on Mondays and Thursdays (the market days of ancient Israel), Shabbat, and festivals so that everyone, no matter how unlearned, can have access to its words.

It takes one year to complete the cycle of Torah portions: On Simchat Torah, the last chapters of Deuteronomy are completed and the first chapter of Genesis begun. Through the Torah, Jews are linked to one another all over the world: Every week, Jewish congregations, wherever they are located, read the identical Torah passages.

Handwritten on a parchment scroll, the Torah includes "stories of the origins of the world, the birth of our people, and the beginnings of the Jewish legal system," explains Rabbi Rebecca Alpert, associate professor of religion and women's studies at Temple University. "It is kept in the ark, a sacred space at the front or center of every synagogue, under a flame that burns perpetually. It is adorned with a special cover and ornaments. It is removed from the ark with great pageantry. . . . To be called to the Torah to recite the blessing for reading from the scroll is a great honor. Blessing and reading from the Torah forms the core experience of the bar/bat mitzvah ceremony."

The Torah passage is divided into sections; before and after each section is read, a blessing is made (see page 45, "Aliyah"). The bar/bat mitzvah may read all or just part of the passage, and another congregant may read the remainder. Then, in an awe-inspiring moment, the Torah is paraded around the synagogue before it is returned to the ark.

MAKE IT A MITZVAH *Although it is too costly for most families to do on their own, if several families or the whole synagogue pools their contributions, a Torah can be purchased as a gift for an underprivileged congregation in the United States or another part of the world.*

Haftarah

Many scholars believe the practice of reading the Haftarah began during the religious persecutions of Antiochus Epiphanes (168–165 B.C.E.), when reading the weekly Torah portion was banned. The rabbis selected portions from the Book of Prophets and other texts that they felt were connected to the corresponding forbidden Torah segments. Even after Torah reading was again permitted in the service, the tradition of reading the Haftarah was maintained.

Dvar Torah

After reading from the Torah and the Haftarah, the bar/bat mitzvah addresses words of learning to the congregation. We discuss this in more detail in "Preparing for the Service."

Parental Blessings

This custom is also explained in "Preparing for the Service."

Blessings by the Rabbi and the Synagogue

In many synagogues, it is traditional for the rabbi to bless the child, and sometimes the whole family, with a few well-chosen words of wisdom. The rabbi may pronounce the ancient priestly blessing from Numbers 6:23–27 ("May God bless you and keep you . . ."), or recite a *misheberach* in honor of the individual's time of joy. In addition, often a representative from the congregation (the president, or someone from the Synagogue Sisterhood) offers a blessing to this newest member of the community, welcoming him or her with a certificate and/or special gift, such as a Kiddush cup or a prayer book inscribed with the celebrant's name.

In addition, the child may conduct prayers and songs from the regular service, and, when permitted, may include some specially chosen additions (see "Can I Personalize the Service?" on page 37).

The Orthodox Bat Mitzvah Service

There are a wide variety of ceremonies in which an Orthodox girl may be welcomed into the community as a bat mitzvah. Mandy chanted from the Torah on Shabbat in a women's prayer group (instead of the sanctuary), while Tovah chanted the Haftarah and gave a *dvar Torah* in the sanctuary on a Sunday. Liz began her celebration at an elegant hotel by reading her Torah portion from a bible (rather than a Torah scroll), and followed with a *dvar Torah*.

THE REGULAR WORSHIP SERVICE

A canopy of mismatched tallitot sheltered a sea of faces, waiting for the ancient bless-ing. This Shabbat was not only the day of Matt's bar mitzvah, but the day Bereishit, or Creation, was read, when all the new babies, nestled tightly in their parents' arms, were welcomed into the congregation, and the prospective bride and groom given a warm send-off. Faces of all colors and many ages, full of hope, all surrounded Matt as they re-cited the Barchu together.

The bar/bat mitzvah is just one part of the regular congregational worship service. Attending services with your family (if you don't do so already) will help your child grow familiar with the communal prayers and become more sensitive to the synagogue com-munity itself—so essential when he or she will have the responsibility of leading the congregation in the service. At the beginning of the *Barchu*, the communal call to wor-ship, we bend our knee, symbolically making us smaller, more humble, before God and the congregation. It is important to remember that the child becomes bar/bat mitzvah in the embrace of a community.

Overview of a Typical Service

The essence of the Jewish prayer service—acknowledging and praising God's goodness, and declaring our sense of wonder at the sacredness of creation—enables us to appreciate the manifold joys of life and sustains us during its sorrows. While most of the prayers express this gratitude and awe, they do so in different ways, coalescing in the unique rhythm of the service.

The morning service begins with a "warm-up": the blessings, songs, and psalms that prepare the congregants for prayer. This is followed by the *Barchu*, the call to worship, and the *Shema*, the declaration of faith in God's oneness. Then comes the central prayer of the service, the *Amidah*, said silently while standing, individual time for personal meditation. Next is the Torah service, as previously explained. The prayers conclude with the *Aleinu*, an affirmation of our belief and trust in God and our hope that all people will recognize the oneness of the world and peace will triumph; and the Mourner's Kaddish, recited by those who have recently lost a loved one. The service ends on a joyful note, with hymns praising God, like "Adon Olam."

MAKE IT A MITZVAH *Volunteer at assisted-living centers and continuous-care facilities to aid seniors who want to attend services. By pushing their wheelchairs from their living quarters to the chapel, or by turning pages in their prayer books, you can help them maintain their lifelong traditions and continue to be counted as active members of the Jewish community.*

When the Service Takes Place

Most bar/bat mitzvahs occur on Saturday, at the *Shacharit* (morning) service, when the majority of congregants are present. As mentioned previously, some synagogues will allow members to conduct the bar/bat mitzvah during the *Mincha/Ma'ariv* (late afternoon) service (the Torah is read again at that time), concluding with Havdalah prayers at the temple or at a separate celebration. Though this service may not be the same as your synagogue's morning service, some families prefer this time as an alternative to sharing the morning service with another bar/bat mitzvah, or, because this shorter service might be best for a child with learning disabilities. There are also *Shacharit* services on holidays and Rosh Hodesh (the day of the New Moon), as well as on Monday and Thursday. (Note: The Haftarah is not read on weekdays, and the Torah portions are shorter then as well.)

In addition, the family may be expected to participate in the Friday evening *Kabbalat*

Shabbat service the evening before the bar/bat mitzvah, and they may be required to host an *oneg*, refreshments for the congregation, at that time.

THE SYNAGOGUE SPACE

Synagogues are sacred spaces, and as such, will have policies regarding when kippot and tallitot must be worn, correct decorum, what is considered appropriate dress. The dress code for those on the bimah or in the sanctuary may differ from what is permitted in other parts of the synagogue. For example, most synagogues require that all males—including non-Jews—cover their heads during services, and some may ask that women do so as well. Or some may require that women cover their heads only at the bimah. Be sure to check your synagogue handbook.

If there will be several young children unaccustomed to attending Shabbat services present, whom you fear may be disruptive, consider hiring a teenager or two from the congregation who would be instructed to baby-sit for them in another part of the temple should they have to leave.

CAN I PERSONALIZE THE SERVICE?

During the bar/bat mitzvah process, while children are finding their place within the community, they are intensely focused on their own highly individual journey, freighted with personal meaning and moments of self-discovery. It comes as no surprise then that many of today's young celebrants want to share their songs, poetry, and philosophical questionings, or add hymns and special readings to the liturgy.

While this may be a legitimate request, some synagogues see it as "privatizing" what should be a communal ceremony, and worry that a service with participants may devolve into a performance with spectators. Rabbi Don Goor from Tarzana, California, encourages children "to start out with the integral part of the religious service, what's already there, and find your connection to that. If you have a real connection to your synagogue and Judaism, you can draw from those fundamentals, rather than start off with 'what new thing can I bring?' Sometimes the less you add, the better."

Before you consider including anything additional, you should be very familiar with the regular worship service. Many elements are set in stone, and the substance and style of the service are, to a large extent, colored by both the rabbi and the congregation. Ask your rabbi and/or cantor whether doing something out of the ordinary for the service or just the bar/bat mitzvah portion alone would be not only permitted, but welcomed by the congregation.

Here are some personalized elements in services we've seen or heard about:

- An older brother chanting the Torah portion along with his learning-challenged brother, the bar mitzvah.
- A bar or bat mitzvah leading the congregation in discussions on the *dvar Torah*.
- Substituting gender-neutral blessings for those in the regular liturgy.
- Calling up someone who had the same Torah *parshah* years before to chant one of the sections in the Torah or to participate in the *dvar Torah* discussion.
- Bar/bat mitzvah children with gifted voices singing solo renditions of Hebrew or English songs that, though not part of the regular service, fit seamlessly into it. For example, Jewish composer Debbie Friedman set to music the Torah portion *Beshalach* (about Miriam, Moses' sister, dancing with timbrels) and the Haftarah portion about Deborah, with which it is paired; a bat mitzvah girl who had this portion sang the songs while dancing with the Torah, as is done on Simchat Torah.
- Although many synagogues do not permit musical instruments at Shabbat and festival services, some make an exception for Simchat Torah bar and bat mitzvah services; we know of klezmer bands and a small Jewish jazz group that played jazz versions of songs regularly included in the service, like "Adon Olam."
- Writings and poems relevant to the child and his or her family, ranging from Albert Einstein's wide-ranging observations on morality, religion, and the nature of the world to Jewish poets like Charles Reznikoff ("Out of the strong, sweetness"), Marge Piercy, and Ruth Brin, or specially chosen psalms such as Psalm 150 ("Praise God with trumpet sound . . .") and the Song of Solomon. The words are usually printed in the program booklet so the congregation can recite them together.
- Group singing always seems to get the congregation involved. In addition to well-known hymns, Jewish songs like those by Debbie Friedman ("L'Chi Lach," "Go Forth," and others) are particularly popular.

At a bar mitzvah in a small synagogue outside of Paris, relatives of the boy's mother, a convert to Judaism, who had traveled all the way from India were polite but uninvolved in the service, which they could not understand, as they spoke neither French nor Hebrew. But when the congregation began singing "Hava Nagilah"—certainly not part of the regular service—the Indian relatives burst into smiles—and song. It seems that Harry Belafonte's album, *Live at Carnegie Hall*, wildly popular in India during the 1960s and 1970s, had made the well-known Israeli folk song a hit there.

PREPARING A PROGRAM GUIDE
FOR THE SERVICE

Although much of the service is in Hebrew, Judaism has always taught that our prayers are heard in every language in which they are spoken, so please feel free to participate in the service in whatever way you are able.
—FROM JAKE'S BAR MITZVAH PROGRAM

In Jewish tradition, prayer is called service of the heart.
We hope that in this morning service
we have shared our heartfelt prayers.
—FROM ZANDER'S BAR MITZVAH PROGRAM

Although it is by no means a universal practice, providing written program booklets for the congregants is increasingly common today. Some families create inserts or additions for the regular program guide the synagogue prints up for Shabbat services, while others prepare a complete booklet themselves. We've seen guides made through desktop publishing (there is a lot of clip art available and Hebrew letters can even be downloaded free from some Internet sites) or handwritten and offset printed. Often a member of the congregation specializes in producing these programs.

The booklets range from the simplest (just the name, the date, and the Torah portion) to those that detail the whole service from start to finish. In addition to explaining the elements of the service for those unfamiliar with them—and thereby encouraging greater participation—the programs afford celebrants an excellent way to include more personal, or simply additional, material they would otherwise be unable to introduce at services. Some families honor deceased loved ones, or mention those unable to attend. Others include meditative questions based on the Torah or Haftarah portions. Note that many synagogues require you to submit a copy for prior approval, especially when you have employed religious terms that must be checked for accuracy.

Here are some of the things we have seen included in personalized programs.

- An explanation of the synagogue rituals, including what you do as you enter the sanctuary (i.e., take a *siddur*, or prayer book), explanation of terms like tallit, *kippot*, and *aliyot*, and what the ark is.
- Your synagogue's policies: turn off cell phones, no videography or photography, no applause; details on the background of your synagogue, perhaps its mission statement.
- What it means to be a bar/bat mitzvah.
- A personal letter to your guests (this may be handwritten, instead of typed) in which you thank the rabbi, the tutor, the cantor, and the congregation, or explain some of the traditions with which guests may be unfamiliar.
- A list of friends and family participating in the service (aliyot and other honors).
- The order of service with page numbers; Torah readings with translations (if the synagogue doesn't have enough *chumashim*, Bibles).
- A copy of the bar/bat mitzvah's *dvar Torah*.
- Alternative silent meditations, alternative gender-neutral blessings and prayers in translation, like the Shema created by poet Marge Piercy.
- Lyrics to songs, verses to hymns, poems, and any other material added to the liturgical service by the bar/bat mitzvah.
- Alternative readings and/or poems: a little take-home memento of writings or prayers you loved but weren't able to include in the service. Rose's program booklet included poems she had written about angels and an essay by Walter Benjamin about angels. So when they sang "*Shalom Aleichem*" as the closing song, everybody understood her allusion.
- Information about the child's mitzvah project; guidance for tzedakah contributions to be given in lieu of a personal gift to the celebrant.
- Remembrance of loved ones.
- Artwork (it is especially nice to include art relating to the Torah or Haftarah portion

or the Jewish calendar): photographs (for example, Noah building his sukkah); desktop publishing using line drawings from Jewish artists; illustrations by either the bar/bat mitzvah child or a sibling (Coryn used the illustrations from her invitation and inserted them into her design with Aramaic writing).

PREPARING FOR THE SERVICE

Learning the Torah and the Haftarah

After weeks spent either nagging Nicky to study his parshah *or suppressing her urge to do so, Sally heard her son's high-pitched tenor rising above the tutor's rich baritone recorded on the CD, and she realized that he had indeed learned it—and beautifully.*

It's a familiar story, but one that bears repeating. Despite moments when the house seems supercharged with top-voltage tension, your child will learn the portion. And it is not easy. The Torah and the Haftarah are chanted according to individual set melodies (except at some Reform synagogues, where they may be recited instead) that must be taught, then mastered, and the Torah is especially difficult to learn because it has no vowels, punctuation, or trope marks (the cantillation, or marks that indicate melody).

In order to prepare, children require assistance even if they are enrolled in Hebrew school or Jewish day school; usually they rely on a tutor or mentor, most often recommended by the rabbi or the synagogue. Because they will be working so closely together, try to find a tutor well suited to your child's personality if possible. Synagogues suggest that the tutoring start about six to nine months prior to the bar/bat mitzvah, and most tutors give the child a CD or a cassette to help him or her practice. There are also multimedia tools available in a range of formats—be sure to check with the tutor or rabbi to make sure you are working with the correct trope version.

MAKE IT A MITZVAH *Return the favor: Encourage your child to tutor young kids in his or her school, or through a community center. In many European communities, a Jewish child's first introduction to education came with licking Hebrew letters painted with honey off a slate, so he would always know the sweetness of learning. Share that sweetness with others.*

Writing the *Dvar Torah*

After working on the Torah and Haftarah portions, reading a translation of them and perhaps a commentary, the child should begin thinking about the *dvar Torah*, or Torah commentary, identifying and formulating some of the ideas and concepts expressed in the assigned passages. Admittedly, this will be easier with some portions than with others. Usually the bar/bat mitzvah child will then meet with the rabbi, the mentor, or the cantor to discuss his or her early thoughts and elicit possible avenues to explore in the *dvar*. The rabbi may suggest additional readings (and you might want to track down a few of the many rabbinic *dvrei Torah* on the Web). Together, they will try to discover one or more areas that ignite the child's interest.

Jews have always felt that the Torah was a living document: What has kept it vital throughout the centuries is that every generation, drinking in its words, could be newly refreshed by its wisdom, bringing contemporary questions to, and finding new answers in, the ancient teachings. As poet Ruth Brin put it, "I agonize over the long descriptions of animal sacrifice, the tedious descriptions of tabernacle building . . . [but] there is always something new to notice, to wonder about, to imagine and think about in that collection of books so densely packed with human experience and the search for God."

The goal here is not simply to extrapolate a pat truism or an oft-repeated life lesson, but rather to inspire your child to embark on a process that will last a lifetime. Urge your child to pose the questions and wrestle with them, without undue pressure to come up with all the answers.

Encourage your child to look beyond the literal. One child, unable to relate to the ritual sacrifices discussed in his portion, decided to approach the topic metaphorically, and explored tzedakah and his mitzvah project, reasoning that charity is another form of sacrifice. Others examined a historical event from a fresh point of view: Mara, whose Torah portion dealt with the story of Abraham and Sarah, imaginatively and lyrically recreated Sarah's life for the congregation, making the ancient biblical mother startlingly real and personal. As Mara concluded her retelling with the question "Who is Sarah?" the audience poignantly responded as one: "She is all of us."

Dvar Torah literally means "words of teaching," and depending on your rabbi and synagogue policies, the child's *dvar* may not be limited to knowledge gleaned from the Torah and Haftarah, but may be expanded to include the significance of the bar/bat mitzvah journey to the child, what being a Jew means to him or her in today's world, or aspects of Judaism that the child has explored in the Talmud. Inspired by his dog, one boy wrote a fascinating *dvar* exploring Jewish thinking in the Talmud and elsewhere on the treatment of animals, and how it spoke to the kosher laws, endangered species, and our relationships to our fellow human beings.

The rabbi or designate will usually suggest guidelines for writing the *dvar Torah*, such as the recommended length and a due date for the outline or draft. Of course, the length and breadth of the *dvar Torah* will vary considerably from one child to another depending on the child and his or her abilities. Most rabbis will want to see the finished *dvar Torah* prior to the bar/bat mitzvah in order to review it, so be sure to leave some extra time in your planning.

DRY RUN

Usually the tutor or synagogue will schedule a rehearsal, or "dry run," for the child and family on a weekday evening prior to the actual service. If you come dressed in your festive clothes, this can be an excellent opportunity to take photos or a video.

Family Support

Become familiar with your child's Torah and Haftarah portions, and initiate conversations about them; there are many Jewish Internet sites that inspire questions for family discussions on the *parshahs*. Focus on what your child is learning, not just planning the celebration. Talk about ways you might be able to integrate the Torah or Haftarah portion into the celebration.

Jacob's Torah portion, *Behalotecha*, provided the motif that informed his bar mitzvah. In it a menorah, or prayer candelabrum, is described. Working with a local artist friend of his mother's, he came up with a visual image: two hands growing out of a Havdalah candle, one white and one black, creating light in the world. This artwork was used in his invitation, on his program book, and became the basis for his explorations of diversity in his *dvar Torah*.

Be sensitive to the palpable pressure your child faces, and realize that some difficult moments are inevitable. As the date approaches, and a serious case of nerves sets in, remind the celebrant that he or she needn't be perfect; the *gabbai* is always standing alongside the reader to help out if necessary.

Advise your child to read slowly and enjoy the moment. It will be over in a flash!

Parental Blessing

At the earliest bar mitzvah ceremonies, the words the father recited did not "bless" his son at all; instead, they absolved him of any responsibility for the child. Today mothers and fathers agonize over the perfect words to say, some lauding the child's accomplishments and painting the fabulous future to come, some sharing words of Torah or offering guidance for the teen years ahead.

Find out if your synagogue has guidelines for the parents' blessings. There may be advice regarding content, time limits, and whether one or both parents are permitted to speak on the bimah. Remember you will have another opportunity to address your guests, should you wish, at the celebration, when you can offer a toast to your child. Do avoid making a long speech: It is your child's bar/bat mitzvah, and the focus should be on him or her expounding words of wisdom before the congregation.

Blessing our children in a Jewish context begins with an awareness of the gift that they are to us. One mother said that though she was supposed to bestow a blessing on her daughter, her daughter had been her special blessing since the day she was born. We bless from the inside out, in our own words, the prayers of poets, or the poetry of liturgy and sacred writings.

As noted theologian Marcia Falk points out, "A blessing turns a moment into an event." Recited slowly and with the depth of feeling this powerful moment invokes, any of the following make an eloquent blessing.

- "May the Lord bless you and keep you . . ." (from Numbers 6: 22–27). This was paraphrased and set to music in *Fiddler on the Roof*, and makes a beautiful song sung to a child either by parents or the entire congregation (the words should be printed in the program); it also may be recited.
- The ancient blessing from Talmud Berahot 17A, "May you live to see your world fulfilled/May you be our link to future worlds/And may your hope encompass/All the generations yet to be . . ." or Danny Siegel's blessings from the adaptation in *Between Dust and Dance*.
- The simple Ladino prayer "We should see you go under the chuppah with your mother and father and every member of the family healthy."
- Jewish poets, including Irving Layton ("You are my best-made poem/The one I labored longest over"), Marge Piercy (from *The Art of Blessing the Day*), and the previously mentioned Ruth Brin's poetry collected in *Harvest*.

- Wisdom from secular poets and thinkers and other spiritual traditions, including Native American poets and Meister Eckhart. Many of these, as well as beautiful alternative prayers, psalms, and poems, can be found in Jewish prayer books like *On the Doorposts of Your House, Paths of Faith,* and *Kol Haneshama Shabbat Vehagim.*
- Additional blessings, rooted in the Torah and Haftarah portions, or in the *dvar,* bring continuity to the service.

SPECIAL HONORS

Assisting in the worship service is an important honor, and there are several opportunities for those who are closely involved in the life of the bar/bat mitzvah child to do so.

Aliyah

The most significant of these is the *aliyah* (plural: *aliyot*), the privilege of coming up to the pulpit, or bimah, to recite a blessing before and after a section of the Torah is read. The number of aliyot will vary by congregation: There may be as many as eight, and the final one (the *Maftir*) is customarily reserved for the bar/bat mitzvah child—the first manifestation of his or her new mature status in the community. Depending on synagogue policy, some aliyot may be reserved for other worshipers (for example, for those who have just recovered from a serious illness, or parents having a baby-naming for a newborn) to enrich the service for the entire congregation, and the remaining aliyot are given to the celebrant's family.

For honorees unfamiliar with the blessings, or those who need a refresher course, write them out in Hebrew (transliterated, if necessary) and/or English, and give them copies in advance so that they will have time to practice. Since they will be called up to the Torah by their full Hebrew names, you will need to find out in advance what they are, as well as their mother's and father's Hebrew names, so that you will have a complete list of the aliyot to give the *gabbai,* the person who administers the Torah service.

Other Torah Honors

In cases where the bar/bat mitzvah is not reading the entire Torah portion, a relative or synagogue member may be chosen to read a section. And though it is not traditional, at some synagogues a member of the family or regular congregation may read the *parshah* in translation.

There are also several "hands-on" honors involving the Torah, some of which may be assigned to younger children. These include opening and closing the ark doors and curtains, taking out the Torah, removing the ornamental covering from the Torah and replacing it after it has been read ("dressing" and "undressing" the Torah), and lifting and carrying the Torah. Make sure you have someone strong enough to lift the Torah: When the scrolls are unfurled at the beginning or near the end of the year, they are unbalanced and difficult to hold steady.

Be aware that some synagogues have policies that exclude non-Jews or women from assisting in the Torah service; others may exclude them only from having aliyot.

MAKE IT A MITZVAH *"Twinning" offers a meaningful way to link your child's bar/bat mitzvah experience with people from other countries and diverse backgrounds. Your funds can help Jewish children from Ethiopia, the former Soviet Union, and other needy kids in Israel without the necessary financial or educational resources to celebrate their own bnai mitzvah. Contact www.emunah.org (Ethiopian and former Soviet children); www.NACOEJ.org (Ethiopian children); or www.amitchildren.org (other underprivileged Israeli children). There are also Holocaust twinning programs. The Jewish Foundation for the Righteous provides financial support to the Righteous Gentiles, now aged and in need, who saved many Jewish lives during the Holocaust. After making a donation, your child selects a rescuer to be twinned with, receives a certificate, and makes a presentation from the bimah (for more information, contact www.jfr.org). The Remember a Child Project links the child with Holocaust victims who were never able to celebrate their bnai mitzvah. A survivor meets with your child, presents him or her with a scroll of remembrance at the ceremony, and the child who perished is memorialized from the bimah. While there is no charge, donations are accepted. Contact your local chapter of the World Federation of Jewish Child Survivors of the Holocaust.*

Honors Outside of the Ceremony

Even those excluded from participating in the Torah service may be assigned these honors: giving out kippot, tallitot, prayer books, and programs, or serving as ushers. Family members and close friends might also help decorate the synagogue, making flower arrangements—especially lovely with homegrown blooms, or bake cakes or otherwise assist with the Kiddush, the celebratory refreshments served after the service. There will be additional honors at the celebration too, like reciting the blessings over wine and bread, and lighting a candle. They are discussed in chapter 11, "Tradition!"

RITUAL ITEMS FOR THE SYNAGOGUE

In 1934, Eva Ferenci became bat mitzvah in a ceremony together with six other girls— the first in the Budapest area. Her father's gift was a prayer book inscribed with the message that she should use it "as often as you can, but with feeling . . ." Somehow, Eva managed to keep the book with her throughout her internment at the Ravensbruck concentration camp. "It was under my armpit the whole time. It was something which brought me home, I think," she said in an interview for Steven Spielberg's Shoah Foundation. "And [now] it goes with me all the time, wherever I am."

Tallit

Symbolically, the Jewish prayer shawl, or tallit (plural: tallitot), represents the Divine Presence that envelops us during worship. The tzitzit, or fringes, at the four corners, call to mind the 613 mitzvot, the commandments we are reminded to keep.

For many Jews, their bar/bat mitzvah marks the first time they will put on a tallit, metaphorically embraced by the mitzvot. (Many Sephardi children begin wearing a tallit from the first time they go to synagogue, while most Orthodox men wear tallitot only after they marry.) Previously, tallitot were worn only by men, but women have increasingly taken on the tradition, and most egalitarian synagogues require all bnai mitzvah to wear one on the bimah.

No longer limited to the customary blue- and black-striped varieties, tallitot are available in a wealth of designs, and can be ordered from Judaica stores, online, or even custom-made by artisans. For more information on tallitot, consult *The First Jewish Catalogue,* edited by Richard Siegel, Michael Strassfeld, and Sharon Strassfeld.

FROM GENERATION TO GENERATION

Hy Zelkowitz wore his father's tallit the year he said Kaddish for him, reliving each day the feeling he had when he was nine or ten, enveloped by his father's tallit-covered arm at Yom Kippur services. After the mourning period was over, he bought a new tallit for himself, but to make the first tzitzit—the fringe that is touched to the Torah, then kissed—he unknotted the tzitzit from his father's old prayer shawl and wove it into his own. A family tradition was born: Strands of his father's tzitzit have since become part of the tallitot of several extended family members. His wife embroidered cranes, a Korean motif, into the mantle of their daughter's bat mitzvah tallit, in tribute to her Korean birth, and wove some of his father's tzitzit in with her new ones. "The memory of my father continues to weave through the generations of my family," Zelkowitz noted.

Kippah

This small head covering (plural: kippot; Yiddish: yarmulke) is worn as a sign of reverence in God's presence "around and above," as Maimonides said. Traditional Orthodox men and boys typically wear kippot at all times; other Jews may put on kippot in the synagogue and when engaged in prayer and religious rituals, like reciting Kiddush or attending a wedding. Though kippot were originally meant for men, we've seen them on more and more women in liberal congregations.

Many families provide kippot at the service. If you decide to do so, find out how many you'll need for your invited guests and the regular congregation, and whether you will need to have kippot for the women as well as the men. They are usually ordered by the dozen, and can be inscribed with the bar/bat mitzvah's name and date, either in Hebrew, English, or both. Standard kippot are satin, but you will find them available in a wide range of other fabrics and designs at Judaica and synagogue stores and online, and some stores will make custom-sewn kippot from a special fabric you have purchased. We've even seen handsome hand-crocheted kippot made by grandmoms and kids, too.

MAKE IT A MITZVAH *Purchase handcrafted kippot by needy artisans through Myriam's Dream (lskantor@snet.net), which provides meaningful work for our elderly around the world, or through www.kulanu.org, an organization that assists "lost and dispersed remnants of the Jewish people." Their kippot sales help support the Abayudaya (Ugandan Jews) and the Benei Menashe (Jews of northeast India, near Burma). For a beautifully embroidered bag to hold your first tallit, contact the North American Conference on Ethiopian Jewry at www.NACOEJ.org. Made by Ethiopian Jews, the bags benefit this grass-roots organization that helps desperately poor Jews survive in Ethiopia, assists them in reaching Israel, and aids in their absorption into Israeli society.*

Other Ritual Items

When visiting Judaica stores to purchase tallitot and kippot, consider buying your child a special Jewish ritual object that he or she will use for the first time on the big day—and for a lifetime afterward. One father, an antiques dealer, found an exquisite eighteenth century *yad*, the pointer used in reading the Torah, on a buying trip to England. His son shared it with his siblings at their bnai mitzvah, and passed it on to his own children.

OTHER SYNAGOGUE-RELATED MATTERS

Decorating the Bimah

It is customary for families to decorate the bimah, the area where the Torah is read, with tasteful arrangements of fresh flowers or greens. Sometimes these flowers can be recycled for use at the reception. (For information on floral arrangements, see chapter 9, "Flowers and Centerpieces.") Remember that any items for the synagogue, including flowers, program books, kippot, and so on, should be delivered by Friday afternoon.

MAKE IT A MITZVAH *As an alternative to the flowers—or in addition to them—some synagogues require that celebrants decorate with "bimah baskets" filled with food or toys to be given away to the needy, either through the synagogue or a Jewish service organization.*

Shopping for Attire

For some of our fathers and grandfathers, their bnai mitzvah marked the day they traded in their knickers for a first pair of long pants; for girls, it was the time to "change from bobby-socks to stockings." Gone now are the ubiquitous jeans: She is achingly beautiful in a real dress and earrings; how handsome and grown-up he looks in his first suit.

FROM GENERATION TO GENERATION

Some parents choose to give their child a special piece of family jewelry they have been saving for that day, such as a mother's gold locket or a grandfather's watch.

Shopping for clothes for the bar/bat mitzvah and the rest of the family is a treasured moment, and you will want to savor it. Although you'll need to leave yourself enough time, don't purchase clothes or shoes for the children too far in advance—you may find they have already outgrown them come the day of the event. Some stores may allow you to order an item, like a suit, far in advance, but to hold off on altering it until shortly before you will need it.

MAKE IT A MITZVAH *Because celebratory clothes are so expensive, and outgrown so quickly, they should be given a second life at another simcha. Create a committee at your synagogue to collect outgrown dressy suits, shirts, dresses, and shoes that are in good condition and send them to needy children participating in bar/bat mitzvah twinning programs with American kids.*

BAR/BAT MITZVAH CUSTOMS
AT THE SYNAGOGUE

Echoing the abiding themes of the bar/bat mitzvah traditions, synagogue customs add a special richness to the service for adults and children alike.

To represent the sweetness of Torah, many congregants traditionally toss nuts and candies (only soft and well-wrapped ones—we don't want chocolate smears on that new suit jacket) at the bar/bat mitzvah child after the service; some congregations throw rose petals at the bat mitzvah girls. Asking younger siblings and cousins to pass out the candies is a perfect way to include them in the service. Rabbis in some Sephardi synagogues traditionally compose a special liturgical poem for each boy, to be sung at his bar mitzvah. And similar to the Ashkenazi chair dance at celebrations (see the description in chapter 11, "Tradition!") in Morocco, the bar mitzvah boy was triumphantly carried, seated in a chair, through the streets to his home after the service.

FROM GENERATION TO GENERATION

At the Torah service, there is a beautiful, relatively new custom of passing the sacred scrolls—literally—from generation to generation: The grandparents hand it to the parents, who pass it on to their children. In some synagogues at bar/bat mitzvah services, the Torah is bound with a wimple, a cloth that incorporates some of the baby blanket originally used for the brit or the baby-naming. Often the wimple is sewn together by a grandparent.

PART TWO

THE
FESTIVITIES

Abraham hastened into the tent to Sarah, and said, "Quick, three
measures of choice flour! Knead and make cakes!" Then Abraham
ran to the herd, took a calf, tender and choice . . .
—GENESIS 18: 5–6

When Abraham learned, at the age of one

hundred, that he was to become the father of the Jewish people, he rushed

with Sarah to put together a feast for the strangers who brought him the news.

It's a story as old as time and as new as tomorrow's bar or bat mitzvah:

Whether it's with a glass of schnapps or a lavish hotel reception, we express

our gratitude for our good fortune in the simcha we share with others.

Yes, putting together a memorable bar or bat mitzvah is intimidating, but

the stories we share here—and the practical details to go with them—will de-

mystify the process and make it easier for you to create your own simcha story.

Hosting a bar or bat mitzvah is unlike other entertaining—it's a unique

party in many ways. First, you will typically have quite some time to plan and

prepare for it; some families even begin scouting locations and checking out

bands long before the bar mitzvah date is set. By planning wisely, you really *will*

have ample time to incorporate many creative ideas to enrich your celebration,

whether you implement them yourself or work with a party professional.

And it differs from the average multigenerational party: Here the honoree—and a substantial contingent of the guests—are teenagers. So you'll want to consider whether to have a menu, entertainment, and a decor that will please everyone, or a separate room or food for adults and children.

This is more than a milestone, or special birthday party: It's a celebration of the culture as well as the child. Both the how-to information, the vignettes, and the festive parties we describe, ranging from simple do-it-yourself to elegant gala, all mark this joyous coming-of-age in a Jewish context. They embody Jewish values and celebrate Jewish ideals. Themes based on social projects and "Make It a Mitzvah" ideas are woven seamlessly into the celebration. In the "From Generation to Generation" sidebars, we emphasize the importance of family and cultural traditions. Using a family collection of china teacups or homegrown flowers to accent a table, giving Great-grandma's strudel recipe to the caterer, or having Dad sing the child's favorite song of long ago at candlelighting time all bring not only a sense of continuity to the celebration, but also make it a more personal, more authentically shared experience.

And we encourage you to borrow from the wealth of Jewish imagery, the treasury of cultural traditions: biblical symbols (the sun, the moon, and stars; the dove and the rainbow); the cycle of holidays and rhythm of the seasons, bringing the food and flowers of the harvest and the spring; the *Gematria* (the Jewish mystical science of numbers); the colors suggested by an Israeli landscape or flag. Let your child's Torah or Haftarah portion inspire an invitation or a centerpiece. To get you started, we've included many ideas, stories, and tidbits from Jewish history and lore in the pages that follow.

Of course, balance is also a fundamental Jewish value. And this is a celebration, after all. For most people, the festivities will mean a harmonious blend of Judaic and contemporary culture. Ultimately, each family decides where that balancing point lies for them.

But all too often, out of balance means a bar/bat mitzvah that is woefully at odds with the basic values of Jewish culture. We wince at some of the overblown bar and bat mitzvah themes we've heard of—perhaps the most egregious example being the Los Angeles bat mitzvah with a stripper theme reported in the Winter 2000 issue of *Lilith* magazine.

FINDING A MOTIF

We've found that the right motif can certainly enhance a celebration and make planning easier by tying together the various celebration elements, like food, decor, and entertainment, with an organizing thread. The motif may reflect a special interest of the child and/or the family. In Julia's story, "In a Butterfly Garden," flowers are not only center-pieces for the table, they figure prominently in the choice of location and decor, food, entertainment, and her mitzvah project.

Or a motif may have a Jewish theme. A Torah portion about the Tower of Babel might suggest a melting-pot menu and a whimsical centerpiece combining flowers with words and letters from many nations. If the Noah portion of the Torah is read at the service, the child's *dvar* might be about Noah entrusted to save the species of the earth, and our own responsibility to protect endangered species. This in turn might lead to a zoo location for the party, or working with an animal theme for the decor (graphically stylized batik animal print tablecloths, for example). The mitzvah project might be "adopting" an endangered species or another project involving endangered animals, or purchasing stuffed animals for children's shelters or hospitals.

Anna Schnur-Fishman wasn't exactly sure what the "theme" of her bat mitzvah should be. "Something," she said, "that hinted at the young woman I was becoming and that helped me see who I was." When three of her four grandparents died within five weeks of one another, her mom suggested that the theme had found her, and it was loss. Visiting Greenwood House, a nearby nursing home, every Shabbos for the previous year, she had established real friendships with Dora, Tilly, Estelle, and many other residents. One day she realized that she wanted to have her bat mitzvah there; then, as she explained in her *dvar Torah*, "In some fashion, I thought my grandparents could come to my bat mitzvah." A resident had told her, "Anna, God gives us memories so we can smell roses in December." In gratitude to the senior citizens who had given her so much, Anna invited them to the auditorium adjacent to the home's large synagogue for a buffet lunch, singing, dancing, and laughing—and creating a wealth of beautiful new memories.

The Norry family decided on a "Streets of Jerusalem" theme that centered on the arty Ben Yehuda district. They chose a sabra menu of falafel, Middle Eastern salads, grape leaves, and other casual foods against a backdrop of outdoor café tables, simulated winding streets, and strolling musicians. As event planners, we have expanded on that theme for other parties, bringing to life Jewish neighborhoods from around the world: rue des Rosiers in Paris; Orchard Street in New York; Whitechapel in London; and the Ghetto Vecchio in Venice.

MAKING IT SPECIAL

For Jews, the joyous songs at a Sabbath dinner or the shimmering crystal and heirloom recipes for the Passover table are the grace notes that, though not commanded, make our experience of the commandments richer and more meaningful. We are not required to have desert flowers blooming in sand-filled clay pots inspired by a Torah portion from Exodus, or a luscious children's drink at a bar/bat mitzvah; but these special extra touches, the *hiddur mitzvah* so intrinsic to Judaism, make this Jewish milestone more beautiful, honoring it and enhancing our enjoyment of it.

We hope that the grace notes that follow make your bar/bat mitzvah celebration all that you envision. And many translate to other festivities as well, so we expect these pages to become well thumbed as you plan lots of joyous occasions, both Jewish and secular, in the years to come.

Now, let the festivities begin!

PLANNING THE FESTIVITIES

*She was the one becoming a Bat Mitzvah and the moment was
certainly hers. But I am a Jewish mother. If the moment was hers,
the obligation to create the moment was mine.
If she was the jewel, my job was to provide the setting.*
—JUDITH SILLS, *TREES OF STRIFE*

HOW TO USE THIS BOOK TO PLAN YOUR PARTY

The chapters that follow are designed to help readers at all stages of preparation for the reception: those at the percolating period at the outset and families who are well along in the process, but looking for fresh ideas and help with details; those who have never planned a large celebration before and those who have already hosted one bar/bat mitzvah and want to do the next one differently; do-it-yourselfers and those working with party planners. In addition to the detailed practical information on the elements of bar/bat mitzvah receptions in the chapters that follow, you'll find interspersed stories of celebrations that illustrate how all of these elements can come together and capture the magic of the occasion.

To put together the simcha that is right for your family, feel free to combine and expand ideas from the various chapters and celebration stories to create your own unique simcha, or to host one of the parties exactly as described from start to finish. We've included parties and ideas to suit all budgets and suggestions to suit every personality.

While you may want to skip over nonapplicable sections (for example, ignoring information on band and DJ contracts if you are not having music), we encourage you to read through all the interspersed bar and bat mitzvah stories that appear throughout the book; a bat mitzvah family, for example, may find the perfect idea for candlelighting, menus, or the wording on an invitation in one of the stories about a bar mitzvah.

THE FIRST STEP: BRAINSTORMING

Wouldn't it be nice if choosing a bar/bat mitzvah celebration were like flipping through a catalog until you happen on one you fancy? But deciding what you want to include is a process, so let's begin with brainstorming to start you on that road. This is an essential step whether you are going solo or working with a party planner.

The bar/bat mitzvah child. What is your child like? What are his/her interests? Favorite colors? Describe the celebrant as if speaking to someone who has never met him or her. Think about your family background and traditions too.

Guest list. What kind of guest list do you need to accommodate? First cousins? Second cousins? Do you feel all the guests should know the child well? How do you envision the interaction among the generations? Will there be a separate area for the kids? How will the adults react to the kids' music, if any?

Location. What type of space do you prefer? Indoors or outside? Your own home, or another special place you are attached to, like your synagogue or country club? Are you looking for something out of the ordinary or an event that's similar to what is usually done in your community? Would you prefer one large or several smaller reception areas (to accommodate special kids' activities, for instance)? Is evening or daytime better for you?

Style. Think of bar/bat mitzvahs and other parties that your family has attended and really liked or disliked. What was it that turned you on or off? What is your style preference: Formal? Informal? A combination of both?

Food. What are your favorite restaurants and types of foods? What are your family's favorite recipes? Are there any food restrictions? Is a sit-down meal with waiter service essential? Do you like or dislike buffet lines? Are hors d'oeuvre or desserts more important than the main course?

Other priorities. What is most important to you at the celebration? Does one element of party planning take precedence over another? Is food most important, or music? Is it a priority that kids have a great time with the entertainment? That adults can converse easily?

Judaism. What is the *parshah*/Haftarah about? Does the bar/bat mitzvah date coincide with a special day on the Jewish calendar, like Rosh Hodesh, a holiday, or a special month? What parts of Judaism are most important to you that you want to incorporate in your celebration? Are there family traditions that you would like to include?

Special family connections. Who will be attending your celebration? A Syrian grandmother who delights in turning out trays of baklava? An uncle who is a gifted storyteller? A family friend who teaches folk dancing?

A FEW WORDS ON "KIDS-ONLY" PARTIES

Some families choose to host a kids-only party, in addition to an extended Kiddush or another larger family celebration, for a variety of reasons. The family may feel that the intimacy of the celebration would be lost if too many kids are invited, or that certain kinds of entertainment would be more appropriate to a special milestone birthday party than to this coming-of-age celebration. Or the child may want to include more friends and young cousins than the space or budget can accommodate.

Kids-only events that we've seen include parties featuring dancing or hired entertainers like magicians; outings to ballgames; skating, pool, and rock-climbing parties; a party in a ceramics studio; and a cooking party at a restaurant. One bat mitzvah girl made her party into a wonderful mitzvah project: Accompanied by great music on her boom box, she and her friends cleaned up an historic synagogue that was in a state of serious disrepair.

Some families host the kids' party in the evening of, or on the day following, the bar or bat mitzvah. Others choose to hold the kids' party immediately following the service while all the child's friends are present (this can simplify making arrangements for the children's transportation), followed by an evening celebration for close family and friends. Some host two separate but simultaneous events in one location: the children in one area, the adults in another. And families may decide to host a "secular" thirteenth birthday party at a time completely separate from the bar or bat mitzvah.

When planning a kids-only event, keep in mind that the weekend is a long one, and that your child has been under a lot of pressure and may be tense. Never underestimate the fatigue factor. You know your child better than anyone else and are best able to decide when to schedule this kind of party. We have observed kids so utterly exhausted at Saturday-night parties that they wanted to leave their own party and head straight for bed. At a children's party scheduled right after the service, the bat mitzvah girl couldn't transition easily from prayer to partying; suddenly the music she had carefully chosen seemed painfully loud, and she collapsed into tears.

While bar/bat mitzvah parties specifically geared to children are really outside the scope of this book, you'll find many ideas for food, entertainment, decorating, and more to help you plan a kids-only event in the chapters that follow.

BUDGET

Begin to figure out a realistic budget that feels comfortable for you to cover all the costs of the celebration: invitations, the festivities (including location, food, flowers, servers, etc.), photos and videography, and charitable contributions. While it is impossible to figure exactly what your costs will be, keep track of expenditures in relation to your budget so that you don't go overboard in one area without trimming another. Set up payment schedules that will work for you. We've included several sample budgets in chapter 15, and you'll find many budget-conscious options in the sections titled "When You Need Less-Expensive Choices."

GETTING ORGANIZED

Guests

Prepare a **master guest list** for addresses, RSVPs, accommodations, and thank-yous. Assembling the correct addresses early on and setting up a good retrieval system will help organize you from start to finish.

Many synagogues encourage children to invite all the kids in their bnai mitzvah class to their celebration. The bar/bat mitzvah is about joining **the community**, and these kids have been part of their community throughout the journey. On the other hand, if you cannot invite all of your guests to every event you have planned (for example, inviting some only to the service and Kiddush, but not to the special luncheon afterward), take care to handle this in a gracious way to avoid hurting their feelings.

Address the **special needs** of your guests: accessibility for the handicapped and elderly, baby-sitting for very young children, and distance from the synagogue for the Sabbath-observant.

If you are planning to have the celebration someplace other than the synagogue or not directly after the service, will you have to provide **transportation**, especially for the children invited? If the event is held in the evening or on Sunday, it will be most difficult for those who live an hour or so away (not the out-of-town guests staying locally) to return for the party. If your synagogue is amenable, consider Havdalah services with dinner afterward.

Will you be having **out-of-towners**, and if so, what kind of arrangements should be made for their accommodations—hotel, or guest rooms at friends' homes? If you are having weekend out-of-town guests, will you provide dinner on Friday evening or Sunday brunch? Perhaps your child's grandparents, aunt, uncle, or godparents might host such events. Will you have "goodie" bags for weekend guests or gifts for hosts/friends who open their homes to your weekend guests? A hospitality suite at a hotel for breakfast or coffee before services?

Making Lists

Buy a special notebook and create a file system for invoices and other paperwork early on. Update budget figures, and keep all receipts and contracts together. Break down what you need to do, using each chapter as a guide. Make lists monthly, until six months before the party, then weekly, and finally, the month before, semiweekly. Cross off tasks as you accomplish them, and revise constantly.

Timelines

Set up a **long-term preparation timeline**. Everyone's party planning path will be different: Some people will book a bandleader three years in advance, others just three months before. Nevertheless, we've included a long-term preparation timeline from Daniel and Rebecca's bnai mitzvah in chapter 15 to guide you in assembling yours—see page 271.

You'll also need to write up a **timeline for the day of the celebration,** noting each activity that will take place: when guests should be called to dinner, when the band will strike up the hora, when coffee and dessert should be brought out, and so on. Because bar/bat mitzvahs are intergenerational parties, you may find you will have more than one activity scheduled for the same time. For example, there may be special entertainment for the kids while adults are still eating. Before orchestrating an element, take the time to visualize where your guests will be: Will the kids be in another room when you want to have the Havdalah service? Where will the guests be when the storyteller begins to spin her tales? You'll find a sample party timeline based on Daniel and Rebecca's bnai mitzvah in chapter 15.

Appoint Someone in Charge the Day of the Event

At the first bar mitzvah we catered, while we were serving the hors d'oeuvre during the stand-up cocktail hour preceding dinner, the DJ suddenly called out "take your seats." Caught completely unawares, we scrambled to butler the remaining hors d'oeuvre to the individual tables. Whether it's you, a party planner, or a friend you've designated, someone should take charge of coordinating the event. You will probably need to consult with everyone involved (caterer, bandleader, etc.) before finalizing your plans. Be sure to give each of them a copy of the timeline highlighting their role (include on it the date, the time, and the address of the event, as well as your contact information). Depending on how elaborate the event is, you may want to schedule a conference call or a group meeting so that everyone is on the same page.

Final Countdown

About one to two weeks prior to the party, get a final guest count. You will need the final numbers for your caterer, for your seating chart (if you are having one), and for any special purchases, like party favors, that you may be making. If necessary, contact any stragglers who have neglected to send in their RSVPs. Confirm all arrangements with suppliers, party professionals, and any friends or relatives who have volunteered to help. Then you're good to go.

GETTING HELP (FLORISTS, CATERERS, ENTERTAINERS, AND MORE)

We've known families who have prepared each morsel of food from scratch and personally arranged the centerpieces, and others who left every detail to an experienced party planner. But most families fall somewhere in between, creating their celebration with help from one or more party professionals like caterers, florists, or bandleaders, or from creative friends.

Planning a bar/bat mitzvah can be overwhelming, so avoid going solo. Use your synagogue and/or your child's bar/bat mitzvah class as a resource. If you are a single parent, consider asking a good friend or relative to help with the planning and preparations. Or trade off favors with another bar/bat mitzvah parent—each doing the other's food and/or flowers, for example.

If you will be hiring outside help, keep the following general guidelines in mind. Consult appropriate chapters for more detailed information on florists, caterers, and entertainers. Party planners, not covered elsewhere, are discussed later in the following section.

- Ask exactly what services the party professionals provide, and whether their expertise extends to other areas as well. A full-service caterer will generally handle renting tableware and may provide centerpieces and displays, and some may function as party planners. Full-service florists often help with decor; and many DJs bring special lighting equipment. In addition, party professionals are usually a valuable source of recommendations for other contractors and suppliers.
- Good party professionals are collaborators, expertly implementing your ideas so that the celebration reflects your vision and sense of style. Let them know to what degree you want to be a part of the decision making—or if you'd prefer to leave most of it in their hands. Read the relevant chapters on celebration elements here

before you meet with them to help crystallize your ideas and communicate them more effectively. The more specific you are about your likes and dislikes, the more they can respond to your personal needs and suggestions.

- Ask to see pictures of their work. If you are interested in something other than their standard service, find out what creative alternatives they offer, and how flexible and open to suggestions they will be. Don't be afraid to ask questions; a good party professional will walk you through anything you don't understand.

- Be an information source: Tell those you've hired about your family and broaden their horizons to include all things Jewish. If they are unfamiliar with some of the many wonderful Jewish customs, traditions, and recipes, share your knowledge and your enthusiasm. Tell them about the Torah portion: Florists or caterers may have special props they can include in their displays or menu items that would complement it (e.g., Jacob's lentils, shepherds' cheeses, and pomegranate sorbets). Print out articles on dishes from your cultural heritage or identify favorite family recipes. Caterers want to hear about new food ideas (a great dish you ate at a restaurant, a recipe from your family file) and florists/decorators love a decor challenge, like the mitzvah flower centerpieces discussed in "Planning Your Flowers Around a Mitzvah" (page 124). Share your music traditions with the bandleader or DJ.

- Let the party professional know about special concerns. Identify guests who will be eating special meals so that they are not served inappropriately. If the family is going through a divorce, mention it to the bandleader or DJ so that uncomfortable situations involving the bill or calling the family up all together during candle-lighting might be avoided.

- Communicate your timeline clearly. You may not want a candlelighting ceremony at the beginning of the reception; perhaps you want to avoid a rushed coffee service and would prefer that cups and candy dishes not be placed on the table before the dessert is served.

- Make sure all payment arrangements—contracts, purchase orders, and so on—are in writing. It's important to save even simple receipts. Be clear about which expenditures require your approval.

Working with a Professional Party Planner

While the degree of their involvement will vary according to your agreement, in general, party planners help plan and manage the celebration, supervise suppliers, and make creative suggestions. Their most valuable asset may be their organizing skills: establishing timelines, working with your budget, and tracking down the best suppliers and resources. They can even save you money by putting the various services you will need out to bid and counseling you on whom to hire. In short, they shoulder many of the planning responsibilities, making the occasion less stressful for the whole family. Because the planner will be so intimately involved with your celebration, it is especially important that you feel comfortable working with him or her. Planners not only represent you, but also make decisions for you: Make sure that they will work to implement your vision—not their own.

Find a party planner through your synagogue network, through personal recommendations from friends, your caterer, the coordinator at the location you are renting, or at bar/bat mitzvah fairs. Try to visit a party he or she has supervised, and, if possible, check references both from other hosts and party professionals with whom he or she has worked.

Such hands-on, personal work does not come cheap. Planners may charge an hourly fee, a straight fee, a commission based on the total costs of the party, or a combination of these charges (try to set a cap, if possible). Be sure to get a written contractual agreement delineating all fees charged, exactly what services are provided (including on-site staff at the party, and their pay schedule/overtime), and the working timeline.

GROUND RULES TO KEEP YOU ON COURSE

Let's not dwell on the installation of a ladder for the fiddler, who along with his Klezmer group, was to be sitting on the roof of our home to play for guests (because if you could have your own fiddler on the roof for the Bat Mitzvah, wouldn't you?). Suffice it to say that somewhere along the way, I had strayed from understated.
—JUDITH SILLS, TREES OF STRIFE

- Yes, homemade is wonderful, but definitely not worth the trouble if it means you'll be too stressed out to truly enjoy your child's bar/bat mitzvah. There's no need to make everything yourself; you can always supplement home-prepared with store-bought items. Bake your own cookies, but purchase the cake; make up bouquets for the tables, but order a large arrangement for the buffet.

- Don't lose sight of the whole as you are planning the parts, obsessing over The Perfect Color of the napkins and other manifestations of the "Bar Mitzvah Crazies." If the panic attacks have started, you know you need to change course! During the last month or six weeks particularly, assess realistically what you can and can't accomplish, and either delegate it to someone else or let it go (Do you really *need* those special candies?). Or consider hiring a person to help coordinate just for two days (day before, day of). Remember to set aside some time for yourself to de-stress, to be available for your child, to make an emergency run to the caterer with your extra key.
- Choose wisely what you can accomplish, and simplify (especially good advice for do-it-yourselfers). Remember the Yiddish proverb: "Before you start up a ladder, count the rungs."

TWINS IN A SUKKAH: DANIEL AND REBECCA'S
AUTUMN BNAI MITZVAH

The twins. Ever since they could remember, that's what everyone called them, as if they were a pair, like peanut butter and jelly. Or Harry Potter and Hermione.

It wasn't that they didn't get along. They were just different. Daniel and his friends were always hiking in the woods, following trail blazes and streams; Rebecca was a member of the swim team. She wanted a party with dancing; he was still shy around girls.

How could they possibly agree on one bar/bat mitzvah celebration that would please both of them? To top it off, a boy in their class had already been given the Shabbat date right after their birthday. If all three had to share the date, none would have a real moment in the sun.

When the family met with the rabbi, he listened to the kids, then stared at the calendar awhile. "Yes, I think it will work out just perfectly."

This year, Monday of that week was not only Columbus Day, he said, but also Hoshana Rabbah, the last of the intermediate days of Sukkot. There was a Torah reading, yes, but none of the restrictions they'd have at the synagogue on Shabbat or the holy days of Sukkot. Weather permitting, the kids could do something fun outdoors during the day *and* dance to a band inside too. And people love to take off Columbus Day to spend time in New England: Fall foliage bursts into peak color then, a leaf-peeper's showy paradise.

"There's a special commandment in the Torah to have fun on Sukkot: 'You shall rejoice in your festival . . . and you shall have nothing but joy' [Deuteronomy 16:13–15]. I'm sure you'll come up with some great ideas." The rabbi smiled.

And after surfing the Web, a few heated discussions, and several e-mails back and forth with the rabbi, they did.

At the service, both kids talked about their mitzvah projects. Daniel joked that "everyone who knows how much I love being a twin will be surprised that I actually chose to have another one." Then he described his involvement with an AMIT project that pairs an American kid with a needy one in Israel; with

Daniel's contribution, his Israeli "twin" could have a real bar mitzvah celebration. (For more on twinning projects, see page 46.) Daniel had been corresponding with his "brother," and hoped to visit him when his family traveled to Israel in a couple of years.

For her project, Rebecca was volunteering at a pet shelter. An ardent animal lover, she had set up "Rebecca's Gleaning Areas" in the temple party space where she was collecting products for dogs and cats—food, little blankets, toys—to take to the shelter.

When they first asked the rabbi about the music at the service, he demurred. But he had been intrigued by recent music-based outreach efforts in all the denominations. And this wasn't a regular holiday service, so there would be fewer congregants than usual, and it *was* a day for rejoicing. Besides, though it was unusual, it was perfectly permissible under Jewish law . . .

So that's how it happened that when the congregants circled the bimah seven times, as required on this holiday, they were accompanied by the twins' cousins' band, playing one of Rabbi Shlomo Carlebach's melodies. The traditional beating of the willow branches—symbolic of the leaves falling in the brisk autumn air, as well as us shaking off our sins—was a blast for the teens as they moved to the beat of the bongo drums. And the service, the music, everything was captured on videotape, since the usual prohibitions against cameras don't apply on Hoshana Rabbah.

The synagogue party space looked out through sliding glass doors to red maple trees and a pine forest beyond. It was here that the congregation built the communal sukkah, using the glass doors as a fourth wall. The trellis roof, threaded with fresh spruce boughs and bayberry branches, was open here and there to the autumn sky. Taking advantage of the fine weather, the caterers set up for hors d'oeuvre and drinks there, with fall vegetable topiaries adding whimsy to the displays.

Seasonal pomegranate martinis awaited thirsty adults, and kids sipped fresh-pressed apple and pear ciders. On Hoshana Rabbah, believed to be the day God's judgment is sealed for the year, kreplach (Jewish ravioli) are traditional fare because they symbolize both our hidden fate and God's merciful decision to cover up our sins. The family, food lovers all, expanded the concept to embrace dumplings and other filled dainties from around the world. So besides Aunt Sarah's recipe for fried potato kreplach with sautéed onions, there were chicken wontons, mushroom tortellini, and little empanadas.

The floral designer had transformed the party room: Using latticework and bamboo poles, she created a magical indoor sukkah. The trellis was entwined with seasonal greens, and hung with Indian corn, clusters of black grapes, and glossy black eggplants, interspersed with bunches of dusty rose dried hydrangeas and pomegranates for color. More greens twirled around the arms of the chandeliers, so that they appeared to disappear into the leafy canopy above. The sliding glass doors remained open, bringing the scent of autumn in on the warm breeze.

The tables were set with sage-green textured cloths to match the synagogue's chairs, and for centerpieces there were straw baskets brimming with fragrant quinces, sumac berries, and cascades of champagne grapes, accented with burgundy and yellow roses and more dried hydrangeas.

Like most Jewish holidays, this one is celebrated with a special festive meal. The adults were served the last of the season's heirloom tomatoes, and a choice of pistachio-crusted halibut, French crisp-crumbed chicken, or lamb chops grilled with Mediterranean herbs. The family figured a buffet would make the most sense for the kids—not only could they choose what they wanted to eat, they'd also be moving around, mingling with one another. Because the twins both adored Asian foods, the caterer prepared an array of selections from kid-friendly to this side of exotic. There were sushi, beef and chicken satés, stir-fries, and noodle dishes.

The bandleader, a music teacher from the local high school, knew instinctively when the kids needed a clever game to get the boys on their feet and dancing. When it came time for the hora, the dance floor was jam-packed, so he orchestrated the hora circle out through the glass doors into the sukkah, and back again. By that time, the two chairs that had been festooned with greens were brought out, and Daniel and Rebecca whooped and laughed as their cousins lifted them up in the Ashkenazi chair dance. Rebecca's friends from the swim team had never seen the custom before, but thought it was a great hoot. They grabbed the chair and sat Rebecca in it again, parading her from one side of the room to the other.

The horse-drawn wagons had arrived, so plain oversize T-shirts were handed out to protect dressy clothes, and the kids went off on hayrides through the nearby fields. Meanwhile, the band turned its attention to the adult guests, playing a medley of fast and slow oldies, even a couple of nostalgic favorites for the grandparents.

When the kids returned, they dipped lady apples into warm caramel, and then feasted on the twin bar and bat mitzvah cakes that had been set out in the sukkah.

The guests left, and the family sat and relaxed in the sukkah surrounded by a few relatives and their closest friends. When sundown came, they lit candles in scooped-out green squashes, and recited the prayer inviting the *Ushpizin*, the invisible Sukkot guests, Abraham and Sarah, and all the other fathers and mothers of the Jewish people to share their blessings and join them for a final nosh before they went home.

6

INVITATIONS AND PHOTOGRAPHY

An invitation to a bar or bat mitzvah is a request to take part in one of the most important days in the family's life. This chapter is about sharing the moment and preserving the memories. We begin by welcoming your guests to the celebration, then turn to photography and videography.

THE INVITATION

In Meknes, Morocco, where he grew up in a family of forty-two generations of rabbis, invitations to Rabbi Joshua Toledano's weeklong bar mitzvah celebration were hand-delivered to the guests' doors. "Mailing them would have been too impersonal," he recalled.

Today we rely on the postal service, but we still want to extend the same warm welcome with our invitations. The invitation not only sets the tone of the celebration for our guests, it also links the ceremony with the reception. Though it may lengthen the process, encourage your child to participate in choosing the invitation, and even designing it.

Think about what message you wish to convey with the invitation—formal, elegantly simple, religious, fun, artistic. Take time to browse at your local stationery store for a wide range of ideas including print styles, paper stock, color, designs, size (oversize, smaller, square, folded), and wording. Decide if you want to splurge on one you've seen—that classic navy-and-white oversize block-print card with raised border and a Star of David; the handpainted irises with script in lavender ink—or simply take ideas away with you. Beautiful custom-designed invitations make a lovely memento when framed, but they can get wildly expensive. We've included many handsome, less costly options, including creating your own, in the pages that follow.

Always order at least ten extra invitations for the guests you decide to add on to your original list, as well as keepsake copies for your family. You will also need additional envelopes in case errors in addressing are made.

Allow plenty of time for decisions, printing, and addressing. You should mail out invitations about six weeks in advance. Note: If the bar/bat mitzvah is scheduled for a holiday or you are inviting guests from out of town, it's a good idea to phone these guests well ahead of time, so that they can make plans accordingly.

Purchasing an Invitation

READY-MADE INVITATIONS, PAPERS, AND CARD STOCK

In addition to made-to-order invitations, many stationery stores sell ready-made invitations on heavy card stock or lovely paper that can be customized. An insert can be printed (on your home desktop or by the store) that attaches to the invitation with ribbon or raffia, or that folds inside it. Sometimes just a change in ink color on a plain invitation, like chocolate on ivory stock, can be enough to create a special look.

Card stock and papers are available in myriad colors, textures, and styles, including parchment, Japanese-style, marbleized, handmade, and other unusual papers. You may find papers with unique designs and special borders that relate to the Torah portion or party motif or you could choose to have something custom designed that is unavailable on commercial paper.

LETTERING

Choices range from the most formal raised lettering, engraved or embossed, to the less-expensive thermography (chemically raised printing), standard flat, and computer printing. All are available at stationery and office supply stores, or discounted through Internet outlets. You can also have a master invitation handlettered (including Hebrew letters, if you would like) or written by a calligrapher, then copied on a laser printer. Very simple and elegant in black and ecru, this is a lovely reminder of the handlettered words of the Torah.

Creating or Customizing Your Own Invitations

GUIDELINES FOR PRINTING
(AT HOME OR AT A COPY SHOP)

- Prepare a master copy, either computer designed on your desktop or handlettered, and print it on good quality paper using a laser color printer. For more sophisticated printing, use "print-shop" software and your own handsome papers or purchase invitation kits that contain software plus fine card stock or paper.
- Don't underestimate the time you will need—complex jobs take a long time to print out. Do test runs on inexpensive paper; it may take several trials to achieve the look you want.
- Be sure the paper you buy is printer-compatible. To avoid paper jams, it may be better to print on standard-size paper, then cut down to the size you want. Feed paper in one sheet at a time. Make sure the ink is completely dry before you insert the invitation in an envelope.

IDEAS FOR PERSONALIZING INVITATIONS

- Use one of the pretty flypapers available at art supply stores (they can even cut them down to size for you), and pair it with a simple invitation.
- Experiment with an interesting fold: Using your computer, print the invitation in

the center of a richly colored sheet of rag paper and fold the sides over the middle, like curtains enclosing an ark.

- Vellum, which is transparent, can dress up plain colored card stock or construction paper. Use an ink that contrasts well with the paper color, and cover with a sheet of vellum. Attach by punching two small holes on top and tying with raffia or ribbon.
- Many families personalize their invitations using their own artwork, either scanned onto their computer, or as design accents directly on the invitation (for example, light sponge painting on the corners of heavy card stock). Maddie painted a lavender scroll, and replicated the motif on both her invitation and the program at the service. Gabrielle personalized a black-and-white print of Miriam by partially highlighting her hem, her tambourine, and her bracelet in metallic gold ink. For her son Eli's invitation, Heidi printed a friend's lithograph of an eagle in black on speckled gray paper, and surrounded it with an excerpt from his Torah portion ("I bore you on Eagles' wing . . .").
- Scan photos onto your computer and add them to the design. We loved Danny's, which included a photograph of him as a toddler perched atop a haystack in France juxtaposed with one as an almost thirteen-year-old, in the same pose.
- Enclose flower petals, small pressed blooms, or confetti-like stamp-outs inside the invitation. Julia (see page 108) used an inexpensive flower press kit available in craft and toy stores, and flowers can also be quickly "pressed" in a microwave.

The Wording

Check and recheck for spelling and other errors. A common mistake is a date that doesn't correspond with the day—for example, writing Saturday, November 21, when November 21 falls on a Sunday that year.

SAMPLE WORDING FOR INVITING GUESTS
TO THE CEREMONY

Please celebrate with us [OR join our family in celebration] when our son Robbie is called to the Torah as a bar mitzvah . . .

Please share our joy as our daughter Sophie reads from the Torah about Joseph and his coat of many colors . . .

Friends and family, the journey from girl to woman is long and beautiful and deeply special. Our daughter Lily will be called to the Torah . . .

Follow this opening with the date, the time, and the place of the services, along with the parents' names. If you like, your child could do the inviting instead, and sign using his or her signature. Many families include the name of the Torah portion or an excerpt from it. You may want to include Hebrew lettering or a prayer. (This may be done professionally, or at home, using a software program or downloading Hebrew characters from the Web.) Or you may want to print a quote from a favorite poem or blessing on the cover.

SAMPLE WORDING FOR THE PARTY DESCRIPTION

Join us in the evening to celebrate at . . .

Please join us as the celebration continues at . . .

Our celebration continues at . . .

Lunch [or Dinner] and Festivities following the service at . . .

Include time, place, and date (if different from the service).

Optional Enclosures

- If you are not inviting all your guests to the reception, you will need an invitation to the service, and a separate card or note for the reception. You may also need an additional invitation if you are hosting a separate kids' party.
- A response card (with a stamped, self-addressed return envelope), specifying an RSVP date at least two weeks in advance of the occasion. There will always be stragglers and those you will have to telephone. We've noticed some people are using e-mail as a convenient way to RSVP, eliminating the expense of the stamp and the response card.
- Directions printed on an enclosure card or photocopied on a small piece of notepaper. Do check meticulously for road signs and exit numbers that may have changed recently.
- A note (included with the first mailing if you're organized enough, but it can be sent later) containing any of the following: a paragraph or two about becoming bar/bat mitzvah (especially nice for non-Jewish guests unfamiliar with the ritual,

and later this explanation can become the basis for a program at the service); information regarding charitable donations or the mitzvah project; a call for photographs to be used on a signing board or for table centerpieces; a request that a guest share stories, make a blessing or a toast, be called up for an aliyah, or receive another honor for which he or she might want to prepare; or special information about attire (for example, one host noted that since their synagogue is not air-conditioned, congregants may dress less formally).

- Tourist information (hotels, local activities, etc.) for guests arriving from out of town.
- A blank card to be used to write a note to the bar/bat mitzvah, then mailed back, and later compiled in a special book.
- A note on the bar/bat mitzvah website, if one has been created for the occasion.
- Transportation information, especially for kids: whether transportation from the synagogue to the party will be provided, and when the party will end, so parents can pick them up.

Addressing and Mailing

- If your invitations are formal, include Mr., Ms., Mrs., or other appropriate titles before the guests' names. For informal invitations, you may omit titles and simply include the guest's full (first and last) name.
- If you don't have attractive handwriting, you can print out envelopes or clear labels using a script font on your computer (practice with inexpensive envelopes first). Many stationery stores can computer-address envelopes in color fonts that resemble hand calligraphy. You might want to splurge on elegant traditional calligraphy, or ask a talented friend or relative to hand-address them. And non-ballpoint pens always seem to make any handwriting more handsome.
- Check out the special stamps available at the post office and online. Be aware that postage is higher for oversize invitations. You may also want to hand-cancel the envelopes at your local post office.

MAKE IT A MITZVAH *Choose a simpler, less-expensive invitation or create your own and use the savings to contribute to a favorite charity or add to your mitzvah project. • Extend your guest list to include a few residents from a grandparent's nursing home.*

THANK-YOU NOTES

Like the fine pens the children receive as gifts, handsome stationery can serve as an incentive to get through the task of writing thank-you notes. If you are having thank-you cards custom printed, it is often cheaper to order them when you order the invitations. Repeating the design motif or color scheme that you used in the invitation in the thank-you will connect the note to the celebration, and might even subtly convey to your child a sense of how important writing the note is. Do consider the size of the thank-you note. For a child who will write just two lines of thanks, order a smaller card: You don't want to emphasize how little he or she has written by using a large folding card or sheet of paper. If guests will be contributing to a particular charity suggested by your child, you might want to have an enclosure card preprinted in the child's words, describing the importance of the charity to him or her.

To help your child get organized, include extra columns when you prepare the master guest list so he or she can write in next to each name whether a gift was received, what the gift was, and check off when he or she sends a thank-you note. Remind your child to mention the particular gift in the note.

It's always lovely to include a photo as a memento with the note.

PHOTOGRAPHY AND VIDEOGRAPHY

Memorable photographs and videotapes eloquently link your bar/bat mitzvah from generation to generation. But preserving those moments can sometimes be a little tricky—many synagogues do not allow photography during services, and observant families cannot be photographed at celebrations that take place on the Sabbath. So some people solve the problem by arranging alternative times for shooting: the week before the ceremony or after the party, when necessary.

When you interview potential photographers and videographers, find out if they have shot other bar/bat mitzvahs, and ask to see their portfolios or sample tapes. Whether you are hiring a professional or relying on a friend or family member, you will want to talk about your options and style preferences: Do you want the photos to tell a story, photojournalism style? Do you prefer the photographer to be as unobtrusive as possible? Do you want photos in color, black and white, sepia, or a combination? An in-

FROM GENERATION TO GENERATION

Create a book of keepsake memories comprised of the invitation, copies of your program book, *dvar Torah*, parental blessings and toasts, and any other special notes you've received from guests. If you have heirloom photos of your parents' or grandparents' bnai mitzvah, include them as well. Maya created a keepsake quilt for her daughter from the fabric squares she had inserted with the invitations. Guests handsewed a special wish, or wrote one in fabric markers, then sent back their squares with their reply cards.

teresting mix of candid, portrait, and table shots? Natural light or supplemental room lighting? Traditional camera format or digital? And consider these video options: photo montages, music accompaniments, guest interviews, titles, and/or special effects.

Get to know the photographer, and make sure he or she knows you. Go over those "not-to-be-missed moments" (put them in writing), and clearly identify members of the family and other special guests you will want in shots. If possible, arrange for a walk-through to acquaint the photographer with the lighting and layout at the location.

Contract arrangements should include:

- Date and time of day (or days, if portraits are taken earlier in the week at the synagogue)
- Fees: "package" or hourly rates
- How many hours of shooting time, any hidden costs (like editing time, for videos), how many rolls of film, how many photographers and/or assistants
- Overtime and cancellation policies
- The end product: reprint and album charges, policy on who owns the negatives
- When the proofs and completed photos or video will be ready

7

THE CELEBRATION SPACE:

LOCATION

Midmorning on the third day, we caught sight of Rebecca's
tent. . . . As we came closer, it became clear that this was
less a home than a canopy, open on all sides to welcome
travelers from every direction.
—ANITA DIAMANT, *THE RED TENT*

Whether it's a community center
or a country club, a banquet hall or your backyard, for a few hours, the celebration space becomes your home, a place where you open your doors to family and friends and make them comfortable. In Judaic terms, it is perhaps even
more like a sukkah, a lovingly prepared, temporary refuge in which to share
your blessings with others, resonating with the rich traditions of your heritage.
In a very real sense, you are welcoming your guests to a sacred space.

SETTING YOUR LOCATION PRIORITIES

After reading the previous chapters, you've probably formulated a fairly good idea of the size of your guest list, as well as the date, the time of day, and the general ambience and tone of the event you want. You may also have chosen a particular caterer or type of entertainment by now. Perhaps you have additional priorities: a separate time and place for cocktails and hors d'oeuvre or the children's entertainment, a band, dancing.

The mythic Perfect Place that will accommodate all your dreams at an affordable price may exist. But just in case it doesn't, figure out areas where your family may be more flexible. Could you forgo the planned evening reception in favor of a more affordable Saturday lunch, or trim the guest list by eliminating the camp friends? Or you might decide that a beautiful room is less important than plenty of space for your guests to walk around between tables.

That said, do maintain a clear sense of what you really need and what is most important to your family. Don't fall in love with a place where you'll start off with too many limitations. As Sholom Aleichem's Tevye put it, if you bend too much, you'll break. For Janet, renting a charming neighborhood restaurant necessitated radically tailoring her son's celebration to suit the space: Painful cuts in the guest list caused family rifts, and there was no room for live music or dancing. Ultimately, she regretted her decision, and next time she chose a more appropriate location for her daughter's bat mitzvah.

LOCATION CHOICES

No place is empty of God.
—ZOHAR

When the boisterous and fun-loving Stein family hosted Ben's late-June bar mitzvah reception at an overnight camp, the unconventional location turned out to be "a hoot and a half," as mother Susan put it. The celebration began with a morning service in their suburban synagogue, followed by a lovely but simple oneg. A few hours later, during a torrential downpour, guests piled into buses and headed a short drive away for Camp Saginaw, arriving in time for supper in the dining hall and activities in the old wooden gym—DJ and all. The adults met in the rec hall to play games, revisiting old favorites like "What's My Line"—no one could guess that Susan's old college friend was a rabbi! Then all the generations gathered together just before lights out for a "Kumbayah" moment, singing and munching on s'mores around an imaginary campfire.

We always suggest beginning the search with a place that has special meaning for your family. For some clients, that may mean the synagogue they attend or their own home. Others follow a personal connection to less-traditional locations. Sara's mitzvah project entailed helping out at a stable that provided riding-therapy sessions to young children. Her family rented the renovated barn there for her fall bat mitzvah luncheon. Another client, the project manager for Philadelphia's Visitors' Center, booked that space for his son's celebration. All eight great-grandparents of the twins, Ricky and Rachel, had passed through Ellis Island, the sweet end to a horrific journey that began during the pogroms in eastern Europe. The family celebrated their bnai mitzvah on a moonlit chartered boat ride around Ellis Island and the Statue of Liberty.

If you have a party planner or have already decided on a caterer, ask her for ideas—she is a valuable resource. Also, ask other parents in your child's bar/bat mitzvah class—it may jump-start a sharing of information and support. Bear in mind that many spaces are booked very far in advance—a year or even two—so if you are considering popular locations, make inquiries early.

Here are some ideas.

- In addition to your own synagogue or Jewish center, consider others in the community that rent out party rooms. Some historic synagogues, no longer used for worship, offer lovely celebration spaces, and rental fees can help offset the preservation and upkeep expenses of these architectural treasures.
- Review other traditional venues, such as country clubs, hotels, and banquet halls.
- It never hurts to ask. Some unusual options that work: corporate spaces where you are employed; handsome retail spaces (for example, one location we have used is a store filled with rugs, carpets, and furniture during business hours, but which metamorphoses on evenings and weekends into a cool party space); historic

spaces; universities (and university clubs); and museums and libraries (some may have an established policy for rentals; others, that have never rented their space before, might find renting out space for a tasteful celebration a welcome, painless solution to tight budgets and cutbacks).

- Look into a favorite local restaurant; gardens, arboretums, and botanical gardens; public spaces; small theaters; and local jazz clubs.

- Inexpensive choices: Consider borrowing the home of a friend or relative. Check off-season rates at local inns and bed-and-breakfasts. Look into neighborhood locations: community centers, the party room of your apartment building or residential complex, basketball courts, VFW halls, gyms and health clubs, and private schools, including Jewish day schools. One family even held a beautiful celebration at the corner church!

Celebrating the Bar/Bat Mitzvah in Israel

Making aliyah is the cherished dream of some bar/bat mitzvah families. Even in times of political unrest, celebrants decide to travel to Israel as a symbol of their love and support. You can hold the entire event (ceremony and reception) there, or take a small group of close relatives and return home for a separate celebration. In their book *Bar and Bat Mitzvah in Israel: The Ultimate Family Sourcebook*, authors Judith Isaacson and Deborah Rosenbloom offer suggestions for both, and include less-familiar locales, like ancient synagogues and nature sites. Celebrants can participate in diverse activities from desert treks, archaeological digs, and camel rides in the Negev, to dancing with a Torah at the Wailing Wall and lessons in writing with quills, ink, and parchment at a scribal arts workshop.

ASSESSING THE SPACE

Whenever possible, try to visit the location at the time of year and during the time of day that the celebration will take place.

Some of the following considerations will be more—or less—important to you than others.

- **Alternative days.** If the space is not available for the date and time of day you want at a price you can afford, is there an alternative time that would work? The Sunday of a Rosh Hodesh, a Monday holiday, like Martin Luther King Day, or the Thursday of a long weekend? A Sunday or weekday bar/bat mitzvah offers several advantages: For the Sabbath-observant, traveling, music, and videography are all permitted; a child who shares a bar/bat mitzvah date with another at the synagogue need not worry about competing for guests; and because these days are usually less popular, rates may be discounted.

- **Capacity.** Is the site large enough to accommodate your guest list with comfort? If possible, check the room capacity when visiting another bar/bat mitzvah or wedding. If the location has not been used for this type of event previously, be sure to figure in room for tables and chairs, buffet tables, and so on, as well as your guests, when assessing it.

- **Food.** If you are looking for a place with on-site catering, is the food served there to your liking? Can they provide kosher food for your guests, if desired?

- **Layout.** Try to envision where everything will take place: eating, drinking, and dancing. Will the kids be in the same room or an auxiliary space? Do you need a lot of space for the kids' activities?

- **Facilities.** Is the space adequate for your needs? Is there room for seated table service, or a band and dancing? Is there a place for coats? Is the kitchen area adequate, is it clean, and does it have the equipment you'll need? Are there sufficient outlets and good acoustics and sound quality? Is the air-conditioning or heating adequate? Are there enough rest rooms and are they clean?

- **Atmosphere.** Does it provide the tone and the ambience you want? Take in the view. Are the decor and lighting appealing to you, or will they require much work or additional expense?

- **Policies.** If the celebration will be held at a synagogue, find out about any restrictions on food and choice of caterer, as well as music, photos, and videography (if the event is held during the day on Saturday). Other places may also have special policies regarding music, liquor consumption, dress code (particularly at country clubs), decorations, burning candles, or the specific time when you may arrive for setup.

- **Privacy and security.** Is the location closed to others during the event? Will your party be the only one, or will others be taking place before, after, or at the same time? If so, what about setup time and sharing facilities, like rest rooms and the kitchen? What is the noise level like if there is another party at the same time? If possible, check out the space when two simultaneous events are going on.

- **On-site help.** Is there a supervisor and/or other help available on-site?
- **Location.** Is the site conveniently located? Is parking available, and how far is it from the site? If the reception immediately follows the service, the site should not be far from the synagogue.
- **Special needs.** Can the site accommodate elderly grandparents and other special needs guests?

What's Provided? What Will I Need?

In addition to the basic cost of a rental site, analyze any other fees, including hidden ones. At first glance, one location may appear more expensive, but a closer look reveals that the cost includes the tables and chairs you would have to rent for an additional charge at a different site. Also take into account whether you will be using what is provided, or will be paying additional money to rent something special.

In your calculations, you should address these issues.

- Flat rate or hourly charge. If the fee is hourly, how many hours will be needed? Is setup time also included? What is the overtime fee?
- Any relevant insurance costs.
- Are tables and chairs, linens, glassware, flatware, and dishes included, or will there be additional fees to rent them?
- Will there be significant decor and lighting expenses?
- Will any additional delivery charges be incurred because the space is on an upper floor (load/unload charges)?
- Bar charges: buying your own wine and liquor in bulk can make for substantial savings, but most restaurants, hotels, and other facilities that sell liquor to the public will not permit you to do so.
- Parking fees and tips.
- Security guards.
- Is supervisory and service staff included? Are there additional charges for cleaning up after the event?
- Is a piano available? A sound system?

PRICE AND CONTRACT

Make sure everything is in writing, including price, add-ons and fees, and due dates for payment. If possible, pay by credit card in case of disputes. Your contract should include the cancellation and refund policy, the date, the hours (including access for setup and cleanup), all services provided, what rooms you have access to, and attendants or other help provided.

AND, OF COURSE, HOME SWEET HOME

Every Passover, folding tables twisted and snaked around the living room to make room for nearly thirty seder guests. David's home was not spacious, but his family loved entertaining large groups of family and friends, and looked forward to celebrating his bar mitzvah there.

Though it is often quite cool on mid-October evenings, they wanted to make use of the oversize patio directly outside the living-room sliding-glass doors. A tent rental company extended the house by constructing a three-sided tent over the patio, leaving the open glass doors leading to the living room as the fourth "wall." The tent's insulation, the heat of the living room, and the warmth of the guests combined to keep the space cozy.

If you are thinking about using your home or summer place, or borrowing a house, consider the following points.

- Visualize the guests in the space. Are there fragile items that have to be moved, areas to be childproofed? Will you be anxious about spills and damage? In addition to evaluating the size of your home, consider whether there are adequate bathrooms (you can rent portable ones, if needed). Is there space for coats? What about local noise ordinances?
- Can your kitchen accommodate a party this size, or will your caterer bring cooking facilities? Can your electrical system handle any special appliances?
- If you are planning to use outdoor space, you will need a tent if the weather turns inclement. Is there enough outside space to accommodate one? If there is heavy rain before or during the event, will the grounds be affected? (By the way, the tent can be used for a children's party later or the next day.)

- Don't forget these possible add-on costs: a dance floor, bathroom facilities, outdoor lighting, and coatracks.
- Plan for extra storage space. You may need an area to store furniture and breakables. If necessary, arrange to borrow refrigerator space and storage room for food and flowers.

Preparing Your Kitchen for a Celebration at Home

- **Organize your space.** Clear all counters in the kitchen. Remove countertop items that won't be used for the event, including mixers, food processors, toasters, and the like. Move nonperishable items from your refrigerator, such as ketchups, mustards, jams, to another location, if possible. Organize setup areas by type: all hors d'oeuvre in one area, all entrée items in another. Store desserts in a cool place. Label all items for easy identification.
- **Prepare the kitchen.** Remove chairs and other unnecessary furniture from the kitchen. If possible, replace a round table with a rectangular one for a more efficient workspace. If you have auxiliary workspaces, such as a garage or a basement, use them for pantry setup (coffee, tea, creamers, etc.) or storing unpacked rental crates and soda and wine cartons. This will free up and neaten the kitchen, which is especially important when guests are using it as an additional party space.
- **Electrical equipment.** Large coffee percolators requiring a lot of energy could easily blow a fuse; plug them into separate outlets. Check other possible energy drains as well. In one house, we kept on blowing fuses until we realized we had to unplug the electric dog fence. Luckily, the well-trained dog didn't run away!
- **Make lists.** Post them on the refrigerator for service staff to see. Include preparation and serving timelines (when to heat/remove things from oven, etc.). Use timers to keep track.
- **Prepare ahead for cleanup.** Dump flatware into a buspan or large roasting pan filled with warm soapy water. Have an extra-large trash receptacle available. Scrape off plates into the trash before stacking. For glassware, use a strainer over a bucket to dump ice, straws, and so on. Don't forget to recycle! (There will be lots of recyclable materials at the party.) And always have upbeat music in the kitchen. It makes the setup and cleanup much more enjoyable, and things move more quickly.

No siren song beckons like the perfume of mouth-watering home-cooked food. Even if all your food is brought in, simmer some spices in a pot on your stove or place a little store-bought bread dough in a heated oven. The warm aromas will make your guests immediately feel welcome.

MAKE IT A MITZVAH *There is no safe shelter from land mines. Ben, whose Torah portion, Korach, deals with fire and rebellions, produced a play for the synagogue, donated money, and lobbied his senator on behalf of the International Mine Ban Treaty.*

AN INTIMATE CELEBRATION AT HOME:
LINDA'S EARLY SPRING BAT MITZVAH

On that same day you shall hold a celebration; it shall be a sacred occasion
for you; you shall not work at your occupations.

—Emor, Leviticus 23:3

It had been a painful divorce, but the weekly Sabbath—an occasion to take
the time to renew and refresh oneself—had helped Barbara and Linda work
through it and had strengthened the mother-daughter relationship. Every
Friday evening, they put the busy week behind them, lit the Shabbat candles
together, and sat down to the fresh challahs they had prepared. After dinner,
they took a long walk with Kasha, their little terrier mix, and watched the
nighttime sky.

When they met with the rabbi to schedule Linda's bat mitzvah, they had a
special request. They wanted the Saturday when *Emor*, the Torah portion dealing with the significance of the Sabbath, is read.

Linda's grandfather bought her a handcrafted tallit, woven of raw silk and
embroidered with green, blue, and purple ombré threads. A few days before
the bat mitzvah, Barbara's Rosh Hodesh women's group gathered together for
a ceremony welcoming Linda's entry into womanhood, as they had done for
the other daughters. The women each recited a special blessing or poem, sang
or shared words of wisdom with Linda, and then tied a knot on the tzitzit of
her tallit.

Wrapped in that tallit, Linda spoke eloquently about Shabbat in her *dvar
Torah*, how she saw it not as a time of "shall nots" and things forbidden, but instead as a time of special "shalls": "Thou shall sing, eat gloriously, and treasure
each other's good company." She told the congregation that she loved to pick
out the constellations with her mother, then walk out of the darkness into the
warm, lit-up house. That was why she had taken the Hebrew name *Lila*, "night."

And night was when she had chosen to have her party, after sunset, the
close of Shabbat.

As a single parent, Barbara relied on close friends for help in planning the small bat mitzvah celebration, and one of them had volunteered her roomy house. The sofa was pushed against the wall, and most of the other furniture stashed in the den and the garage to make room for the three large folding tables and twenty-four chairs they had rented. But the big white room looked stark, with its enormous picture window staring, uncurtained, into an inky backyard. To create a warmer, more intimate ambience, they replaced the bright-white bulbs in the table lamps and torchères around the room with pink, lavender, and soft amber bulbs of low wattage. Then they threaded red and yellow string lights through the patio railing until the window glowed like a hearth. Even more inviting was the fragrance of freshly baked bread that greeted guests. An old caterers' trick, the source of this aromatherapy was a lump of raw bread dough purchased from a local bakery, left slow-warming in the oven to scent the house.

Barbara had found some butter-yellow rayon fabric at a remnant store and cut it into three table toppers; instead of hemming them, she attached dusty rose ribbon trim around the edges, using double-sided tape. Beneath the toppers, pink twin-size bedsheets lined the tables, hiding their unsightly legs. Three friends supplied the dishes, the flatware, the glasses, and the cloth napkins: Each brought her own service for eight. Though the unique patterns and colors made each table slightly different, the coral votives, the candleholders—large globe artichokes that were scooped out, dried, and sprayed gold—and the softly shimmering yellow tablecloths gave a beautifully unified look. Grandma Molly cross-stitched challah covers for the homemade onion challahs at each table. After the party, Barbara presented them as gifts to her friends in appreciation for all their hard work.

Ficus trees, entwined with tiny white lights, were placed on top and on either side of the massive pine dining table, pressed into service as a buffet. The early spring menu was long on fresh, seasonal tastes, but short on preparation time. Most of the dishes were made ahead, and either heated through just before serving, like the four-cheese, green-and-white lasagne, or served at room temperature, like the well-seasoned egg barley with artichokes and mushrooms. Even the salmon pinwheels had been cut into strips, rolled with a melange of garden herbs, and tied with a purple chive blossom late that after-noon. They went into the oven when the first guest arrived, and were on the table just twenty minutes later.

Out on the sunporch, Great-aunt Yasmine gave Linda's friends a quick les-son in *mehndi*, and soon the girls were applying henna in fine tracery to one another's hands and feet. Then they dipped and decorated candles until sweet beeswax perfumed the room.

After Grandma's fudge-luscious brownie cake and Magda's signature plum tart, Maryellen, an Irish friend of Barbara's said, "We all are so thankful for tonight, for all our blessings. Can I sing a traditional blessing my family sings? Would that be all right?" When everyone vigorously nodded "Of course," she sang "May the Road Rise to Meet You," and taught them the harmony.

Then, one by one, they began picking up plates and carrying them into the kitchen, where they took turns washing and drying the dishes, and nibbling on the leftovers.

Early the next morning, before Grandma left with Grandpa for Florida, she baked a few trays of her brownie recipe with Linda, but this time they pressed pastel-colored candy flowers into the icing. It was Easter Sunday, and for her mitzvah project, Linda had volunteered through Project Ezra to work at a local church soup kitchen "so a Christian volunteer there can take the day off and enjoy her holiday, knowing she isn't disappointing anybody." As she raced out of the house with the carefully packed brownies, Linda said, "I don't know what else they're having, but their dessert will be awesome!"

8

DECOR AND LIGHTING

ANNA'S EARLY SPRING BAT MITZVAH *would take place at one of the oldest synagogues in the city, but the small party room there could not accommodate her large guest list. Just a short walk from the synagogue, the family found a school gymnasium—it was spacious, the ceilings were extra high, there was plenty of natural light, and the floors would be great for dancing. Draping the entire room to disguise the gym proved to be too costly; instead, the family hung inexpensive white muslin panels, hand-painted by an artist friend with spring flowers in blues, lavenders, and greens to match the invitations. Some of the panels incorporated Hebrew words from the Torah portion, painted vertically like Japanese calligraphy, amid the flowers. Rented standing fans provided cross-ventilation and kept the panels swaying, gently diverting the eye from the walls and the sports equipment. White, yellow, and blue irises, daffodils, and narcissus in oversize glass fishbowls were wrapped in loosely woven grapevine wreaths on the guests' tables. Anna's friends sat at a long table beneath a grapevine trellis woven with greens, fragrant herbs, and white buds.*

Transforming a space—whether in your home, the synagogue, or a sophisticated hotel aerie overlooking the twinkling lights of the city—so it greets your guests with a promise of festive celebration and warm welcome may entail nothing more than tables set with gleaming cloths, spring flowers, and the soft glow of candlelight. We will talk about flowers and tables in chapters to come.

But more often than not, as in the example above, you may need to address the larger picture—walls and ceilings, carpets, chairs, curtains, lighting, and other preexisting design elements—to make the space more attractive and inviting, to create an atmosphere, or to develop a motif. In this chapter, we'll begin with decor and discuss lighting separately later on.

DECOR

Assessing the Space

How awesome is this place!
—GENESIS, 29:17

Stand in the corners of the celebration space and examine the room from every angle. Then look at it from the center. Stepping back, get a sense of the energy, the traffic patterns, and the proportions of the room. In a large banquet space, will decorative black-and-white photo blowups of family members look better on the walls than your intimate photo montages or collages? Is there a mood or ambience suggested, such as light and airy, high-tech, or elegant? Are there views to play up or hide behind closed drapes? Design problems like ceiling ducts or inappropriate wall art that you will need to work out? If you're having difficulty visualizing the area "all dressed up," visit your local library or bookstore to browse through illustrated books on entertaining and parties.

Find out the decorating policy of the space: If necessary, will you be able to move plants, floor lamps, tables, wall art, temporary displays, and so on? We always suggest revisiting the space a few weeks before the celebration. The luxuriant harvest cornucopias that decorated the room when it was booked last September may be replaced by a Christmas tree or other seasonal decorations come December.

Working with Existing Decor

Whenever possible, try to incorporate the existing decor, not to fight it. Stained-glass windows, or other architecturally distinguished features, make wonderful focal points; you can train a spotlight on glorious old wood beams or surround columns in a city loft with twinkle lights or artificial trees made of canvas.

Work with the walls, drapes, and floors not only when choosing tabletop design, but other decorative elements as well. Don't worry too much about matching, but do try to harmonize and avoid obvious clashes in color and style, like busy patterns with bright printed wallpaper and carpets. Before you bring in a special design element, consider how it will work with the existing decor. For example, in a space filled with glass, chrome, and lucite, a stylized Garden of Eden, created with handsome oversize papier-mâché trees and flowers, may be a better choice than one incorporating natural elements.

Special Decor Elements and Motifs

When clients ask us what special design elements they should look for, we suggest they think of the decor in terms of the purpose they want it to serve. Then we ask them to consider whether their design choices feel right for their child and their family, and whether they work with their Judaic values: a sense of balance and moderation, an awareness of tradition and community. For example, Sandy's family wanted the decor to express his passions, yet remain appropriate to the celebration. He had devoured every baseball book from John Tunis to Roger Angell, memorized stats of legends, old and new, and visited Cooperstown with his grandfather annually since age four. For Sandy, baseball was the story of teamwork, of fighting for fairness and racial justice. His family decorated the synagogue space with beautiful sepia blowups of the historic teams of the

Boys of Summer. Rich chocolate-colored tablecloths, topped with centerpieces of wheat grass and leather baseball gloves (later donated to a boys' club) completed the picture.

Ask yourself if there is an organizing thread or motif that you might want to develop for the bar/bat mitzvah, if you haven't already done so. Many families like to focus on a motif not only because they prefer the unified quality it lends to the event, but also because starting out with a motif can make choosing decor, food, entertainment, and other elements easier, as it did at Sandy's party. Jeremy's family used his Torah portion, *Tetsaveh*, as a starting point: *"And the decorated band that is upon it shall be . . . of gold, of blue, purple and crimson yarns, and of fine twisted linen worked into the designs."* They draped grosgrain ribbons in these colors over the ark during the service; more ribbon decorated the *oneg* room, forming a backdrop for a candlelighting ceremony featuring a colorful family menorah on a table adorned with ribbons in the same hues.

Don't be afraid to discuss your ideas with your party planner or caterers: They may take the theme and run with it. They may have props on hand to create visual interest, or they may suggest items you already have in your own home, or others that can be rented from a theme factory.

Here are some suggestions for motifs and decorative touches. But remember, less is always more. Decorations that interfere with your guests' comfort—no matter how fabulous—are never a good idea.

Holiday themes. Holidays make wonderful themes: Cloaked in its own array of delicious aromas and treats, each offers a panoply of decorating and entertainment ideas. For Purim: masks, costumes, noisemakers, scrolls, storytelling. For Hanukkah: menorahs, dreidels, gold coins, to name just a few.

Jewish traditions and culture. Do you simply want to reflect Jewish culture and traditions? An excellent resource is *The Encyclopedia of Jewish Symbols,* by Ellen Frankel and Betsy Platkin Teutsch (Jason Aronson, 1992); browsing through, you're sure to come across evocative visual images that resonate for you and your family. Some ideas: the golem, the huge superhero created out of a mound of earth by a rabbi of Prague to defend the Jews against a pogrom, has great kid appeal (think foam-core cutouts made from blowups of golem drawings; instead of a DJ's "dance motivator," how about a golem entertainer on the dance floor?); a lacelike paper-cut, a piece of traditional Jewish folk art like the design that graces the cover of this book (lovely hung like clothesline art on a fish wire and made into table decorations; and for entertainment, a skilled paper-cut artist could lead children in a workshop); or a lion's den for a child named Ari or

Aryeh (lion), Ariel (lion of God), or, of course, Daniel, after the prophet sent to the lion's den, with an arch of lion balloons, a mustard-yellow draped wall, and shaggy yellow tablecloths.

Secular themes with Jewish values. Is there a secular image that has great meaning for your child and is consistent with Jewish values? For Steve, an avid hiker committed to cleaning up our national parks, his parents found a painted backdrop of the Grand Canyon rented through the Internet to decorate one of the party-room walls.

Emphasis on a special area or activity. Do you want to highlight that mouth-watering food buffet or enhance a head table with one-of-a-kind, hand-decorated chairs? At one event, wide streamers in every color of the rainbow were attached to the top of a tent; released at the start of the hora, they fanned out across the dance floor—a glorious finale to a June bat mitzvah.

Decor geared to entertainment. At a luncheon at a charming synagogue space too small for dancing, the party planner suggested that the instrumentalists become the focal point. The musicians played conga, bass, and amplified harp. Dressed all in white, they looked wonderfully hip against the checkered black-and-white floor and huge urn of red flowers on the little platform that was set in the center of the room.

Ideas to Help Define and Decorate a Party Space

Draping options. We love draping, so reminiscent of tents, furled scrolls, and ancient robes, and we use both loose fabric and "pipe-and-drape." To drape loose fabric, you will need something preexisting in the space to anchor the fabric, like ducts or pipes, beams, curtain rods, the metal arms of sconces, chandeliers, or other fixtures. Drape one section of the room to set it off; use tented fabric over buffet tables (suggesting food markets), sheer gauzes, tulles, or cheesecloth swagged through poles over a dance floor. Pipe-and-drape, available from rental companies, supplies its own frame, so it can be used anywhere, either as a solid curtain or pulled back for a more open effect, or even arranged as a special portal or entryway, or a canopy. "Walls" of pipe-and-drape can enclose a children's area; set up pipe-and-drape walls behind buffet tables to highlight them; arrange pipe-and-drape to set off a dance floor. Or use transparent fabric to separate a cocktail area from the dining space, where candlelit tables beckon guests to supper within. Use nonflammable cloth to drape large areas.

Ornamental hangings and special backdrops. Foam-core backdrops—ranging from your city skyline to scans of your child's artwork—work well; hang runners of lace, beautiful embossed saris, or other unusual fabrics or rugs in colors to match table decor or flowers; suspend bird feeders wired with cut flowers (and later contribute them to a nature conservancy).

Separate but coordinating decor for adults and children. For a bar mitzvah we did during the Passover holidays, we took our cue from the Haggadah, which enjoins us to relax on pillows as a visible sign we are no longer slaves in Pharaoh's Egypt. On the dining chairs in the adult section, we tied pillows in sand, ocher, and brick, desert colors to match the table linens. The children reclined on huge floor pillows on the carpets, Middle Eastern style. (See Balloons below and "Lighting," page 103, as well as chapter 10, "Setting the Table," for many other ways to highlight a children's area.)

An inviting entry to the celebration. Instead of the ubiquitous foam-core sign-in board, consider having guests sign in on something playful but useful for the child's room. One idea: an eminently cool metal locker (the kind used in schools and gyms), signed in graffiti style with magic markers. Or welcome guests with an elegant table set with flowers, a guest book, and photos, or hanging wind chimes threaded with tropical flowers, and soft birdsong playing in the background.

Props. Pillars, urns, gazebos, sculptures, and other large props can be rented from prop-rental companies, theme factories, or some florists. We've used Jacob's ladders, drums, oversize Chinese parasols, and even weathered barn doors and windows! At one event, we rented four faux stone (fiberglass) columns and placed them around what remained of the little linoleum floor after the tables were set up. Then we dimmed the lights. The synagogue basement cafeteria metamorphosed into a tiny dance pavilion.

Balloons. Forget your preconceived ideas about balloons. Buoyant, metaphorically spirited, and uplifting, they can be surprisingly handsome and a quite reasonable way to decorate a space. Incredible sculptures in fanciful shapes, like underwater sea creatures, zebras, flamingoes, and creatures of the earth in fantastic patterns, and huge, Gaudiesque flowers are just some of the creative balloon ideas you'll find at local party stores or from searching on the Internet using the keywords "party balloons." Don't limit balloons to tables. We've used clusters of giant twenty-four-inch balloons to surround a dance floor, tied them to wall sconces with pretty wide ribbons, and decorated children's chairs with zany balloon sculptures.

Lighting. We will discuss this in detail in the "Lighting" section later in this chapter.

Solving Some Common Decor Problems

It is not always possible—or even desirable—to cover up a room of unattractive walls or other unaesthetic design elements. We often prefer instead to play up a strength, highlighting a beautiful aspect of the room, creating a new, attractive focal point, or brightening up drab spaces with dramatic touches.

Accentuate the positive. Highlight lovely deep windows with candles, flowers, or balloons placed on the sills. Festoon a grand doorway or handsome chandeliers with greens and roses. Capitalize on those tall ceilings by hanging large Japanese lanterns that evoke sunken moons.

Divert attention to buffet areas and focus your decorating budget there. Some ideas: umbrella tables and/or pushcarts, readily available from rental companies, with fun food for kids, or old-fashioned treats like pickles and knishes for all; fabulous dessert tables, like an ice cream bar covered with a bold-striped or polka-dotted cloth (in colors that contrast with the room decor) and fitted out with a fun balloon arch; a bar, unusual in length or curve, with colored lights directed on the glassware (these could be simple canister spotlights) or different colored flower petals under each stack of glassware. (For more on great buffets, see chapter 14.)

Adorn nondescript or barren spaces and hide flaws. Use pipe-and-drape walls or backdrops to cover up a kitchen doorway or disguise unattractive art and signs on walls. If the view from the windows is really unappealing or distracting, consider draping them with a sheer, inexpensive fabric like scrim or cheesecloth to let some light in. Hang baskets of flowering plants from tent tops.

Transform defects into decorating assets. If there are columns or poles that break up spaces, center a buffet area between two columns swathed with fabric, then arrange the fabric above to form an arch or inviting market canopy. Or lash spray-painted branches to poles and hang with giant paper flowers. Metamorphose those tacky ultramarine cafeteria chairs into a treasure, creating a symphony of blues in linens, lighting, and flowers.

Camouflage institutional ceilings that have fluorescent lighting by using strings of metal cutouts (cut fun shapes from disposable pie tins and hammer out holes with nails to mimic Mexican tinware). Or cover the area with balloon arches suspended from the ceiling. (For more on fluorescent lighting solutions, see page 102.)

You'll find many other ideas in chapter 9, "Flowers and Centerpieces," and sprinkled throughout the book.

MAKE IT A MITZVAH *After the celebration, don't forget to bring the paper flowers, balloons, backdrops, and other reusable decorations to a children's center, a hospital, or other facility for others to enjoy. • Adorn a sukkah or set up Hanukkah or Purim decorations at a nearby Jewish assisted-living or nursing home. Or sound the shofar there on the High Holidays. • Decorate the bags and boxes in which your synagogue or soup kitchen delivers hot meals to make them look as good as they taste.*

LIGHTING

Jonah's family loved the New York City loft they had rented—especially its mesmerizing views of the Hudson. But the large, open, nearly square space was a decor challenge: Inelegant ceiling pipes lent an industrial, even impersonal air, and there were no naturally defined areas for eating, drinking, and dancing. Estimates for renting functional space dividers and furniture to "warm it up" proved exorbitant. Then a friend suggested consulting a lighting designer since the party was at night.

With "Jonah and the Whale" as the organizing motif, everything fell into place. The dance area, created with a wash of lights, changed from blues and greens to yellows and back again—underwater colors to simulate a gently rippling ocean. Lit with warm pinks and corals, the buffet tables were outlined by forty-eight-inch-high metallic paper fish wind socks in blues and purples; tied to the ceiling pipes, they formed an arch that suggested the Great Whale's mouth. At the tables, named for different fish, glowing tea lights floated inside variously shaped clear glass vases and other containers filled with different colored waters (tinted with food coloring)—eliminating the need for, and expense of, fresh flowers. Near the entrance, bathed in soft orange-amber lights, a lucite beverage bar, lit from underneath, beckoned with freshly made colorful blender drinks, both nonalcoholic and spiked.

What we see and how we experience it depends on the light we see it in. Looking at snappy umbrella tables in a sun-drenched botanical garden or the local library done up in party lights and candle glow, we see the promise of good times. Light has a spiritual dimension, too: In Judaism it is the symbol of Divine Power, source of the holy sparks within us all. Through our awareness of light in the space, a celebration is transformed into a more spiritual event. Think of lifting your glass before the gray light of a snow-filling sky or lighting a Havdalah candle, eloquently twisted strands of light and dark, to start an evening celebration.

The buffet tables for the Kiddush at Noah's synagogue were traditionally placed against the dark, wood-paneled wall, making the fluorescent overhead lights necessary even during the day. But on the May morning we were setting up, the sunlight streamed through the wall of windows opposite, and we could almost smell the lilacs pressing up against the panes from the garden outside. We moved the tables against the windows, and we were able to turn off the bright lights. The spring sun lit the food and the flowers.

Look at your party space carefully at the time of day you'll be using it, so you can evaluate the existing light, whether natural or artificial. Is it adequate? Does the light change as day shifts to night? If you're renting the space, familiarize yourself with all the lighting sources available: In addition to track lights, there may be chandeliers and sconces. If you are celebrating at home, you'll need to check light levels there, too. Locate the power sources and find out how much power is available.

While party lighting, like flowers and tabletops, can establish a mood, complement a theme or event, decorate, or even solve decor problems, most hosts think about lighting only when there isn't enough—or, less often, when there is too much. Whenever possible, take advantage of the existing light. Set up buffets, bars, dessert stations, and so on in front of good natural light or under chandeliers, sconces, and other light sources.

We suggest here several lighting ideas for do-it-yourselfers. For more professional and site-specific advice, rely on your contact at the location, the party planner, the caterer, lighting companies, or a lighting designer from a local theater or the theater department of a nearby school or college. We have found that the cost of professional lighting services may be at least partially offset by savings in other decor areas, especially when dealing with big spaces.

Lighting to Create Warmth and Ambience

Subdued light is the most comfortable and conducive to good conversation and relaxed dining. Here are some simple steps you can take to achieve attractive lighting.

Light levels. Play with the light levels in the room. Do you need all the lights on? If you turn off the track lights, will other sources, like chandeliers, sconces, candles, or spotlights be adequate?

Dimmers. Experiment with the dimmer, if there is one, to find the optimum light level. If there is no dimmer for the overhead fixture, and you are handy, perhaps your synagogue would appreciate you installing one in the party room. For plug-in lights and lamps, you can purchase a dimmer that plugs directly into the outlet without installation; it's inexpensive and can be reused in your own home.

Lightbulbs. We often change lightbulbs to ones with lower wattage or warmer colors, like pink, amber, or gold, which resemble candle glow or firelight. Inexpensive novelty bulbs with low wattage are fun, too; we used a faceted hexagonal bulb in an overhead fixture to create a star pattern over a buffet table.

Strings of lights. Lights nestled in tree branches illuminate softly, like little glimmering spotlights peeking under large leaves; tiny twinkle lights, or even chili pepper lights, add a little spice when hung over the dance floor, around poles, or strung across the room.

Fluorescent light. So harsh and unflattering, this is often the only light available in party rooms and cafeterias in synagogues and schools. Because fluorescent fixtures are relatively cool to the touch, we drape them with gauzy fabrics, netting, and voiles to softly diffuse the light. You can also use inexpensive colored gels, available at theatrical equipment and supply houses in easy-to-cut twenty-inch by twenty-four-inch sheets in a slew of colors. (Be aware that the darker the gel, the less light will come through.) Cut the gel to size and either lay it inside the fluorescent light cover or attach it to the outside of the cover with Scotch tape. (Gels are made to withstand intense heat and can be used for incandescent lighting fixtures, too, with a specially designed black aluminum tape. But always test first or check with a professional before using gels on any lights other than fluorescent.)

Daytime lighting. During the day, artificially lit party spaces call for brighter lights than at night. Perhaps it is our internal clock, accustomed to more light during daylight hours, but we find very subdued lamplight oppressive at daytime parties.

Lighting as a Decor Tool

- Highlight architectural details, like friezes and columns. Uplight beautiful old wood beams by placing gooseneck lamps in the room corners and focusing them upward, or by directing a small group of canister spotlights from the floor to the area. Tip: Always check that lights are directed so that they neither shine in guests' eyes nor are aimed at their eye level.

- In recreation or basement spaces, make unattractive walls "disappear" by turning the lights in the area off to black the walls out and redirect all the lighting to the center of the room.

- Use novelty lights to create separate eating, dancing, or children's sections. Make a "dining room" by placing battery-powered red paper lanterns on tables in a softly lit area. Separate a children's section or define a dance floor using lights: Envelop columns with twinkle lights (we love not only clear or white, but blue and gold, too) or place clusters of trees threaded with lights around the dance area. String up twinkle lights, Chinese lanterns, or other special lights, or press adhesive light strips onto the floor to outline the area. Highlight a wine bar, surrounding it with grape-cluster party lights. Or bring a sno-cone cart to life by wrapping the umbrella with twinkling fruit-shaped lights.

Lighting Splurges

Here is just a sampling of options often available through DJ packages, as well as lighting companies and designers. Look under the keywords "lighting design" on the Web or in the Yellow Pages under "Theatrical Equipment and Supplies."

- **Color washes** (using colored gels). Bathe walls or dance floor with colors: Matt's family played up the jazz band they hired with a dance floor in cool blue-greens. Use color washes to separate two areas with different lighting needs: soft ambers in the dining area; dramatic blues and purples for the dance floor. Change the gel colors so a different color wash signals dessert is served, time for the hora, or the end of the party.

- **Pinspot lighting** (light focused tightly on a small area). This is a wonderful complement to floral arrangements on buffet and dining tables and an excellent way to draw attention to challah and candlelighting ceremonies.

- **Laser, mirrored disco ball, and strobe lighting.** These lights add drama to the dance floor. Use **black lights** to illumine the white gloves the DJ brings for your dancers' hands.
- **Gobos.** By projecting words or an image on walls using a stencil called a gobo, you can create a silvery moon and stars, or gorgeous green trees in delicate tracery for a memorable Tu B'Shevat bat mitzvah. You may want to design your own gobos—perhaps Judaic symbols or others meaningful to your family.
- **Light shows.** Sarah, who spoke at her service about the shadow portion that dwells within each of us, hired a local puppeteer to put on a shadow play.
- **DJ lighting effects.** If your DJ is bringing a lighting booth, don't be afraid to ask exactly what he or she will be using: colors, gobos, flashing messages, or a preprogrammed light show. Often these special effects can be changed, and certainly tell the DJ if you prefer not to have them at all.

Outdoor Lighting

- **Tent lighting.** Ask the rental company about lighting options. Many of them offer a choice between chandeliers and canister lights. If you are planning to string twinkle or other decorative lights, double-check power sources and company policy.
- **Outside lighting.** A city nightscape etched in glittering gems, soft-colored lights dancing in the country club pool—sometimes beautiful outside lighting just comes with the territory. But if there is a view of outdoor space or the celebration is held outdoors, it's easy to create a little light magic on your own. Twinkle lights or little lanterns can be strung in trees or around a pool or fountain. Float candles in the water or create a path with tall tiki torches or candles in paper bags filled with sand. And don't forget citronella candles to shoo away the bugs!

Candle Glow

For thou wilt light my candle, my God will enlighten my darkness.
—PSALM 18:29

At Lauren's bat mitzvah celebration at home, when her father turned off the track lights, the large living room was lit entirely by glowing candles: fat pillars of varying heights on the mantel and in the wraparound windows; masses of votives crowding the tall plate stands on the buffet; fragrant, soft beeswax tapers on the tables. The difference was palpable: The thoroughly modern room grew more intimate and comfortable, conversations easy and everywhere.

We love the metaphor of lighting candles. It always preludes a special occasion—ushering in the Sabbath or a holiday, making a birthday wish, the start of a celebration. At parties, candles warm up a room and invariably make guests feel more relaxed.

Though they are rarely bright enough to light up a space alone, candles can provide an effective supplementary lighting source for your party space. In general, taller candles, like pillars and tapers, will give the most light; tea lights and votives provide a soft, ambient glow. But whether we set menorahs burning in windows on a moonless night or use subtle candle glow on the tables to create a special ambience around the room, for us candlelight, like summer fireflies, is inextricably linked with sunset and beyond. That is why we prefer not to use candles during the day. If you're a candlelight lover, consider planning an evening event or lighting your candles toward the close of day.

Before you raid the candle store, however, check the policies on candlelight. Many places do not permit uncovered candles; they may require that candles be placed in hurricane lamps (we've sometimes put pillar candles in inexpensive large florists' vases) or special candle lamps with lampshades; votives and tea lights set in jars or pretty glasses or floated in bowls or vases. Be mindful of potential fire hazards when burning candles, like raffia tied around napkins or dry leaves decoratively carpeting the table, which can easily catch fire, and keep candles away from drafts. If you are unsure whether your kids will play with burning candles, err on the side of caution and limit the candles to the adults' tables and buffets.

TIPS ON BUYING CANDLES

- Candles are usually a better bargain at large stores, online, and from catalogs than at specialty shops. They are often on sale, especially after holidays.
- Candles are available not only in every hue and size, but in myriad designs as well. Just some of the fabulous ones we've seen on the market recently: elaborately carved, stamped, mosaic, rainbow, and spiral candles; beeswax candles from a local greenmarket, plain or rolled in glitter; fragrant flower candles made to float in shallow bowls, either alone or with real blossoms.
- There are loads of candles with a Judaic feel, available from Judaic stores and Judaic

websites: Hanukkah and Havdalah candles; scroll-like spiral candles that suggest a Torah; fanciful Rebecca the Water Carrier, dove, moon, star, or candles braided like challahs.

- Subtly fragrant candles can be delightful; perfumed candles can spell disaster. No one wants to smell patchouli or coconut when tucking into a salad.

CANDLE LOOKS WE LOVE

- Candlesticks from **family collections.** These can be supplemented, if necessary, with additions from relatives and friends. If you want a unified look for a diverse group of candlesticks—ceramic, silver, crystal, brass—use the same candles for all.
- Candles set in front of **mirrors** around the room or votives and other short candles arranged on antique framed mirrors for a soft, reflected glow. Tie clusters of fat candles with French ribbon and set them on mirrored trays or tiles.
- Votives in holders or pillars directly placed on a bed of herbs or fresh pine branches so their heat releases **fragrance.**
- A **variety of candle types,** shapes, and heights. On dining tables, we often place votives on cake plates and footed dishes to raise them up. Make sure candles on buffets are out of guests' easy reach. If you don't have plate stands, invert three tall stemmed glasses and set a plate on top, attached with florists' gum or candle adhesive (usually referred to as candle stick-um); then arrange the candles on the plate.
- **Votives** have become increasingly popular as more places prohibit open candle flames. Some of our favorite arrangements: a generous number artfully grouped in the center; a swiggle of votives in an S shape down the middle of a long, narrow table; or just a few of them clustered at each table setting. Votive candles can get very hot, so we put a little water, table salt, or sand inside each holder. In very warm weather, we sometimes freeze tapers for a few hours prior to use.

CANDLEHOLDER IDEAS

- Some of the prettiest candleholders we've seen are **nature's gifts:** artichokes, dried and hollowed out, then sprayed gold or colors; hollowed-out gourds or small pumpkins; and scooped-out lemons and oranges that emitted a delicate, haunting scent as the candles burned.
- **Small drinking glasses or jelly jars,** plain or decorated with paint or glued-on little beads, make fine holders for votives and other short, stubby candles. Hillary's

family borrowed traditional gold-etched tea glasses in blues and greens from her Moroccan relatives—a wonderful complement to the couscous on the menu.

- Stand candles up in **wide glass bowls** filled with sand or salt. Steve's wiggly blue-and-white candles (menorah sets, purchased on sale after Hanukkah) looked great anchored in coarse salt in shallow blue glass bowls.
- **Candle lamps,** usually used with tapers, are an excellent option for full-size or cocktail tables, when candles must be covered. And pretty candle lamps can eliminate the need for flowers. Often available from the same suppliers that rent tableware and linens, they come in a variety of lampshades: with or without fringe, in silver and other metallics, exquisitely patterned, embossed, beaded, or art deco.
- **Candelabra,** perfect for the candlelighting ceremony or for dining tables, as well as candlesticks, can also be rented.
- **Pillar candles** need no candleholders. Stand them on simple saucers, a bed of fresh leaves, mirrored tiles, or flameproof trays.
- Don't overlook **fun, offbeat holders.** Slip metallic Slinkies over narrow beverage glasses filled with tall spiral candles and use to decorate a dessert bar, then put additional Slinkies on the children's tables. One child used recycled bicycle gears made into holders for taper candles.

CANDLE CRAFT SUGGESTIONS

- A simple **candle craft set,** containing sheets of wax to roll and decorating materials. This is a great way to keep kids—especially younger ones—occupied during cocktail time. Later their creations can be used in the candlelighting ceremony.
- **Dress-up ideas** for plain candles: Wrap pillar candles with a bit of ivy or other vines, even pencil-thin asparagus, and attach with straight pins; glue colorful legumes, beads, sequins, or dried herbs, like lavender, on candles.
- **Sticker decoupage:** Apply stickers of flowers, butterflies, flags, and more to votive cups or other glasses.

MAKE IT A MITZVAH *Light up the world with literacy. Lovers of the written word, Jewish volunteers combat illiteracy through the National Jewish Coalition for Literacy. Their outreach extends to local libraries, public schools, and community centers. Contact the group at www.njcl.net.*

IN A BUTTERFLY GARDEN: JULIA'S BAT MITZVAH

Julia had followed Lesley into the gardens from the time she was a toddler, dragging her tiny hoe and playing hide-and-seek among the foxgloves as her mother weeded and transplanted cuttings. One spring Lesley even set up an area for butterflies, choosing special blooms like buddleia, joe-pye weed, and flowering milkweed to attract them. There was no question but that Julia's bat mitzvah celebration would be here at home. "A remote, commercial space is just not us," Lesley explained. Set on a private street reminiscent of a French Norman village, with stone houses and tiled roofs, the yard seemed to extend past its own borders to the wooded lane beyond.

They had already been given a date for early the following May—a glorious time of year if the sun would just cooperate. Planning ahead, Lesley, Julia, and her sister Rose collected dozens of blossoms and buds during the summer and fall, and hand-pressed them to enclose with the invitations.

Julia is a vegetarian, and strongly felt there should be neither meat nor fish at the party. While this was not an easy decision for Lesley and Richard, they decided it was Julia's day, and with careful planning, a menu highlighting the earth's bounty would work well, especially in the garden setting. They decided to do two menus: one featuring an array of teen favorites, the other with more sophisticated adult selections.

Behar, Julia's Torah portion, was about the Year of the Jubilee, and she explained that the section from Leviticus was a call for freedom. "Those are the words engraved on the Liberty Bell here in Philadelphia: 'Proclaim liberty throughout the land unto all the inhabitants thereof.' " Julia told the congregation she believed that Jews have a special obligation to ensure that all people everywhere are truly free. And she read from the famous poem written by a young man at the Theresienstadt concentration camp, about how he found his people among the white chestnut flowers in the ghetto, but never saw another butterfly.

When the guests arrived at Julia's house after the service, they were ushered past spring ground covers—Solomon's seal, Jacob's ladder, and silver-green lamb's ears—into a serene garden. Knee-high boxwood edged the clean-cropped grass where the caterers had arranged a few small tables for cocktails under leafy canopies. On top of the bar, wine coolers brimmed with wisteria, lilac, and delphiniums.

Adults snacked on international hors d'oeuvre, including vegetarian sushi and mini herbed latkes. The caterers set up their kitchen in the garage to leave the house undisturbed, plugging in two electric fryers to make sacks of French fries to order for the kids' starters. There was a little lemonade stand covered in floral chintz, with a kitschy sign offering cool drinks at five cents each.

The weather had indeed cooperated, so that morning the largest tables were pushed outside the dining tent, providing more room for the smaller tables in the center. Surrounded on three sides by lush woodlands and on the fourth by a storybook garden of fantasy flowers, the tent required little in the way of decoration.

The tables looked extravagant, but were actually quite easy to do. Round, of different sizes, they were covered with sherbet-colored underlays, then vivid flower petals were strewn over them, and "tea-stained" net overlays were placed on top. (For details on putting together these cloths, see page 133). Large glass service plates permitted the flower petals to peek through. At a slumber party a few weeks earlier, Julia and her friends had tied small pot-pourris of dried petals in net trimmings for the party favors/place-card holders.

Simple centerpieces best complemented the table settings and views: loose bouquets of peonies in inexpensive glass vases on some tables, and ceramic pots of fresh rosemary and sage on others. At Julia's table, miniature Heritage roses tumbled out of her grandmother's lead crystal vase.

Between bites of thin-crusted pizzas and Caesar salad flavored with blue borage flowers, Julia's friends created a memory glass, filling a wine goblet with petals, place cards, and little notes, then covering it with netting and sealing it with candle wax.

The adult guests were still finishing up their tasting plates while the caterers moved the wisteria bouquets and cocktail tables onto the driveway for the dessert buffet. Draped in plain, floor-length white, the tables were topped with square damask cloths that had belonged to Lesley's grandmother. Fresh pansies scattered over the cloths camouflaged any telltale signs of age. Lesley and Julia had specially selected the pedestal cake stands from the family's collection for the pastel-frosted butter cakes, specially iced Betty Crocker–style to look homemade. Fresh violas, little sisters to pansies, ringed the cake plates, and tiny Johnny-jump-ups, the baby of the pansy family, garnished the cakes. There were many other May birthdays to celebrate besides Julia's own, both of friends and family.

While the kids lined up for fresh vanilla ice cream served from a hand-cranked ice cream maker, Julia's aunt brought out a surprise: live butterflies. She had seen them at a friend's wedding and loved them. Julia's friends opened the containers and released the butterflies into the garden. Several lighted on nectar flowers, and lingered awhile before finally fluttering off. (Butterflies indigenous to your area are available on the Internet. Order them at least two weeks in advance.)

Julia had not yet come up with a mitzvah project, but as she watched her grandmother Sophie, an active octogenarian, enjoying a piece of cake near the flowers, she had an idea. She could set up a butterfly garden for the nursing home nearby, transplanting some of her mom's buddleia and joe-pye weed, as well as the potted herbs from her party.

When the flowers bloomed in midsummer, she'd bring iced cakes to celebrate with the residents. And wait for the butterflies to show up.

9

FLOWERS AND CENTERPIECES

*In order to serve God, one needs access to the enjoyment of the
beauties of nature, such as the contemplation of flower-decorated
meadows, majestic mountains, flowing rivers, etc. For all these are
essential to the spiritual development of even the holiest of people.*
—ABRAHAM BEN MOSES BEN MAIMON, EGYPT (1186–1237)

Moving with the rhythms of the natural

world is part of the Jewish spiritual tradition. There is even a special blessing

to mark the first time we see a fruit tree bloom in spring. Watching the earth

renew itself fills us with an awareness of creation. "The earth is full of thy

riches," David said (Psalm 104:24), and each time of year offers us different

gifts, from casual spring bouquets of lupines and phlox to dahlias, marigolds,

and blush-tipped sedum in the fall.

Bar and bat mitzvahs call out for these riches, on the bimah, at the table,

in your daughter's hair or your son's lapel. The metaphor is not lost on us: The

child we nurtured has grown, and it's time to celebrate the blossoming.

We love centerpieces and buffet arrangements that tell you about the child, and we often rely on branches and trees, seasonal fruits and vegetables, grasses, herbs, and other natural objects to create handsome tabletop decorations that are unique and personalized. Sometimes we combine flowers with nonfloral elements—a layer of fresh lemons placed on the bottom of clear glass vases filled with purple, white, and yellow Siberian irises—or we dispense with blossoms completely: A centerpiece composed entirely of candles and seasonal greens can be simple and elegant. One bat mitzvah girl, who treasured memories of winter beach vacations with her grandparents, included her cache of seashells, stones, and rainbow-colored sea glass in the centerpieces. Pots of Elijah's bluegrass proved ideal centerpieces for the eponymous bar mitzvah boy wild about its vivid color because it matched the team color of the Miami Dolphins, his favorite football team.

With advance planning, home gardeners can plant and cultivate specific flowers with their children so that blossoms are ready in time for the party and/or for decorating the synagogue. Homegrown flowers, like lilies of the valley and garden roses, often unavailable at commercial flower markets, bring a sense of your family and your home to the celebration—no matter where it takes place.

In this chapter, we begin by sharing information and ideas to help you envision the kinds of flowers and other arrangements you might want to decorate the synagogue and celebration space, to adorn the dining tables and buffets. These insights will help crystallize your ideas and enable you to make more informed choices, whether you will be working with a florist or tying every bouquet yourself. Then you'll be ready to check out our guidelines for working with professionals as well as our tips for do-it-yourselfers, plus details on how to incorporate your mitzvah project into the centerpieces.

FROM SIMPLE TO ELABORATE

At Rick's bar mitzvah reception, food was the main event, but the dining tent in the backyard was uninvitingly low and dark. So we set up the serving area in a corner of the tent, piling bales of hay on top of and alongside the buffet tables to create various levels of height. Over the hay, we arranged dozens of loose fall flowers in big copper buckets and sheaves of broomcorn tied with raffia. The result was an autumnal still life that drew attention to the buffet area and gave an illusion of depth to the space. Simple, low arrangements of Indian corn, pumpkins, and gourds, and cranberry colored cloths, decorated the guests' dining tables.

Well-thought-out floral arrangements can transform even nondescript places. And you can create the focal points you want by using flowers to direct your guests' attention. Consider how differently flowers were used at another tent party, with a more lavish budget, where the focus was on the dancing:

Samantha's Saturday evening bat mitzvah celebration took place in a large, high-ceilinged tent. Though spacious, the tent looked unappealingly bare and cold, so to highlight the music and dancing and give that area of the tent a more intimate feel, we hung three huge burlap-covered buckets of flowering quince and dogwood branches above the dance floor. We arranged one of them high and two slightly lower down, and spotlighted them, creating a suggestion of movement. Small terraced "gardens" blooming with delphiniums and foxgloves were set up on either side of the band. Adjacent to them, flowering trees wrapped in burlap echoed the branches above. The effect was of an enchanted bower enveloping the dancers. (The trees and gardens were later planted on the family's property.)

FINDING FLOWERS THAT WORK FOR YOU

Begin by visualizing the area and the movement flow from room to room. Decide what and where your focus should be (it may change at different points during the event): dining, dancing, candlelighting, and so on. Then consider the design of the room and work with the existing palette and textures.

If your focal point is in the larger space, the table flowers may prove less important. Big items—branches placed in urns around a bandstand, little bushes threaded with twinkling lights circling the cake table, topiaries on the buffets—make big statements. They are often less expensive than is assumed, and are even more affordable if they allow you to cut back on centerpieces.

Masses of wildflowers overflowing straw baskets at an outdoor summer party make a soft, casual, less-static statement, while more formal arrangements like floating gardenias say elegance. Let your floral arrangements express the ambience of the space, the mood and tone of the event, and—whether you grow every single blossom or just contribute your ideas to your florist—the preferences of child and parents.

TO EVERY THING THERE IS A SEASON

Using seasonal flowers and greens brings a heightened sense of our place in the universe and connects us to the Jewish calendar. And these blooms are likely to be fresher and less expensive, too. We've put together a list of seasonal ideas to share with your florist or local nursery, or do on your own for centerpieces, larger arrangements (used for buffets and other special tables or for decorating the room), and arrangements for the synagogue bimah.

Fall

CENTERPIECES

- Coxcombs in autumn crimsons, pink sedum, orange physalis (Chinese lanterns), hypericum berries, and red grasses. Burgundy corncob candles.
- Early fall or late summer: splatterware bowls of red and yellow cherry and pear tomatoes, set off by crimson, gold, and chartreuse zinnias.
- Clusters of champagne grapes, lady apples, thistles, bittersweet, and bunches of cinnamon sticks presented on grapeleaf-lined trays. Tablecloths in a variety of fruit colors. (These are also beautiful on buffets.)

LARGER ARRANGEMENTS

- Pale bushel baskets filled with a palette of fall blues: spiky sea holly (eryngium), salvia, gray-blue globe thistle (echinops), Russian sage, and metallic blue viburnum berries.
- Some or all of the following: magenta flowering kale; purple, white, and slender lilac eggplants; artichokes; glossy green and purple peppers; and sweet-smelling

basil (the opalescent variety is especially lovely) or purple-flowering sage. Purple and emerald candles of varying heights intermingled with the vegetables. (Small groupings make great centerpieces, too.)

ON THE BIMAH

- Japanese painted ferns, hostas, and astilbes for a native woodland effect.

Winter

CENTERPIECES

- Potted winter jasmine or pots of paperwhites and pale grape hyacinths, nestled in cobalt-blue glass bowls piled with chestnuts instead of pebbles.
- Japanese-style rock gardens with miniature bonsai trees.
- Orchids: white, fuchsia, or yellow, in stems or potted in speckled, dark-olive clay containers. A tangle of ivy, embellished with a few orchid blooms tucked here and there, cradling tall candles. (Orchids are no longer as costly as they used to be; a spray of orchids or a potted plant may be less expensive than a traditional floral arrangement.)

LARGER ARRANGEMENTS

- Baskets of pomegranates, Seckel pears, black grapes, and pinecones. Pots of orange amaryllis for height. (Make smaller scale versions for centerpieces.)
- Small citrus trees, with a few clementines, lemons, and limes scattered on the table. Matching trailing organza ribbons or raffia tied around the trees or pots. Lemon, lime, and orange sherbet–colored tablecloths.
- Birds-of-paradise and tropical ti leaves to conjure rain-forest lushness in the dead of winter.

ON THE BIMAH

- Winter branches decked out with nosegays tied on with thin silver ribbon.

Spring

CENTERPIECES

- Moss-covered baskets filled with pots of chive blossoms, lavender, and fresh mint leaves. Garnish with little spring lettuces, like ruby-tipped or plain bibs or frisées, that resemble blossoms.
- A variety of nodding daffodils, from cream to butter yellow to saffron, some cut and interspersed with green asparagus, tied with raffia; others potted.
- Individual nosegays of sweet peas or delicate bouvardia at each place setting.

LARGER ARRANGEMENTS

- Flowering topiary trees, like viburnum and azalea, either singly or an assortment. Topiary trees are lovely in other seasons too: Miniature roses, hibiscus, and lantana are just a few ideas. And they are very attractive on the bimah as well.
- Large arrangements of forsythia and pussy willows on buffets or in urns around the room; yellow and white tulips and ranunculus in silver and pewter teapots at guests' tables. Charcoal, ivory, and yellow repeated in table linens for a handsome effect.

ON THE BIMAH

- Branches of mountain laurel or flowering spring trees, like peach, plum, cherry, or apple blossom. Or branches of purple and white lilacs.

Summer

CENTERPIECES

- Varying shades of pink and purple sea heather and fragrant beach roses in round glass vases that are layered on the bottom with a collection of colored sea glass; vases may be tied with trailing pink and purple ribbons. Or tall glass vases of sea grasses in blue-tinted water, with a few exquisite large shells set decoratively on the table. Stands of tall silver-plumed reeds placed around the room.
- A late summer cornucopia of colorful peppers and pattypan squashes. Nasturtiums in a family collection of little pitchers or teacups.

- Silver pedestal bowls filled with Queen Anne cherries; pink- and orange-streaked garden roses (inserted in flower tubes) and fresh spearmint tucked in among the cherries as garnish.
- Bright blue bachelor's buttons or cornflowers, and white bellflowers or anemones.

LARGER ARRANGEMENTS

- An assortment of casual loose arrangements: stone jugs with Queen Anne's lace, ox-eye daisies, and black-eyed Susans or loosestrife on buffets; masses of cosmos and flat baskets or little wooden crates of simple lawn grass at dining tables.
- Tall vases of pink or white peonies.

ON THE BIMAH

- Rose bushes, to be replanted later in the synagogue garden. "Roses of all kinds filled the temple and a carpet of rose petals covered its beautiful marble floors," Edda Servi Machlin poignantly describes her bat mitzvah in Pitigliano, Italy, on the eve of World War II in her book *The Classic Cuisine of the Italian Jews*.

FLOWERS OF ALL HUE

Whether selecting bold, dramatic hues, shy pastels, or a combination, playing with colors is a surprisingly simple way to achieve striking effects. Try these ideas.

- Flowers in a single range of hues, like roses from blush to hot pink.
- Monochromatic palettes: different varieties of blossoms all in a single color, such as irises, roses, calla lilies, and freesias, all in yellow, with perhaps a few glossy lipstick-red anthuriums to accent the trace of crimson you may find in many of the blooms.
- Variegated flowers to tie two different color choices together: streaked hydrangeas paired with matching sky-blue tablecloths and pistachio napkins; birds-of-paradise with coral and periwinkle linens.
- Groups of three bud vases arranged together, each filled with a different color of the same bloom: try tulips, roses, or ranunculuses.

- Sunflowers in cornflower-blue pitchers, the colors echoed in a butter-yellow or apricot tablecloth with cobalt napkins for an easy Provençal look.
- A variety of colors, heights, or even types of floral arrangements instead of a uniform look at all the tables: a rainbow of potted primroses at smaller tables with the same colors mirrored in tall bouquets of snapdragons at the larger tables.

THE LANGUAGE OF FLOWERS

At each moment, the knowing heart is filled with wonder.
—AMIDAH PRAYER

To encourage conversation among your guests, consider these centerpiece ideas to break the ice.

- **Plants with biblical names.** Wandering Jew, Jacob's ladder, Solomon's seal, Elijah's bluegrass, and so on. Attach labels to identify them and include something on the origin of the name—fact or fiction!
- **Flowers that carry a message.** Irises symbolize wisdom, anemones sincerity, zinnias goodness, and peonies happiness. If your choices symbolize a trait or embody a wish for your child, let your guests know.
- **Family photos in the floral centerpiece.** Place flat baskets filled with strips of simple lawn or wheatgrass on long, rectangular tables; fashion miniature "clotheslines" out of wire and anchor them in the grass, then hang old photos on the line with tiny clips. You can continue the family heritage motif in the decor with blowups of some of the pictures, and a few favorite family recipes on the menu.

FLORAL RUNNERS AND CARPETS

Add color and texture to dining areas and buffets with a bas-relief of low potted plants, flowers in near-invisible containers, or branches, leaves, and blooms placed directly on the table.

- For rectangular or square tables, cluster small pots of blooms like African violets down the centers of tables. Or arrange tiny glass vases of assorted cut flowers.
- "Carpets" that sit flat on the table, like fruit runners (garlands of grapes and flowers or vines or grasses studded with figs, dates, and nuts), grapevines threaded with cut flowers that have woody stems (for a Havdalah-time celebration, add cinnamon sticks and other spices, and tiny dried rosebuds), or aromatic herb runners (rosemary is especially pretty when blooming with tiny blue flowers).
- Clusters of lemon leaves or ivy with flowers like fragrant white freesia tucked here and there (if water tubes are necessary, they can be hidden under leaves). Or line tables with a variety of vibrant fall foliage.

FLORAL CONTAINERS

It was important to Hannah and her family that younger brother Nathan be included in her bat mitzvah, but his autism was severe enough that even his presence at the service was called into question. But as guests entered the celebration space for the luncheon, they smiled to see that Nathan had obviously been given an important job: hand-coloring the clay pots on the dining tables. The magic marker designs were . . . magical.

Like a frame for a painting, a floral container should form a complementary setting that showcases the flowers. Choose a container proportionate to the arrangement, whose material, shape, and style harmonize with the bouquet and the decor. For dinner tables, select arrangements that are not too high or compositions that are more horizontal. The containers, when filled with flowers, should be low enough to allow guests to see the people sitting opposite or raised high on pedestals above guests' eye level. An unattractive plastic vase will not only detract from your pretty flowers, but also may be the one item directly in your guests' line of vision throughout the meal.

For full, lush arrangements, choose a container that is as tall as it is wide, like a fishbowl. And remember, the wider the mouth of the container, the more flowers you will need.

If you are giving away the flowers or centerpiece to a single guest per table, avoid confusion by discreetly indicating the lucky recipient beforehand. For example, place a note on the table or in their seating card advising guests to look under their plate for the message saying that they have been "chosen."

Florists' containers. Many florists have lovely containers that they will loan or rent, and they can design an arrangement with a removable insert. Or simply tie the bouquet together. That way, the guests can take the flowers home when the vases go back to the florists.

Dress up inexpensive or plain containers. Do what florists do. Cover that underwhelming pink plastic vase with sticky floral tape and glue on large leaves, moss, ivy, or scattered blossoms. Wrap with fabric, ribbon, or raffia. Attach beads or fringe to glass containers with a glue gun. Line the inside of clear vases with large, flexible leaves. For an attractive, inexpensive container, rinse empty half-gallon milk cartons, cut the very top off each, and gently pull the edges so the carton is completely open. Wrap with double-sided tape, then attach fresh green leaves in layers, pressing to smooth them, and overlapping as necessary, so the carton is covered completely. Tuck the ends of the leaves under the carton, tape flat, and if you'd like, tie a raffia or ribbon belt around the middle. Keep it fresh overnight by wrapping with moist paper towels.

Look beyond vases. Uncover many intriguing containers in your own home, and use them alone, or to supplement a florists' collection. Anything that holds water can be used as a vase: tin buckets, champagne coolers, watering cans, brandy snifters, and eclectic jars of all sorts, including mason, jelly, and baby-food jars. Many bottled waters, liquors, and perfumes come in interesting vessels. Mix and match your containers: low and tall; one large and clusters of three or more small ones. You can use containers that aren't waterproof, too: Just place a small water-filled vase or bottle, or a bowl fitted with dampened floral foam, inside. We've used baskets, decorative tins, flowerpots—even scooped-out pumpkins. Recycle the small wooden boxes from clementines and other fruit: Line them with plastic, and fill with potted impatiens or other little plants like pansies. Later, the flowers can be replanted.

MAKE IT A MITZVAH *Set up a cupboard at your synagogue where members can donate vases for all to use. This is a great idea for all those vases that accumulate from flowers delivered by the florist.*

IF YOU ARE WORKING WITH A FLORIST

While many florists focus primarily on flower arranging (simply delivering the bouquets to the doorstep), some will set up the displays, and others include floral and room decorating—even event planning—among their customized services. If you are unfamiliar with the florist's style and the quality of flowers used, visit the shop to see sample displays and photos. Discuss the look you want to create and the blooms you prefer. You can order a sample flower arrangement to make sure you are "looking at the same picture."

Ask for a contract from your florist for whatever services he or she is providing; flower prices can vary seasonally, and yearly (if you are booking in advance). A contract is an assurance that the date and time are reserved, and that the only arranging left to do is the flowers!

PUTTING TOGETHER YOUR OWN FLOWERS

If you'd like to arrange your own flowers, try to enlist a few friends to help, or consider hiring an art student from a local college or design school for assistance. If you are not confident about your design skills, you may feel more comfortable limiting yourself to one or two colors or kinds of flowers, and making a sample arrangement first. Having a sample is also a good idea if friends are helping you out. Here are some tips to help you on your way.

Preparing the flowers. Strip stems so no leaves will sit below the water line. The bacteria they create not only damages flowers, shortening their life span, but also discolors the water. Cut stems on an angle with a sharp knife. Don't cut flowers and foliage to a uniform length; a variety of heights will look less contrived and add texture and dimension to your arrangement. Immerse the stems in warm water mixed with floral preservative.

Loose bouquets. Some flowers—a bunch of zinnias or a mass of daisies and black-eyed Susans, for example—practically arrange themselves; in the right container they require nothing more than cutting their stems diagonally before placing them freeform into water. Other bouquets may need more structure, especially those that contain several flower varieties. For these arrangements, insert foliage or the heavier-stemmed flowers first, crisscrossing them as you go to create a gridlike framework that will support the lighter flowers you add next. Leave some stems an inch or two taller and place them toward the center. Add smaller, more delicate flowers last.

More structured arrangements. Make lattice grids using tape to give your flowers more structure if needed to keep them in place or to permit a wide-mouthed container, like a crock or a pitcher, to accommodate a too-sparse bouquet. Form a lattice over the top of the container using floral or even plain-old Scotch tape. Make sure flowers and leaves cover the tape when inserted through the grid.

Tied bouquets. If you need to make up arrangements in advance and transport them later, you may prefer to make the bouquets at home and tie them so they're ready to place in containers at the site. Should it be necessary to change the water, it's easier if your flowers are bound together. Binding is also a good idea for flowers with stems that are easily bent or broken, like daffodils. Lay flowers out on a flat surface. Tallest blooms usually work best toward the center, unless they will curve and arch over the rim of the vase. Line up all the stems and gather into a bouquet; for a fuller-looking arrangement, spread into a spiral by twisting the bouquet one turn clockwise or counterclockwise. Secure with long twist ties or kitchen string. If you're using clear glass containers, choose a tie that blends in with the stems or cover it with raffia or colorfast ribbon.

Smaller arrangements. Even if your centerpiece consists of a single bloom or type of flower, it should never look skimpy. Choose a narrow bud vase to showcase a solitary flower. To make a sparse bouquet look fuller, lusher, don't be afraid to cut the stems short, bunch the blossoms tightly together, and use a smaller vase. Shorter stems always focus more attention on the blossoms of flowers.

Dried arrangements. These are not only long-lasting, but can be prepared well in advance of your celebration. A quick search on the Web, using the keywords "dried flowers," will familiarize you with some of the many kinds available, from flowers and grasses to pods, from simple to stagy. One of our favorites is echinops (blue-purple and gray globe thistle) with golden wheat or millet and yellow billy buttons. Other intriguing combinations include green wheat or barley and lavender, lunaria (Chinese pennies) and physalis (Chinese lanterns), and fresh or dried pepperberries with silver green sage.

Arranging flowers in advance. If you are preparing your arrangements a day or two ahead, mist with cool water, cover loosely with thin plastic, and keep in a cool place, away from drafts and direct sunlight. (Misting with cool water will also perk up flagging arrangements.) Change the water if it looks cloudy. If someone will be arranging your flowers for you at the synagogue or the celebration space, leave clear instructions or a diagram, explaining what you would like to have done.

Transporting flowers. Carry bouquets in a large flat box. If you need to transport arrangements in vases and other containers, place them in milk crates and insert crumpled newspapers between the vases to protect them. If you will be delivering your flowers early, make sure they will be stored properly.

When You Need Less-Expensive Choices

- **Buying loose cut flowers,** even retail, is much cheaper than buying arrangements because you eliminate the floral designer and setup charges. Order flowers online direct from growers. The California Cut Flowers Commission website (www.ccfc.org) features links to several commercial growers willing to sell to retail customers and ship overnight via FedEx. And many large cities have wholesale flower markets that might sell to retail buyers if the order is sizable.

- **Potted plants and bushes.** If you have a large space to decorate, renting small trees or large potted plants may be more affordable than purchasing flowers. Choose potted flowers and greenery, trees, and bushes that you want to replant or use as houseplants. If you don't have a garden, share them—and perhaps some of the cost—with a close relative or friend who does. If there is a bar/bat mitzvah reception either the week before or after yours, buy your potted plants and bushes with the other family and split the cost.

- **Ready-to-bloom bushes** like roses or hydrangeas, can be bought, then planted in your garden and snipped when needed. A florists' tip: Those garden roses will look more abundant if you combine them with carnations in the same shade.

- **Floating blossoms.** Reminiscent of miniature reflecting pools, the refined look of blossoms swanning in shallow glass bowls, bubble vases, or other clear vases is very easy to assemble. Though each flower must be beautiful and in perfect shape, since every one is showcased, you get a lot of bang for your buck here, and you'll need fewer than you would for other arrangements—not to mention that you won't have to worry about broken stems. Choose fully opened blossoms with full, wide, flat heads that will float easily, like gerbera daisies, dahlias, sunflowers, peonies, garden roses, and camellias.

- **Save substantial delivery charges** by asking a friend or your older child to pick up your flower order.

- If you have adequate storage, **it's never too early to begin collecting** vases and other containers at tag sales and flea markets. One family set aside twenty classic one-quart glass milk bottles from their regular milk purchases over a six-month period. They looked charming filled with yarrow and Queen Anne's lace on blue-and-white checkered tablecloths. After the bar mitzvah, the bottles were returned for the original bottle deposit they had paid. Cost of vases: zero.

PLANNING YOUR FLOWERS AROUND A MITZVAH

Many families want to create an arrangement that speaks to their child's mitzvah project. When done with whimsy and panache, decorations that embody a sense of purpose will delight your guests, and, in the best-case scenario, might even enlist them in your cause.

But too often we've seen a heavy-handed approach. While a book drive, for instance, is certainly laudable, haphazardly stacking a pile of books as a centerpiece doesn't add anything to the table. And the books might equally inspire guests to get more involved in the project if they were collected at a clever display in a designated corner of the room.

Jane Carroll, a floral designer and event planner with offices in New York and Los Angeles, has helped scores of families incorporate mitzvah projects into innovative, attractive centerpieces. Her creative designs invariably combine practical items to be donated with fresh flowers and greens, bringing simple elegance and humor to her arrangements. She created a Warhol still life from pyramids of Campbell's soup cans (destined for a food bank), accented with little bouquets of red and white zinnias set in empty matching soup cans as vases, and she transformed muffin tins, measuring cups, and cooking pots into floral containers for an agency that collects kitchen equipment for homeless people moving into permanent housing.

With Jane's help, we've put together some tips and guidelines to help you create your own mitzvah centerpieces.

Think of your centerpiece as a way to **"tell the story" of the mitzvah project,** not merely display items you are donating. All storytelling entails careful editing to keep the focus sharp and everyone interested. Jane told how to keep the needy warm in winter by dressing styrofoam long-necked head and hand mannequins with new ski hats, scarves, and gloves, adding eyes and earrings of real flowers and other whimsical touches; later, the winter woolens were taken to a shelter.

If your mitzvah project includes items you are giving away, **select only those that are good-looking,** eye-catching in color or shape, to display as part of your centerpiece. Limiting what you put out leaves your guests not only space to dine, but room for their imagination. For example, if you are collecting children's shoes (for an organization like Shoes That Fit; www.shoesthatfit.org), stash away the sturdy, less exciting lace-ups. They will be included in your delivery to the charity, of course, but why put them on the table? Instead, buy shiny kids' rain boots in primary colors. Tuck glass jars inside the boots to protect them, and fill them with bright flowers. Picturing the puddle-jumping child who will receive them will make your guests smile.

Or **tell the story through suggestion and metaphor.** If your child is completing a bike-athon as a mitzvah project, you're not going to put a bike on each table, but perhaps you can scavenge some attractive used parts or accessories at garage sales or flea markets. For centerpieces, you might combine handlebars with flower arrangements in a "spoke" formation; have flower-studded pedals at another table; and mannequins adorned with a blossom necklace and dressed in a cool helmet and biking glasses at another. For a Habitat for Humanity project, one family arranged their table flowers in paint cans, and we placed ladders on the buffets, setting flowers in clean plaster buckets between the rungs. We've previously mentioned Sara's mitzvah project, involving horseback-riding therapy for young children. For her buffet centerpiece, her family created a beautiful pastiche of wooden horses, prize ribbons, bunches of carrots with greens, small bushels of apples, and country flowers.

Practical Matters for Mitzvah Centerpieces

- If you are working with a florist and/or a party planner, share your ideas with her. She may not know what a mitzvah is, but she knows how to nurture a budding project. She has great resources, and may take on your concept as a creative challenge. And you'll all feel good about the work you've done. Or visit your local home improvement store for advice. Better yet, put your fix-it friends to work.
- Coordinate your displays with floral and plant material, as Jane does. Keep your

designs clean, uncluttered, and, most important, playful. Sort by color or shape, and cluster like items together to maximize their visual effect. For a kid's hospital, Jane grouped colorful picture books by size and shade and enclosed them between bookend vases holding matching flowers. For a donation of art supplies, you might fill a paint can with paintbrushes and flowers that echo their shape: erect, narrow-blossomed carnations or calla lilies.

- When purchasing materials, shop wholesale or at discount stores. Your local retail merchants may offer a discount if you explain that the items will be donated to charity. That will give you more money to put into the project.

- You may need to buy additional items for the display because the ones you have already bought or collected for the mitzvah project will not work well as a centerpiece. More to donate!

- Leave background elements simple: white or neutral-colored tablecloths, and so on. Extravagance would serve only to distract, rather than enhance, here.

- Include a little note on the table, nicely worded, explaining what the mitzvah project is all about. Make sure to mention if you plan to donate any of the centerpiece items, and request that guests leave the display intact—or you may find that the baseballs and gloves you carefully stacked in a pyramid are being used for a game of catch in the corner!

MAKE IT A MITZVAH *Hand out seeds of an especially beautiful or unusual flower from the party for guests to take home. • Recycle or replant potted plants, either in your home garden or a windowsill or in a community garden space. • Plant a garden with fruit or flowers to be used on special days: greens and flowers for Shavuot, the first fall fruits for Rosh Hashanah, or the first spring vegetables for Passover. • Plant a tree, a rosebush, or even a window box of ivy that can be used for another life-cycle event—even a chuppah (a wedding canopy), one day.*

10

SETTING THE TABLE

MICHAEL'S TORAH PORTION, Vayigash, *was about Joseph,
his many-colored coat, and his responsibility to his brothers: "God did
send me before you to preserve life, the life of my brothers. I too accept
responsibility for them." Building on this imagery, the family decided
on an intimate homespun reception, 1960s style. The rainbow-colored
cloths covering the large round tables were fringed at the edges, reminiscent of the tzitzit on a Jewish prayer shawl, representing the
mitzvot, or commandments. Though the table setting was simple—
inexpensive glass plates, tie-dyed napkins to match the tie-dyed
yarmulkes, and bright woven bread baskets—it all held together. The
potluck foods were set in simple vessels at each table, family style.*

*After dinner, guests circled around the tables in an original square
dance choreographed by Michael's aunt called "The Tzitzit," which
symbolically brings together the four corners of the earth. (Gathering
the tzitzit can be interpreted as a call for repairing the world, and for
his mitzvah project, Michael asked everyone to bring warm coats,
which he matched up with colorful scarves and gloves, then donated
to a local shelter.) When the guests returned to their seats, the tables
had been reset with colorful pottery mugs to match the family collection of kooky teapots from around the world.*

There used to be a very good custom in Jerusalem," a

scholar recalled in the Talmud. "A tablecloth was spread at the door. So long as it was in place, guests would enter the house; when it was removed, they would not."

Centuries later, things haven't changed much. Today a tablecloth—and attractive tableware—still makes guests feel welcome. Whether it's a treasured lace cloth for the traditional synagogue Kiddush, a family collection of soup tureens on colorful buffet tables, or square dessert plates at a seated dinner, a lovely table says slow down, this is not about casual eating and drinking, but something more. The festive table invites your guests to share a leisurely meal and good conversation. And even simple food becomes special.

WHAT'S PROVIDED?
WHAT WILL I NEED?

Sarah's family decided to hold her bat mitzvah luncheon at the synagogue, and booked a charming local restaurant to cater it. The agreed price included a light, delicious menu, and even flowers for the tables. What was not included, her mother learned at a tasting of the foods to be served, was china: The restaurant was set to serve the meal on paper plates. Fortunately, the family was able to stretch its budget to rent standard china from a local party supply store.

· · · · ·

"If it were any other color," Justin moaned when the country club displayed their only tableware: pastel pink cloths with floral dishes. His family asked

what other bar mitzvah boys had done: Had any come up with a clever solution that wouldn't break the bank? One boy, they found out, had covered all the tables with denim toppers, and replaced the floral china at the kids' tables with the country club's poolside service: clear glass plates. Blue glass vases filled with wildflowers completed the casually handsome look.

When your caterer or full-service location is providing the table items, always find out exactly what you are getting, and ask to see it. Ask if there are other options, and what other families have done. If there is a separate charge for the tableware, request a line-by-line breakdown, so you'll have an idea of costs should you want to substitute something nonstandard. If the tableware is part of an all-inclusive flat fee, but you want to use outside sources for some or all of the items anyway, ask whether you can be credited for items you won't be using.

If they are not supplying your tableware, caterers and other party professionals will still be able to detail exactly what you will need to have. Do-it-yourselfers often depend on rental companies and other parents in their child's bar/bat mitzvah class as their information sources.

Even when it seems you have no options—when the caterer has just a single set of linen and china, for example—you can still personalize your table and make it your own.

TABLE LINENS

Table dress can set a tone, add color, character, and warmth, and even move along the "story" your celebration is telling.

If you haven't already chosen colors for the celebration—based on the colors at the party space, for example, or the invitations you've selected—now is the time to do so. It might simply be your child's favorite colors, or shades and patterns that seem to define him or her (like crisp navy and white for a child whose tastes run to preppy); or colors you and the rest of the family are drawn to, inspired by a special vacation spot or a beloved family painting.

You might choose colors suggested by the Torah portion or the theme of the celebration; the desert colors of Exodus, for example, or gold hues from the song "Jerusalem of Gold." Perhaps there is a palette you associate with Judaism, like the stained-glass windows of your synagogue or the exuberant shades of a Chagall.

Or take your cues from the calendar. Dina's bat mitzvah fell in the spring, so her family selected a variety of greens—including huge monstera leaves as place mats. Stevie chose cool water shades for his late-summer celebration.

When selecting your linens, keep these guidelines in mind.

- **Consider the room.** Take into account the room colors, what time of day the celebration will take place, and how much light there will be. Hannah chose her son's favorite colors—navy and powder blue—in a fabric with a slight sheen to reflect the shimmering candlelight at their evening reception. But as she unwrapped the linens the night before, she realized they appeared murky black and gray in the dark banquet room. Last minute pinspot lights for the tables recaptured the true blue.

- **Stay true to your own taste, and your child's.** Deep, vibrant colors can be dramatic and fun, and we've seen unusual combinations that worked beautifully: lime-green tablecloths and lilac napkins bridged by a table arrangement of green-and-purple orchids; striking tables covered with floral toppers and contrasting striped underskirts. But this is *your child's* big day, and he or she must feel comfortable with the choices. For children like Sarah, for whom a subdued, cream-colored cloth with a slight weave to add textural interest was just different enough, whites and pastels may be the safest options. Other families prefer different table coverings for adults' and kids' tables (see "For Kids Only," page 139).

- **Don't lose sight of the big picture.** There may be a lot going on your table and around it: China, flatware, glasses, centerpieces, and chairs will all obscure some of the cloth. If very little of your tablecloth will be visible, you may want to choose a less-expensive one, saving the money for something else that's more important to your family. Heidi, a landscape artist, selected a white linen because there was so much on the table already, and she didn't want the gorgeous flowers to be upstaged.

- **Use patterns effectively.** With a highly patterned cloth, you'll need to take special care in coordinating with everything else. The batik scarves (sold as pareos) Sharon found on sale proved attractive toppers for the buffet tables, complementing the wooden serving bowls, bread boards, and baskets. But solid-colored cloths looked best with the gold-and-blue-rimmed china on the dining tables.

- **Cloth length**. We prefer a tablecloth with a longer drape. It is more attractive, not that much more costly, and will hide unsightly table legs. Or use a long underskirt with a topper.

Renting Linens

If you are not working with a party professional (many floral designers and caterers offer this service) or a full-service location, it's easy and efficient to get a sense of the great variety and range of linens available by searching on the Internet under the keywords "party linens" or "table linens" or in the Yellow Pages under "Party Supplies or Rental." Or walk into a linen rental or party supply store. Many companies offer unusual choices, in addition to the standard linens. Often they have linen books available for browsing, sometimes organized in color schemes, or in coordinating patterns (same color and weave, but different pattern). The price range is enormous: from under $10 to well over $50 per cloth, with fabrics that include traditional cotton, polyester, and other blends, plus linen, velvet, organza, and more.

When you find something you like, request a sample whole cloth for inspection. We've found that small swatches can be misleading: They don't show repeats in patterns, and faded cloths (especially cotton) may not even resemble the swatch. If they can't send you a sample, ask if the cloths have been laundered often.

Never leave soiled tablecloths in plastic bags. It not only promotes mildew, but as we can attest, it's all too easy to toss them out with the garbage.

Ideas for Unusual Linens

We often rely on an unusual cloth to accent a special table: a Renaissance still life of gorgeous fruits printed on a black background for a table of fine wines and winter fruit; a taffeta plaid shot with a whisper of metallic ribbon to brighten up a table filled with seating cards. You can put some unique cloths on just a few of the dining tables, too, if they are placed well throughout the room. Some families play up the "head" table, where the bar/bat mitzvah is sitting, like Sally, who spread her table with her great-grandmother's Sabbath cloth from Poland. Here are more out-of-the-ordinary linens.

- **Couture cloths.** Luxury linens for rent include sheer overlays, in stunning patterns like embroidered gold scroll (dazzling over a royal-blue cloth, more subtle on pale yellow) or lavender swirl (to top a deep-purple linen); lush new damasks in sage green or deep sienna to complement the fragrant herbs or spices at Havdalah time; elegant silks and luminous satins in soft candlelight or hot electric colors; exceptional textured weaves, like puckered striped cotton in samurai red.

- **Luscious prints.** Eye-catching patterns are available in chintz and a host of other fabrics: antique maps, toile, color-saturated botanicals, rich Moroccan rug patterns, and more.

- **Unique toppers and accent cloths.** Placed over full-length liners or on cocktail and dessert tables, these cloths are easier to find or make up because of their smaller size. We've seen them in brilliant duppioni silk, rich velvets, and fabulous flea-market vintage fabrics. Jodi, a theater director, dyed accent cloths to match the funky stage screen she was recycling as a backdrop for the band at Lily's bat mitzvah.

- **Simple white cheesecloth as overlays.** The wonderful nubby dimension cheesecloth gives to undercloths in palettes from sand and mocha to dusty rose and turquoise and brings to mind ancient biblical weaves. Equally at home as cool sophisticate or casual nature child, it plays well with both boys and girls. We find it especially handsome over best-quality, fine-textured burlap. Buy it inexpensively in fabric—not kitchen—stores, and simply cut to size, no hems needed: The delicate tracery of threads is part of its charm.

In addition to the ideas we list in this chapter, there are many other unique table toppings described throughout the book, especially in chapter 9, "Flowers and Centerpieces."

When You Need Less-Expensive Choices

- Form a buying co-op with the families in your child's bar/bat mitzvah class. One co-op bought a set of parchment-colored cloths and napkins for all the boys and girls to use at their celebrations. The neutral linens could be dressed up easily with unique table decorations when desired. One bar mitzvah boy's mother pinned colorful decorative paper leaves (available in many stationery stores) to the cloths around the front of the buffet tables, then coordinated dishes and napkins to the leaves.

- Flat bedsheets can be cheaper than renting tablecloths, especially when purchased during white sales. Available in 66 by 96 inches (twin), 81 by 96 inches (full), 90 by 102 inches (queen), and 108 by 102 inches (king), the sheets will look crisp and fresh right out of the package. They can be laundered at home and then reused or donated to shelters.

- Look for inexpensive remnants. Remember that not all tablecloths (or napkins) have to be identical, and you can coordinate colors and patterns when you use smaller remnants.

Ideas for Do-It-Yourselfers

- For buffet tables, arrange a king- or queen-size solid-color sheet as a liner and place a patterned sheet on top. Now swag the top sheet: Drape the bottom edge of the sheet at equal intervals and secure with pins. Camouflage the pins with fresh flowers.
- Silkscreen simple images on plain white muslin or sheets, or use muslin with colorful runners. Judaic art kits are available, offering user-friendly stencils in Hebrew lettering and Jewish designs for table runners, banners, and ritual items.
- If you can't hem cloths, trim the fabric with pinking shears or glue ribbon or felt around the borders. Or gather the edges of the fabric, twist it into a "ponytail" or "bun," and secure it tightly with a rubber band; hide the rubber band with ribbon or raffia, and tuck the fabric edges underneath, using pins if needed to keep the edges up and out of sight.
- Create the overlays we used at Julia's party (see page 109). Use bolts of netting with a tea-stained appearance, available at fabric stores. The grids on the netting make it easy to cut into fifty-four-inch squares. If you wish to use these overlays again for other parties, hem the squares with ribbon, but they are also lovely when they're simply cut using pinking shears. Tulle, inexpensive lace, or other open-weave or sheer fabrics also make good overlays. For the liners, use plain white or pastel tablecloths.

NAPKINS

Like tablecloths, napkins come in every hue, from delicate lace-edged varieties to textured weaves. Always check prices. Rental fees can be surprisingly moderate—in some cases, not only less expensive than paying to have your own laundered, but cheaper than many types of paper napkins. To add verve, it may prove more economical to splurge on printed napkins, paired with a solid tablecloth, than on a printed tablecloth.

When budgets permit, we always suggest cotton or linen napkins to those using cloth—even if the tablecloths will be synthetic—because these natural fiber napkins are more absorbent and pleasant to the touch.

Here are more napkin ideas.

- We often "paint" dinner and buffet tables by playing with napkin colors. Instead of matching napkins to the tablecloth color, we contrast them: For a fall bar mitzvah, we arranged cranberry napkins on butterscotch tablecloths on some tables, and inverse colors on others, then finished with vases of celosia and burgundy and striped ivory roses, and sprays of red maple bedded on deep-hued fall leaves. You can create a pattern of colors with napkins: for round tables, a circle of sun colors, from straw to fire; or a forest palette from palest leaf to pine green in a basket on a buffet. Or use a different napkin color for each table.

- To dress up napkins, tie them with bows of beautiful ribbons or ribbons inscribed with fun sayings or the child's name (available at party, stationery, and balloon stores, where you can also purchase inscribed cocktail napkins). Wrap ivy around the napkins, then slip a flower through the greens if you like. Or use cookie cutters or inexpensive ethnic bracelets as napkin rings.

MAKE IT A MITZVAH *Purchase table coverings that can later be donated to your synagogue or soup kitchen. Pretty oilcloth—very popular in Europe—is perfect for buffet tables and need only be wiped down before it is used again. • Cut accent cloths for small square cocktail tables out of lightweight polar fleece; no hemming is needed. The little squares will make soft baby blankets for a women's shelter. • Inexpensive or closeout kitchen or tea towels in gingham, waffle weave, or floursack cloth make colorful, fun napkins, and they will look crisp and sharp the first time you use them. They're easy to launder (don't bother ironing them), and would be welcome donations at soup kitchens like ours that prefer them to paper towels.*

TABLES

Tables are available in an assortment of sizes, shapes, and even heights. Sixty-inch rounds (seating eight to ten) are the standard size provided by most facilities, like synagogues, hotels, and banquet halls. Many spaces also offer rectangular tables in six- and eight-foot lengths (seating six to ten)—known as banquet tables, these are typically used for bar and buffet setups, too. Seventy-two-inch round tables (seating ten to twelve) are another option. Tablecloths come in specific measurements to accommodate different table sizes. Check with your linen provider to ensure proper fit. For eight-foot banquet tables, you might need to overlap two or more cloths.

Since guests often end up talking only to their neighbors when seated at large tables, whenever possible, we like to have some smaller tables too to allow for more intimate conversation: forty-eight-inch rounds (seating six to eight), or thirty- and thirty-six-inch round cocktail-size tables. Besides, a mix of tables or an unusual configuration can add pizzazz to a room. We find that kids prefer rectangular tables because it's easy to talk across their narrow width. Combine half-round ends with banquet tables to make ovals or extra-long tables. High tops (forty-two-inch tall tables) are a fun flourish for nonseated parties and perfect for beverage setups. Lay out tables in creative ways to suit your design needs: horseshoe, diagonals, even serpentine.

To estimate how many tables you can comfortably fit in your dining space, add approximately six feet to the diameter of each table. That will allow room for chairs and space for guests and servers to circulate. For each place setting, estimate about twenty inches of linear space.

CHAIRS

Though often ignored, chairs are an important decor element; not only will they affect the look of the tables, but usually there will be quite a few of them in a room! If they are not provided with your location, or if your budget permits you to consider other options, there are many rental chairs available, from plastic to ballroom chair, natural wood to forest green. Chair covers can be rented from most table linen companies to camouflage unattractive chairs or coordinate a design scheme. More important, how does the seat feel? Your guest will remember the comfort of the chair more than its good looks.

PLACE CARDS

At seated parties, most families assign guests to a table, not to specific seats, displaying cards with the guest's name and table number on a table near the entryway to the event. If you have many guests, always alphabetize the names. Here are some unique place-card ideas.

- Instead of arranging place cards on a table, display them pinned on screens, on burlap draped over doors, or on an easel. For fun, lay the cards out right to left, mimicking Hebrew lettering, on a scroll of paper.
- Instead of cards, use guests' photos inscribed with their table number; or bookmarks (with the guest's name written on back, either computer printed or written in calligraphy), that double as party favors and tie in with book-drive mitzvah projects.
- Use a metallic gold-ink pen (available at art supply and many stationery stores) to write names on pretty leaves, fall fruits, or vegetables (like tiny crabapples or miniature pumpkins set in hay). Or try white ink on black poster board, putting names on postcards, or, for Purim, inscribing masks from the dime store.

TABLEWARE: CHINA, STEMWARE, AND FLATWARE

As with renting tablecloths, if you're renting tableware, take the time to check out party rental services and Internet sources for different options and creative ideas. Most renters decide to use the same supplier for all their tableware needs (dishes, glasses, and flatware) because it is more convenient and often saves on shipping charges. Kosher caterers will usually supply their own certified tableware, but there are kosher rental companies available, and many general rental companies offer kosher lines as well.

We often mix-and-match china patterns and achieve striking effects inexpensively by using just one or two nonstandard items in a place setting: martini glasses for mashed potatoes while the rest of the meal is served on basic white china; black dinner plates to contrast with white linens; a unique service plate that can be reused for dessert. At one memorable synagogue bat mitzvah luncheon, jewel-colored wineglases sparkled on otherwise pristine white tables, echoing the stained-glass windows in the spring sun.

Here are more ways to add impact with tableware.

- **Besides standard white,** choices in china include white or ivory with a variety of rims in all colors and prints, even a rain-forest one; glass, round and square-shaped, plain or embossed with flowers, in sapphire, ruby, or emerald; casual plates like country splatterware or elegant etched glass with antique gold borders. And deep pockets can consider beaded glass plates, Japanese pottery, Asian celadon, and fine Sevres porcelain.

- **Splurge on a single special element for the table.** Place a large, pretty plate in the center of the table, like a cabbage leaf majolica platter to hold dips or spreads, for instance. Or put a pressed flower, petals, or a small leaf between clear glass and china plates.

- **Flatware options** include not just silver, silver plate, and stainless, but handles made of bamboo or handles that are twig- or rope-shaped, or painted in every color of the rainbow.

- **For glassware,** you can set your table with clear or tinted, stemmed or not, delicate and graceful like Baccarat or sturdy as a beer stein. Wine lovers should steer clear of stemware that is too small (for example, six-ounce capacity).

MAKE IT A MITZVAH *Organize the bnai mitzvah class to collect tableware, pots and pans, and other kitchen equipment and deliver them to a local Jewish Family Services program for redistribution.*

Tips on Renting Tableware

Order extra quantities to allow for accidents or unexpected guests. When the rented merchandise is delivered, check to ensure you have everything that you ordered and that you received everything on the packing list. Make sure rented equipment is in working order. Note any items that are damaged or chipped on receipt and keep track of any damaged merchandise while it is in your care (you will probably be charged replacement value on these). If you are working with a catering company, they will typically perform these services for you, as well as repack the merchandise for return.

USING PAPER AND PLASTIC PRODUCTS

Before buying disposable products—not only paper or plastic, but miracle fibers that look and feel like linen—check prices: Renting or buying the real thing may be as cheap or nearly so. We avoid using disposable products whenever possible because reusing and recycling the earth's resources seem more in keeping with Judaic traditions, and so many of today's mitzvah projects speak to environmental concerns.

But you can set a very pretty table with paper and plastic. And there *are* times that they will be your best option because they are less work, easy to find, cheaper, and will save you money on service staff.

- When possible, look for eco-friendly choices. Spray eco-friendly plain brown wrapping paper in gold or autumn colors, using leaves as stencils, or purchase inexpensive vellum ends at a printing shop, and cut into overlays for the tables.
- Paper plates and plastic cutlery are best suited for foods that are not too heavy or wet on the plate. Try to plan your menu accordingly, or reserve paper for your cocktail and finger foods, and other light fare, and serve the heartier food on china.
- Paper plates and napkins come in a remarkable array of colors and prints. Add interest by mixing patterns with complementary solids or combine two coordinating prints: Our fish-print plates (great for brunch) looked lovely with a geometric pattern in the same black-and-tan color scheme.
- For meals, paper napkins should be large; consider colored or patterned ones if paper plates are solid, especially white.

MAKE IT A MITZVAH *Set up a recycling program at your synagogue, if none exists.*

SIMPLE TOUCHES TO DRESS UP
THE PLAIN VANILLA TABLE

White linen topped with white china can be ho-hum at children's celebrations. If you want to dress up an all-white table, try one of these ideas.

- Place small toppers or heirloom doilies under the centerpiece.
- Arrange flowers, herbs, or leaves directly on the cloth (see Chapter 9, "Flowers and Centerpieces").
- Scatter colored orzo or fanciful stamp-outs decoratively in the center of the table (avoid glitter and similar decorations that can easily get into the food).
- Create pretty, computer-printed menus on colored paper (either just a couple, framed, for the buffet or dining tables, or one rolled and tied with ribbon for each guest). Combine with place mats made out of handmade papers, available at art stores. The torn edges look wonderful. Use Hebrew letter stamps for extra fun.
- Think color when choosing flowers and candles: a burst of periwinkle cornflowers, radiant marigolds surrounded by a cache of little gourds, a flame-braided Havdalah candle. (See chapter 8, "Decor and Lighting," and chapter 9, "Flowers and Centerpieces," for more ideas.)

FOR KIDS ONLY

Recognizing that a bar/bat mitzvah is a multigenerational party, many families decide to dress the kids' tables more playfully. Look for fun ideas—decorations that might serve as party favors or tie in with the entertainment, yet work well with the rest of the room decor and the spirit of the celebration.

Here are some suggestions.

- Shiny colored cellophane over white tablecloths; clear plastic plates and cups in bright colors; rainbow cellophane flowers as centerpieces and party favors.
- Pink- and purple-striped tablecloths; clusters of little pink and purple balloons with streamers, anchored with rocks that have been painted with purple glitter and

inscribed in white marker with words or phrases such as: *Peace, Friendship, Shalom,* and *You Rock!* Rocks can be used as party favors or later "planted" in the child's garden. Alternating pink and lilac china or paper plates and napkins.

- Potato prints: Carve out triangles and squares on potatoes, brush them with yellow, orange, and blue paint, and use the patterns to print designs on brown wrapping-paper tablecloths. Use the same potato prints on invitations. Square paper plates in a denim pattern. For centerpieces, fill vases with daffodils, then place in short brown paper bags; pinch bag with a raffia bow or fold down the top so the bright blooms are clearly visible.

ADDING A JEWISH FLAVOR

A bar/bat mitzvah is a wonderful time to begin a family collection of Judaica, if you don't already have one. The family Kiddush cup or new challah knife can be used in the traditional ceremonies, while other Jewish objects, like a group of beautiful spice boxes or tzedakah holders, can be supplemented by some borrowed ones and become part of the table decor. At a recent autumn bar mitzvah, two pearly gray shofars (rams' horns), crisscrossed in front of the family's silver candlesticks, formed an eloquent still life on a charcoal silk-covered buffet table.

Here are some additional suggestions.

- Look for unusual Judaica. We've used quirky Jewish figurines, like our windup guy who dances to his own hora music, or a couple celebrating Shabbat. And we've displayed a miniature jewel-like sukkah, made of a thin wire frame; inside, its ceiling hung with delicate glass fruits, and a tiny table set with harvest foods.
- Use the same fabric for the kippot and small accent cloths or napkins for the tables. Brian's kippot were made to order inexpensively out of a blue-and-gold cotton sun, moon, and stars print. The same fabric was decoratively cut using scalloped scissors and placed under the centerpieces on the tables.
- A grandmother appliquéd blue stripes on off-white raw silk to resemble a tallit and sewed the symbolic fringes in each of the four corners. The family used this to cover the synagogue table for the Kiddush served following services; three years later, the bar mitzvah boy passed it on to his younger brother for his Kiddush.

FROM GENERATION TO GENERATION

Grandma's Fiestaware teapots or heirloom sterling serving spoons, a favorite aunt's zany salt and pepper sets, one of your fine china dinner plates placed under the centerpiece at each table—using personal objects and special collections like these opens the door to your family stories, bringing a special intimacy and charm to the table. You can supplement your own personal items with additions from friends' and relatives' collections, if needed, or use some treasured objects at just a few tables. Even something simple—the family's holiday tablecloth or platter—can suffuse an ordinary restaurant buffet table with the warm ambience of your home.

Consider some of these other touches of home at the table.

- Place small framed family photographs around the centerpiece. Or buy the popular photo holders made of curved wire and designed in styles from antique to whimsical. Each can hold several photos of family members.
- If you or the bar/bat mitzvah child has started a collection, incorporate it into the centerpiece: miniature tea sets for a bat mitzvah dessert party; a collection of tops and dreidels at Hanukkah time.
- Involve siblings in creating the table decorations. They can help with place cards, napkin rings, party favors, and centerpieces.

- Tables covered with sunny Provençal cloths printed with black olives and their silvery green leaves continues the story told in the *Tetsaveh* Torah portion: pressing olives for the purest oil to light the *Ner Tamid,* or Eternal Light.
- Cut cobalt-blue felt into triangles and fit them together to form a large Star of David topper to cover a white tablecloth.
- Instead of numbering the tables, many families choose Judaic names for them. We've seen tables named after Noah's animals, the Twelve Tribes, and Jewish heroines, from ancient figures like Sarah, Miriam, Ruth, and Esther to modern-day people like Emma Lazarus and Hannah Senesh. Peter, whose portion was *Bereishit* (Creation), labeled his seven tables for the Days of Creation: Light and Dark; Oceans and Sky; and so on.

CELEBRATION OF HANUKKAH AND THE NEW
MOON: SAM'S BAR MITZVAH

B y the age of two, he was asking for crepes at breakfast instead of pancakes. At eight, he was spray-painting autumn fruits for Mom's centerpieces. But that comes with the territory: Sam is Lori and Jon's son, and
growing up in his mom and dad's catering business, he chose to work in a
soup kitchen for his mitzvah project and developed his own very definite ideas
about food and parties. When it came time to plan his bar mitzvah celebration, he wanted a say in all the decisions.

First was the location. Sam really wanted to be in the new synagogue
space. Trouble was, it wasn't ready yet. In fact, the congregation had been
renting space at the nearby Unitarian church for services. But the family decided to take a chance that the renovation from former textile mill to spacious
temple would be completed just in time.

Sam's bar mitzvah date was quite unusual: Because it fell on a Rosh
Hodesh (the New Moon) during Hanukkah, the congregation read from three
separate Torahs—to honor Shabbat, the New Moon, and Hanukkah. His *dvar*
on the Torah and Haftarah from Zechariah was wide-embracing, too.
Beginning with Pharaoh's dream of seven fatted and seven lean cows, he led
the congregation from an exploration of Joseph's relationship to God and
Judaism to the Maccabees and the desecration of the Temple. Just three short
months had elapsed since the terrorist attacks of September 11, and Sam re-
fracted the discussion through the lens of recent events. At the close of his
commentary, he invited everyone to consider thoughtful questions like "Who
is our Joseph today, guarding us from destructive forces and evil?" and "Could
you forgive the terrorists as Joseph forgave his brothers?"

"As evening falls," the invitation read, "join us to light Hanukkah candles,
eat heartily and dance a hora or two in honor of this day." Sam and Lori had
visited several Judaica stores before they finally saw four menorahs handcrafted
by the same Israeli artist. Each represented a different, potent Jewish symbol:

a dove, a ram, Jacob's ladder, and the Tree of Life. And then, quite organically, Hanukkah became the organizing thread of the party, and things just fell into place.

For the food, there would be mini latkes among the hors d'oeuvre, including Aunt Jayne's special chickpea recipe, and Israeli fritters for dessert. They would play a dreidel game, with a fun reward system they devised, entailing gold and silver gelt, Maccabee candies, and bookstore certificates. In keeping with the Festival of Lights, there would be candlemaking for the younger guests (including sister Sophie and Sam's many cousins), using kits, and supervised by a couple of hired teenagers from the congregation.

The handsome new menorahs would decorate the kids' tables. Sam proposed that guests light menorahs in lieu of a traditional candlelighting. The family asked relatives and close friends to bring a menorah from home, so that each table could light a menorah and set it in the window to blaze its presence, the first Jewish synagogue in this neighborhood.

That evening, arriving guests were ushered upstairs for drinks and hors d'oeuvre at the latke/potato bar (Sam's idea—guests spooned every imaginable topping onto his favorite, blissfully rich mashed spuds). An accordionist played familiar Jewish melodies; the family had won his services at their synagogue's fund-raising auction.

Rosemary and sage were passed around in a fragrant Havdalah ceremony lit entirely by the glow of braided candles. It was an important prayer because it was the first in the new synagogue, so afterward the rabbi recited the special *shehecheyanu* blessing reserved for the unique, joyous occasions of life.

Then guests walked downstairs for dinner. The new space *was* ready in time, but just barely; the carpet had been installed the night before. The original overhead lighting was harsh and glaring, inimical to the candle-glow ambience they were trying to achieve, and the family had budgeted for a lighting designer. He turned off all the lights in the room and replaced them with indirect lighting: pinspot lights to bathe each table in a separate pool of light, and a buttery color wash on the walls. The effect was subtle—only a theatrical friend noticed—but the warm glow flattered both diners and dinner, and played up the old wood beams and other architectural details.

The synagogue had no tables and chairs yet, so the family rented round tables and fruitwood ballroom chairs. To avoid long lines at the buffets—anathema to Jon—three separate buffet areas were set up, one for every forty people. Each was set in the center of a cluster of tables covered in dusky blue with brick-colored napkins. The bronze moiré cloths, copper serving pieces, and wooden bowls on the buffets picked up the wood tone of the beams and fruitwood chairs. Close by, large farmhouse tables, made from old barn doors balanced on trestles, groaned with wine, grapes, cheeses, and, later, desserts.

An avid carnivore, Sam had wanted meat, but the synagogue rules insisted on a pareve menu. So they settled on family favorites from Peachtree & Ward's recipe file, like slow-roasted salmon with a tomato compote, toasted orzo, and, for the kids, gnocchi with pink tomato sauce. And no meat meant that in addition to the fritters, there could be lots of dairy-rich desserts, including a chocolate roll and a buttery tarte tatin. As a special treat, tiny homemade ice cream cones were butlered to the guests.

Sam, whose taste in movies leans toward Mel Brooks's *History of the World—Part I*, was looking for some offbeat entertainment. He came up with the idea of hiring character actors to dress up as long-lost Jewish relatives. And characters they were—straight out of *Fiddler on the Roof:* a baker who proffered challahs that were glued to a tray; Yentl, who tried to marry the baker's daughter off to Sam's friends. They were great fun, and some guests may still be wondering whose side of the family they came from!

Then the band got white hot, and everyone got into serious dancing.

In the dead of winter, the family lit Hanukkah candles against the darkness and placed huge pillar candles everywhere—on tall iron stands, on terra-cotta tiles—some decorated with a few seeded eucalyptus leaves, some with black grapes. How could they have known that the candles' glow that evening would also represent the spirit of a dear family friend, Max, who had passed away in Boston just as Sam was finishing up his service in Philadelphia?

TRADITION!

Kiddush, Motzi, Candlelighting, and More

THE MOTZI, THE HORA—*in fact, all the familiar old blessings and traditions that Harriet remembered from her childhood—took on a joyous new life in her congregation. The richness of these Jewish traditions nourished her family from Shabbat to Shabbat, especially during her husband's recent illness. And Matt's October bar mitzvah would celebrate this richness.*

Trouble was, Matt had invited seventy of his friends. How would the ceremonies she wanted to include at the party go over with all those adolescents, so many of whom were unfamiliar with their traditions? What Matt enjoyed alone with his family was one thing, but how would he react in front of his cool teenage buddies?

At the party, when a swath of stars winked from the nighttime sky, the family rabbi called the guests away from the hors d'oeuvre for the Havdalah service. She explained that the ceremony bids farewell to the Sabbath and ushers in a brand-new week. She lit one of the twisted candles, and asked for volunteers to light the eight others on the table. Eight boys rushed up, took a candle, and touched it to the flame. Tin foil collars on the bottom of the candles protected their hands and caught any wax drips.

The rabbi inhaled the lavender, rosemary, and cinnamon sticks. "This fragrance will give sweetness to all the days of the coming week. Who else wants to sniff these herbs?" Girls and boys, Jewish and of other faiths, crowded around her, grabbing for the aromatic bundles; laughing, they too inhaled deeply, then passed the herbs to the other guests.

"Cup one hand in front of the flame," the rabbi demonstrated. "Do you see how the reflection of the light on your fingernails makes shadows on your palm? The play of light and dark, new and old, past and future—separation, that's what Havdalah is all about.

"Who knows," she asked the now-enthralled teenagers, "who knows? Maybe this week will be a week of peace? Maybe this week will be a week of joy? Maybe this week will be a week of love. Shavua tov. A good week."

In a world where nothing seduces like the high-tech and future-forward, it may surprise many parents to learn that their children, thirteen-year-olds going on twenty-five, still feel a strong connection to centuries-old customs and traditions. Just try serving chicken on Thanksgiving or eliminating the finger-flicks of wine for each plague at the seder. And, of course, some Jewish customs are just plain cool by any measure. Think of adolescents kicking with wild abandon as they circle the room in an exuberant hora, or a teenager, arms extended in the air in a blissful parody of Rocky, as he is carried around by the strongest men in the room in the Ashkenazi chair dance.

At life-cycle events, rituals connect us to the enduring rhythms of the natural world: A song or a morsel of bread, invested with new meaning, tastes richer. These shared customs and traditions create a "we-ness": "We sniff fragrant herbs at Havdalah," "We light candles." By inviting others to share in our rituals, we connect them to our community, and, even more intimately, to the warm embrace of our family.

MAKING TRADITIONS MEANINGFUL

Rituals and traditions that speak to us add depth to our celebrations. They come alive in the personal stories we bring to them and share with our families: your grandmother's raisin challah at Rosh Hashanah, the Kiddush cup your son made in nursery school, the way Uncle Sam always mumbled the Motzi so no one was ever sure he knew the words.

But don't stop at memories. Breathe in the aroma of the challah; savor the wine today. Explore the traditions to see how you can invest them with new life; create vivid new memories. Taking a cue from an old Syrian custom in which children traditionally escorted the bar mitzvah child by candlelight, have your child make a memorable entrance, walking into the darkened celebration space accompanied by friends holding votives to illumine the path. Or twist fragrant lilacs around the chair that will hold your daughter for the Ashkenazi chair dance.

For a culture to survive, it cannot remain static. We cherish our traditions for their timelessness, but what keeps them alive is the way they continue to unfold in our changing world. The Torah has been compared to an unripe fruit of Divine Wisdom. It is our job to participate in its ripening.

. . . . .

Taking one's place in the community as a bar/bat mitzvah is all about continuity: Linking the past to the future, the streams of time become timeless. We love to weave customs and traditions, so integral to this milestone, throughout the celebration. They form an essential part of our party planning, touching on everything from design choices for the table and decor to food, music, and dance.

The purpose of this chapter is to highlight some of the most important blessings, traditions, and customs, revive a few from the past, and perhaps even inspire you to create some anew. We begin with the best-known blessings and traditions, then go on to

Havdalah and others that, though less familiar, will equally enhance your simcha. Finally, we talk about the rhythm of the rituals, and how the traditions can work organically to orchestrate the bar/bat mitzvah celebration.

GETTING IN TOUCH WITH YOUR TRADITIONS

As a family project, research your own treasury of family customs. While interviewing older family members, you may discover intriguing information about their upbringing and history: how they celebrated Shabbat or a bar mitzvah they remember from long ago. This is a wonderful way to get siblings involved in the simcha and invite participation by grandparents and other relatives. In interviewing their Sephardi great-aunt, the Israels learned about *desayuno,* the brunchlike meal traditionally served following Saturday services, and at their Kiddush buffet decided to feature the delectable Turkish recipes she remembered as a girl.

Rabbi Nancy Fuchs Kreimer created a family history book for her daughter's bat mitzvah, writing about each grandparent and all eight great-grandparents as well. Partygoers felt a deep sense of the family's roots when they read one of the many xeroxed copies of the book available at the reception; each family member was given a copy to take home.

If you don't have a large family, or if your family members were not born Jewish, interview members of your synagogue about their Judaic customs. We have previously mentioned how important it is to recognize the multicultural background of children with non-Jewish relatives or birth parents at the bar/bat mitzvah. Make it a family project to explore the culture of your child's ancestors; there are many ways to incorporate other traditions into the celebration that would not conflict with Jewish practices. At the bat mitzvah of a girl whose birth parents were Guatemalan, the family covered buffet tables with the traditional, colorfully embroidered cloths from that country.

Food traditions are perhaps the easiest to include: kosher fried chicken and corn bread to honor a bar mitzvah boy's African-American dad and his southern roots; mini egg rolls, chow fun, and fortune cookies with wise Jewish sayings—all kosher—in recognition of an adopted bat mitzvah's girl's Chinese birth parents.

THE KIDDUSH (BLESSING OVER WINE)

There is no holiness except with wine, there is no blessing, except with wine,
in a place where joy dwells.
—Zohar, Bamidbar 189b

It was Louise who introduced the family to the Friday night Kiddush ceremony when she began Hebrew school. Her father, who had not chanted the blessings since he was a teenager, found the silver embossed goblet his grandmother had given him more than thirty years before at his bar mitzvah, bought a bottle of kosher wine, and encouraged the eight-year-old as she stumbled over the words the first time.

Before long, Louise was singing the Kiddush every Friday night, in the honeyed alto that always reminded her mom of gospel singing. Afterward, Louise would take a sip, scrunch up her face as the sweet wine trickled down her throat, and pass the goblet. Mother, father, and little brother, each in turn, took a sip and, mimicking her, grimaced, too. And Shabbat dinner began.

So when it came time for Louise's bat mitzvah, it was only natural that she would chant the benediction over the wine. A waiter wheeled the table to the center of the dance floor. Set on an amethyst-and-emerald cloth, surrounded by clusters of purple and green grapes, was the family Kiddush cup. Louise stood next to her family. After she sang the blessing, she took a sip, made a face, and passed the cup. Mother, father, brother scrunched, and the party began. L'chaim!

L'chaim! To life! The familiar toast says it all: From the beginning of Jewish time, wine has been a potent symbol of life's blessings, as well as its sacredness. Kiddush, the prayer over wine, actually means "sanctification"; it is chanted or recited not only to consecrate the Sabbath and holidays, but to mark every joyous milestone, from the brit to the wedding. Many families choose to have a wine blessing at the bar/bat mitzvah reception in addition to the Kiddush said at the synagogue directly after services. This benediction, completed by the requisite drink of the wine, symbolically sanctifies both the child and the meal that follows.

Fruit of the Vine

The goblet is poured with a sweet kosher wine, a fine contemporary dry kosher wine, or grape juice. Red, rather than white, is the color of choice, and sweet wine is more customary because kids find it more palatable.

The Kiddush Cup

The cup can be a simple wineglass, perhaps one decorated by a sibling, or an heirloom Kiddush cup from the family's collection. Often, the bar/bat mitzvah child receives a Kiddush cup as a gift from the congregation or one of the guests.

Who Says the Kiddush

The family decides who will chant the blessing: It may be a grandparent, a parent, an older sibling, or the bar/bat mitzvah child. The honor may be shared: For instance, all the members of the synagogue bar/bat mitzvah class may say the prayer. If the rabbi or the cantor is present, he or she may be asked. In the Orthodox tradition, if there are men available, a man will be chosen to say the blessing. Some recognize both sides of the child's family by giving one the Kiddush and the other the Motzi to recite.

Drinking the Wine

Only the person who recites the Kiddush blessing is required to drink some of the wine; but in small groups, it is lovely to pass the goblet around so each may share the taste of life's joys. For large groups, glasses of wine or grape juice are usually made available.

Imaginative Kiddush Ideas

- One father computer-generated beautiful labels, detailing his daughter's name, the date of the bat mitzvah, and both a transliteration and a translation of the Hebrew blessing, and pasted them over the original ones on bottles of wine and grape juice. Every table was set with a large goblet that would serve as a Kiddush cup, filled with wine or juice from one of the specially labeled bottles. After the rabbi chanted the benediction, the guests tasted Hannah's happiness as they passed the goblets around.
- To make the Kiddush more festive at stand-up buffets, servers can pass glasses

filled with wine or grape juice on trays. One wine enthusiast served cordial glasses of sauternes to make a sweet blessing for his daughter.

- At Danny's bar mitzvah, the last one in his synagogue class, the children brought the Kiddush cups the congregation had given them to the reception. Together they all said the blessing, clinked their silver glasses, and swallowed their juice.

MAKE IT A MITZVAH *Grapes growing in a cluster are a symbol of community. Sign up to work on community projects, such as cleaning vacant lots and parks, creating gardens, or rebuilding playgrounds that have fallen into disrepair.*

And Every One a Kiddush?

The term *Kiddush,* which is familiarly used to designate the blessing recited over wine on special occasions, may confuse some people, because Kiddush usually refers to the well-known wine ceremony on Friday night (which Louise chanted; see page 149) and holidays like Passover.

To make matters even more bewildering, *Kiddush* is often used to denote the collation following synagogue services on Saturday morning (which is preceded by the prayer over wine). Many congregations also refer to this collation as the *oneg.* This type of Kiddush or *oneg* is described more fully in chapter 13, "Celebration Food and Drink" (see page 200).

THE MOTZI (BLESSING OVER BREAD)

From the immense, burnished gold twists at a chic Paris banquet to the *haimishe* whole wheat braids at a potluck *oneg,* nothing announces a Jewish simcha more than the iconic fragrant challah. And why not? Fraught with symbolism, the braided strands of dough represent not just the staff of life, but unity and peace as well. The delicious egg bread nourishes the soul as much as the body.

Since biblical times, bread has been at the heart of the Jewish meal. When we break bread at any Jewish festive occasion, someone leads the group in the Motzi, a blessing that gives thanks for the feast we are about to share with family and friends. While there are separate blessings for meat, vegetables, and other foods, when the benediction over bread is made, it is unnecessary to recite prayers over any of the other foods eaten. The exception is the prayer chanted over the wine. When Kiddush is said, the challah is covered by a cloth, which, according to some traditions, protects the bread from embarrassment at seeing the wine blessed first.

FROM GENERATION TO GENERATION

Lovely challah covers, traditional in many Jewish homes, remind us to be sensitive to another's feelings. If you have your own family cover, use it at the Motzi ceremony. Or buy or make one, and create an heirloom for your child.

Although challah is the festive bread of the Ashkenazim (descendants of eastern and central European Jews), today many Jews of other backgrounds make a Motzi over challah at their celebrations, too. Of course, you can use any bread for the Motzi: pita, Yemeni kubaneh, an Indian sweet chapati, and, at Passover, matzo.

Who Makes the Motzi over the Bread?

The image of a beloved grandparent blessing the bread at a bar/bat mitzvah speaks eloquently of continuity, the oldest generation linking the youngest to tomorrow. So, many give the honor to the eldest, or the most respected, member of the family. But there is actually no hard-and-fast rule about who can make the Motzi and cut the challah. The choice rests completely with the family, and we do encourage you to include your child in the decision. It may be someone who is especially close to the child: an uncle, a rabbi, a teacher. Or sometimes the bar/bat mitzvah child makes the Motzi as a symbolic gesture of his or her new maturity.

In the Orthodox tradition, the honor of making the Motzi, like the Kiddush, is reserved for men only (unless there are no men present). However, in other traditions, women are increasingly asked to make the blessing as well. The honor may also be shared—by all the grandparents or siblings, for example. If you don't do a candle-lighting, including both sides of the family in the Motzi is one way to avert ruffled feathers.

Dividing the Challah

After the blessing, the bread may be sliced and then passed around so that everyone may eat some before beginning the meal. Among some Jews, however, it is customary to break the bread by hand-tearing it into pieces instead of cutting it with a knife. Recalling the verse in Exodus 20:22 comparing a knife to a weapon of war, as well as Isaiah's prophecy ("And they shall beat their swords into plowshares"—Isaiah 2:4), they believe that using a metal knife would profane the blessed bread.

Salting the Challah

After blessing the bread, some people traditionally salt it before eating it—a reminder, some say, that salt accompanied every sacrifice at the Temple altar in ancient days, and that since the destruction of the Temple, the dinner table has become our present-day altar. For others, salt evokes the admonition in Genesis 3:19: "By the sweat of your brow shall you get bread to eat."

A Challah Bank

You might want to get together with the other families in your child's bar/bat mitzvah class, or with a group of friends, and form a challah co-op. Take turns baking fresh challahs for each bar or bat mitzvah celebration or other simchas as they arise.

MAKE IT A MITZVAH *Numbers 15:19 tells us: "When you eat the bread of the land, set apart a portion for a gift to God." Bake an extra challah on Friday, set it aside, and take it to a nursing home nearby. Or bring fresh bagels there once a week.*

Break bread with those different from you: Start a series of Shabbat home dinners where you invite people from other cultures, other faiths, or different walks of life to break bread with you. Or contribute to an organization that unites people of different cultures, like Seeds of Peace, a summer camp that brings together Israeli and Palestinian kids.

THE CANDLELIGHTING CEREMONY

Diehard Bob Dylan fans, the Kayes knew they could create no finer parental blessing than the one the songwriter had composed for his own son in "Forever Young." They, too, wanted their son to stay surrounded by the light and love of friends and family. Dovetailing the candlelighting with this blessing would be pure magic: The jokes and rhymes they'd heard so many other people use to call up their candlelighters were not their style.

At the celebration, after the hors d'oeuvre were served, the bandleader asked the guests to come up, take a lit votive candle from one of the trays the waiters were passing, and gather around Robbie. Then, as friends and family held their candles in the darkened room, the Kayes blessed their son, reading the lyrics to "Forever Young," and, with apologies to Bob, added a stanza thanking the guests for being present. Afterward, as the band played a slow rendition of the song, guests carried the candles to their tables to light up the rest of the room, and then sat down to a wonderful meal.

. . . . .

Much loved, and too seldom seen,
Light a candle, Aunt Irene.
—ALLEGRA GOODMAN, *THE FAMILY MARKOWITZ*

The bar/bat mitzvah candlelighting ceremony is a relatively recent Jewish American tradition, probably dating back to the early 1950s. Commonly, thirteen or fourteen people, chosen by the family, light candles on a cake, and perhaps make a special blessing for the child. Most likely, the ceremony was a way of investing the celebration with more meaning and spirituality, but it has resonated powerfully among many Jews because it mirrors the commandment to kindle lights that is at the heart of many enduring Jewish rituals, and allows the family to honor relatives and friends. It is optional, and generally not included in Orthodox celebrations.

We've seen candlelighting ceremonies that brought tears to our eyes: At one, a handicapped boy asked his two special-aid teachers to light candles for him—the only way he could honor them at his bar mitzvah, since his synagogue did not permit non-Jews to be called up for aliyot at the service. And we've witnessed others that were commandeered by a DJ with canned music. So when Debbi came to us saying, "I'm not a fan of most candlelightings, but for sentimental reasons, I want Jesse to have one because I remember mine from my own bat mitzvah," we suggested they take a fresh look and come up with a ceremony that would work for them, and fit in with their plans for the evening.

Connecting the festivities to the service. In rethinking their candlelighting ceremony, some families decide to put it in a more traditional Jewish context—emanating from the commandment to kindle, evocatively ushering in a special spirit—rather than like a birthday—that is, lighting candles on a cake and then blowing them out so the wishes come true. (Besides, we personally do not like to bring out a cake until it is to be served.) At these celebrations, glowing tapers on a great-aunt's old candelabrum or a shining rainbow of pillar candles form a transcendent symbol of burning lights. In Michigan, Jennifer combined her candlelighting with Havdalah: Each table had a fragrant homemade spice box, and everyone called up was asked to say something special to the bat mitzvah, then use the beautiful twisted Havdalah candle to light another candle. Many families choose to light one or more candles as *Yahrzeit*, a memorial that honors beloved family members and friends who have passed away.

For everything, there is a time. While most people begin candlelighting just before the meal is served, we encourage families to choose the most appropriate time for their particular party. After a long morning synagogue service, guests may be too hungry to enjoy a candlelighting ceremony, especially if it is lengthy. We tend to think of candles as illuminating darkness, so for a luncheon bar/bat mitzvah, we prefer to light the candles just before dessert or at the close of the meal, as day nears dusk.

The setting. If the candlelighting takes place at the furthest end of the dance floor, guests cannot get caught up in the moment. Consider placing it closer to your guests, or, at small celebrations, ask the guests to gather round.

Calling up the candlelighters. Many people use music to create a special ambience or signal a change in tone as the candlelighters are called up. You may want music that is meaningful to the child, or songs that capture something about each candlelighter. Whether your musician is family, friend, or professional, discuss your ideas and let him or her know if there is anything specific you want in or out of the playlist. Or you may prefer to have no music at all.

Decide who will announce the candlelighters—the bar/bat mitzvah, a relative, or the DJ—and how to do it. You might choose rhymes or simply a no frills approach, which may prove more refreshing when overwrought introductions have been featured at everyone else's bar/bat mitzvah. After you and your child have worked out and written down what you'll say, practice the ceremony at home, adding time for guests to come up from their seats, and make cuts if it runs too long.

Candles. Think about what kind of candles and candleholders you would like to use (for more information on this, see "Candle Glow" on page 104).

You'll find several examples of unique candlelightings throughout the book. Remember, the tradition is still evolving, and many people enjoy personalizing it because it is not writ in stone. And for those who cannot have a candlelighting because of Sabbath restrictions, please see "Wine-Pouring Ceremony" on page 163 for an interesting alternative. Here are more candlelighting ideas.

- During a time of crisis, the Levy family asked the guests at each table to light a candle for peace. Another family provided a different candle and candleholder to match each person lighting a candle.
- After calling up all her family members at her recent bat mitzvah, Maddy began summoning ever-larger groups of people to light a candle. Eyes and ears then riveted on the ceremony, lest they miss their turn, guests watched as everyone in the room was eventually called up. Maddy lit the last candle. Her mother concluded, "I know it sounds like a cliché, but it really does take a village to raise a child. Thank you all for being here."
- One winter evening, just before the last dance, the lights were dimmed, and Ellie's grandmother asked the guests to light individual tea lights and make a wish for the bat mitzvah girl. The band followed with "Sunrise, Sunset," and everyone got up to dance in the soft candlelight.

MAKE IT A MITZVAH *Instead of a traditional candlelighting service, one bat mitzvah girl wanted to "give back" something to those who had given so much to her. She carefully selected a charity that would have special relevance to each person or group of people she wanted to honor, and made donations using a portion of her gift money. As she called her loved ones up to light their candles, she announced the gift, and why she had chosen it.*

THE HORA

See chapter 12, "Music, Dancing, and Other Entertainment."

THE CHAIR DANCE

Following the hora, at many Ashkenazi bar/bat mitzvah celebrations, the child sits in a chair and is lifted by family and friends high above their shoulders, and "danced" to the Jewish music being played. Usually the parents are held aloft next as well. Brothers and sisters also love being invited into the chair—grandparents, too!

It is an indelible moment for the child and friends as he or she is lifted up, laughing and shrieking, feeling exalted, empowered, and vulnerable all at once. The joyous dance embodies the individual/community construct in Judaism: The individual is hoisted above the crowd, alone, in a starring role, and yet it is only through the support of the community that he or she is kept aloft. The custom most likely evolved from a similar tradition at eastern European weddings: Bride and groom sit in separate chairs and are lifted up, "attached" to each other by the handkerchief to which each clings.

A word to the wise: We have seen kids fall out of the chair during spirited bouncing. Make sure the person being lifted is tilted back in the chair for balance, not sitting upright or leaning forward. If possible, use a sturdy chair, not a folding one. To make the dance even more fun, the chairs can be decorated with streamers, ribbons, flowers, or other adornments.

TOASTS, ROASTS, AND WELL-WISHERS

"Jake, this Kiddush cup holds fine wine. When we drink it, we taste sweetness, strength, spiciness, and many more flavors developed slowly through a complex process. May you age gracefully like a fine wine, through teenage years and into the fine young man I already see in the grape harvest of your bar mitzvah today."
—Bob's toast to his nephew

Parents often deliver words of welcome or offer up a toast at the celebration. At some bnai mitzvah, this may be the first time they are addressing their guests; personal speeches by one or both parents during the synagogue service may be limited or even eliminated because of regular synagogue policy or the time constraints of the service. And some parents prefer to save the parental blessing until the excitement of the service is over, at the relaxed reception of family and friends.

Grandparents, siblings, and other well-wishers may also want to deliver a few words (this can be another way to spread out the special honorific duties, especially among those who could not be called up to the Torah for an aliyah), and the bar/bat mitzvah's friends may want to give a toast. Everyone is brimming with good feeling, and it is easy to go overboard here, so we suggest that you approach your speakers in advance, not on the spot, so they have time to prepare and polish their remarks, and gently remind them that "brevity is the soul of wit."

HAVDALAH

When the first star appeared in the sky, we lit the havdalah candle, a long multi-colored candle, plaited from thin strips like a girl's plait. We said farewell to the Sabbath.
—Karel Lamberk, *Memoirs*

Included more and more in Saturday night bar/bat mitzvah celebrations, Havdalah is one of the most poetic Jewish ceremonies. The word itself means "separation": When Shabbat, metaphorically described as the Queen, departs, we are once more "separated," thrown into chaos and darkness. So, as Freema Gottlieb puts it in *The Lamp of*

God, we strengthen ourselves by taking "light and fragrance and wine and all the symbols of *Shabbat* for the *Havdalah* ceremony, and comfort ourselves with 'songs of the night.' " With these symbols, we carry a taste of heaven with us as we step back into the workday week.

The Ritual

When night falls and Shabbat draws to a close, we bring the light back into the world with either a special single candle made of several braided strands of wax or two candles with flames touching, expressing separation and union at the same time. After lighting the candle(s), the leader of the service (this may be the rabbi, a family member, or the bar/bat mitzvah child) often hands it to the youngest child present to hold. Then a cup of wine is filled to overflowing, symbolizing a week full of joys to come, and the blessing over wine is recited. (Because the ceremony includes this blessing over wine, no separate Kiddush is made at a celebration that includes Havdalah.) Next, we say the blessing over sweet-smelling spices, like cinnamon, cloves, fennel, and vanilla beans (often in a special ritual spice box), herbs, or even flowers, and pass them around for all to inhale. The fragrance not only consoles us at Sabbath's end, but also evokes the dream of a world as sweet and peaceful as the first Sabbath, when God found all things good and rested from the work of creation. The leader takes the candle again and, holding it up, makes the blessing that thanks God for separating light from darkness, Sabbath from weekdays, sacred from commonplace. At a bar/bat mitzvah, it is a special reminder of the bittersweet separation of youth and adulthood.

The cup of wine is passed around for sips. Then the flame is immersed in the cup (or in a few drops of wine that are spilled into a saucer). A cloud of smoke, and Sabbath is over. We close with blessings for the week to come.

BIRKAT HA-MAZON
(GRACE AFTER THE MEAL)

Dessert had been served, and the big band was taking a break before the final hour of dancing resumed. The bar mitzvah boy's godmother, his mom's college roommate, who had flown East from San Francisco for his coming-of-age celebration, made her way to the empty dance floor with her acoustic Gibson guitar. Strumming, she began a home-spun song of gratitude for all the blessings we, the warm and well-fed, share. The chorus was very simple, and by the second stanza, everyone was singing along.

Considered by Jews to be a mitzvah, saying grace at the conclusion of the meal not only expresses our gratitude for the sustenance we have been given, but also sensitizes us to those who have nothing to eat. Sometimes called *bentsching*, from the Yiddish word *bentsch*, "to bless," and based on the commandment in Deuteronomy 8:10, "When you have eaten your fill, and are satisfied, give thanks to God," the actual content of the *birkat ha-mazon* has been developed and modified over the ages. Among observant Jews, the *birkat ha-mazon* consists of a series of four prayers, plus additional psalms and blessings. The service may be led by the bar/bat mitzvah, a family member, the rabbi, the cantor, or another congregant. Booklets containing the prayers can be borrowed from the synagogue; some families have lovely personalized prayer books printed for their guests.

Others who include grace after the meal may choose to have a less formal one. This might be the perfect place for a favorite poem you had to cut from your speech at the service, like e. e. cummings's "i thank You God"; a simple prayer like "We praise You God, Creator of the Universe, for the earth and for our sustenance"; or a more elaborate one, offering thanks for our blessings and calling attention to those less fortunate. Look for more ideas in your synagogue's prayer books.

You can order pretty *bentschers* (small prayer books containing just the after-meal blessings) at Judaica stores and online, or you can create your own with desktop programs. Some families have beautiful place-card bentschers made, combining the guests' names and table numbers with the grace transliterated or translated. Besides providing seating information and a memento of the celebration, they offer your guests the opportunity to recite a silent prayer if they wish. Or the bar/bat mitzvah might lead some or all of the guests in the grace.

Traditionally, the *birkat ha-mazon* blessings conclude with a prayer for peace. Calling the guests together to bless the world is a wonderful way to bring the meal to a close.

MAKE IT A MITZVAH *Express your gratitude for the abundance you and your guests have enjoyed by contributing to the Mazon charity. After the meal, tell your guests, "We've taken care of your hungry bodies, and now we would like to feed your souls. In accordance with Jewish tradition, we are sharing our simcha by contributing 3 percent of its cost to Mazon. Mazon, which means "food" in Hebrew, allocates donations from the Jewish community to nonprofit groups providing food, help and hope to hungry people of all faiths and backgrounds.'"*

HOLIDAYS

From the first fall fruits of Rosh Hashanah to the heady deep-spring flowers of Shavuot, the Jewish calendar revolves around the holidays. Each festival arrives arrayed in its own set—or sets—of customs and traditions, and if your child's bar/bat mitzvah falls on or near a holiday, it can be especially fulfilling to incorporate those customs into your celebration. Tu B'Shevat, for example, though a minor festival, has inspired many lovely customs that would enhance a bar/bat mitzvah reception. Connecting Jews to the land of Israel, it occurs in early February, when branches there begin to bud and the sap rises in the trees; in fact, it is known as the New Year for the Trees. It is traditional to eat lots of different types of fruit, nuts, and grains on this day, especially those indigenous to Israel. For a Tu B'Shevat bar/bat mitzvah, decorate with flowering tree branches. Have a challah baked with dried fruit and nuts for the Motzi; and for dessert, set up a do-it-yourself fondue station, featuring warm chocolate and caramel syrups, and as many fresh or dried fruits as you can buy.

Elsewhere in this book, we mention several other holidays whose traditions can be adapted to a bar/bat mitzvah taking place either just before or during the holiday; and we urge you to explore the many books written on the subject (we've included some of our favorites in the bibliography) for more holiday ideas to enrich your celebration.

OTHER LOVELY CUSTOMS

Some customs usually performed before or at the service may not be practicable at the synagogue, or are so much fun the family wants to reprise them. These include tossing soft candy or rose petals at the child when he or she enters the party space the first time or addresses the guests. And it's always a delight to repeat the *Shehecheyanu*, the prayer reserved for the wondrous moments of life. It is the blessing author Anita Diamant calls "the Jewish version of 'Wow.'"

CREATING TRADITIONS ANEW

While there is a blessing for everything, "every blessing has not already been written."
—TAMARA COHEN, *CONTEMPORARY JEWISH RITUALS*

It had been an especially beautiful service: Lily's moving dvar Torah, Dan's poetic words to his daughter, the congregation's animated singing. Intoxicated by the day's magic, Lily and her mother found themselves unable to wind down before the bat mitzvah party that night. The last-minute preparations had been finished the day before, and the caterers would take care of the rest.

What to do? A long walk? A bubble bath? Jodi was inspired. She remembered reading about women reclaiming the ancient ritual of mikvah in their contemporary lives. So they filled the hot tub with warm water, sprinkled in mineral salts from the Dead Sea, and mother and daughter climbed in.

"Lil and I made seven wishes and dunked ourselves under the water and had such a great time together. It was an absolute highlight," Jodi said.

The *Mikvah* Revisited

For years many modern Jews had abandoned the *mikvah*, or ritual bath. To them, the ritual immersion required for a bride prior to her wedding, and for married women after menstruating, implied that menstruation, and therefore women's bodies, were unclean. Certainly more enlightened thinking and contemporary hygiene, they thought, made such rituals outdated.

But now, as we've come to learn more about the healing and transformative effects of water, many feminists are reinventing the *mikvah*. The Sephardi custom of celebrating a bride's prewedding ritual immersion in the *mikvah* waters with wine, sweets, song, and a profusion of rose petals is being revived, but today it celebrates her spiritual purification. In the same way, Jodi and Lily connected to the ancient ritual and brought new life to it—in a backyard hot tub.

Rap to Wrap Tefillin

Men like Ed are creating rituals of their own for their sons, too. A bar mitzvah boy traditionally lays tefillin on his thirteenth birthday, so Ed gathered a group of uncles, older cousins, and friends for the morning minyan on the Thursday prior to David's bar mitzvah to honor the boy's coming-of-age. Each of the men present sang a prepared "rap," blessing the young hip-hop enthusiast, then wrapped the tefillin strap once around the boy's arm. The men then laid their own tefillin, some winding the same leather bands used by their fathers—the ties that bind, from generation to generation.

Wine-Pouring Ceremony

When religious restrictions preclude candlelighting (because either the family is observant or the celebration takes place in a space that adheres to Sabbath restrictions, such as many Conservative synagogues and Jewish Community Centers), a special wine-pouring ceremony is a wonderful alternative. At Matthew's bar mitzvah, relatives and friends were invited up to make a wish for him, just as might be done at a candlelighting. But then, instead of lighting a candle, each person poured a bit of wine into a special glass. After everyone had been called up, Matthew and his family sipped from the goblet, drinking in his guests' good wishes.

The Challah Connection

Because the twisted bread evokes humanity linked together, holding hands, in some congregations, while the challah is being blessed, everyone connects to the blessing by either holding hands with or touching the person just in front of him or her, until this human chain they have created reaches the one reciting the Motzi.

HOW RITUALS FIT INTO THE CELEBRATION

Just as rituals create the rhythms of our lives, so they set the cadences at our celebrations. They are not just spiritual "action-directives," but physical action-directives as well: Rituals gather us together, focus our attention, even change the energy in the room.

Remember, you can group blessings and traditions together, beginning with Havdalah, Motzi, and even candlelighting, if you wish. Or you can space them apart, to establish the individual rhythm of your simcha.

To Gather Guests Together

- When the party atmosphere feels diffuse, with guests entering the celebration space absorbed in separate conversations, gather them for Havdalah, a toast, or a blessing.
- If guests are scattered around the room, direct them to their tables for the Motzi before calling them up for the buffets, or for a toast before dessert is served.
- At a candlelighting, asking all the guests to surround the child for the last candle is a great way to get everyone up for a crowd-pleasing dance.

Transitions

- Rituals can exert a calming influence when energy is high. After a round of exuberant dancing, start the Kiddush service so people will take their seats for dinner.
- After kids have been dispersed at various entertainment activities—working on crafts projects, watching jugglers, and so on—seating them for a candlelighting helps refocus their attention on why they are there.

To Heighten the Moment

- To prevent a blessing from being a rote exercise, make it a face-to-face experience, performed table by table. Appoint someone at each table to be in charge of a blessing (you can do this by placing a little note near their plates). This might be the Kiddush, as we have described previously, or the Motzi.
- Ask each table to prepare a communal blessing for the child. This helps to gather the guests together for a meaningful moment, which is useful since often the groups at the tables break off into smaller conversations, especially at larger tables of ten or more people.

A TIME TO DANCE:
RACHEL'S LATE-SPRING BAT MITZVAH

This story begins in the late 1960s, when a young girl watched her family reconnect with their Algerian traditions at her brother Philippe's bar mitzvah in Paris.

Brigitte can still taste the *couscous au beurre* lunch they shared at home after the services, and she remembers the Arab band sitting on her living room floor at the party that night. "Yuyu, yuyu," the women yelled, swaying their hips to music that sounded wonderfully exotic to her ears . . . relatives and friends laughing, dancing . . . her stern grandpa suddenly moving in tune with the music, expressing himself in a way she could never before have imagined.

The memory has always been bittersweet, though, the recollection of a girl looking in, who wanted to participate but couldn't. A year and a half older than Philippe, she read Hebrew just as well, and longed to be tutored like him by the student who, they would learn, later became a renowned singer-songwriter in Israel. She, too, wanted to chant from the bimah. But you are a girl, her parents had said. *Girls don't do that.*

Philippe's bar mitzvah brought the forgotten customs of her mother's family back into her home, and Brigitte loved being a Sephardi: the food, music, and joie de vivre of her people. Now, as an adult in California, she re-created those Paris memories with the music she taught. And Brigitte was determined to keep alive the family traditions when it came time for her own daughter Rachel's bat mitzvah.

Using the theme of reconciliation from her Torah portion, *Behalotecha*, Rachel's dad designed invitations with a border of olive branches edging down the left side. On the bimah, Rachel discussed the anger she was surprised to find in her *parshah*. The Hebrews, unhappy and probably frightened at wandering in the desert so long, are no longer satisfied with the manna God had given them: "We remember the fish we ate in Egypt . . . the cucumbers, the melons, the leeks, the onions, and the garlic; but now our strength is dried up."

Moses, the intermediary between the Children of Israel and God, feels over-whelmed by his burden. And God, understandably, says the Hebrews are un-grateful, and tells Moses that they will have meat—quail—to eat for an entire month, so much that it will come out of their nostrils and be loathsome to them. All have legitimate gripes, she pointed out, and even peaceable people get angry, just like God. Extending the metaphor, she talked about Seeds of Peace, an organization that originated to bring together Israeli and Palestinian kids, but now convenes children from other areas of world conflict as well. For her mitzvah project, in addition to donating money to the group, Rachel had put together information about the organization and presented it to the rabbi, convincing him to invite one of their representatives to speak at the synagogue.

Months before, her grandmother and aunts had prepared huge trays of *pasteles*, savory cheese and spinach pastries, for the Kiddush and frozen them. Paired with fresh summery salads of smoky peppers and tomatoes, and avo-cado with toasted cumin vinaigrette, they made a delicious lunch for the con-gregation and Rachel's guests.

During the afternoon, relatives, some of whom had flown in from as far away as Israel and France, gathered around the pool at her house to catch up with each other, while sipping mint tea and nibbling *betzels aux amandes*, al-mond pastries that tasted of home.

As the sun lowered in the southern California sky, everyone got ready for the celebration that night. Rachel put on the little pearl-and-diamond earrings from Oran that her mother had given her. At dusk, when guests arrived at the beach club, they picked up their seating cards at a table adorned with olive branches and a stack of the Seeds of Peace newsletter, *The Olive Branch*. The event planner had converted the dining room into a North African food mar-ket. Strung with twinkling lights, the tented canopies set up over the "food stalls" served not only to decorate, but also to delineate each buffet area, di-vided into "Manna" (tagines including lamb with coriander seed and chicken with olives, couscous pyramids, and salads) and "Quail" stations (spiced quail and grilled tuna), with a dessert table of Algerian treats, chocolate fondue with tropical fruits, and citrus cake for dipping, and a very French bat mitzvah cake.

The buffets underneath the canopies comprised round, square, and rectangular tables, decorated with jars of preserved lemons and olives, baskets spilling a tumble of purple figs, apricots, and black grapes, and menus on parchment scrolls. The markets were arranged around a makeshift well that served as the Oasis Bar, equipped with piles of lemons, limes, and oranges for the fresh-pressed kids' drinks.

Cloths in the deep, vivid colors of the desert draped the dining tables: dusty mauve, brick, cinnamon, Nile green. They were topped with center-pieces of blooming sabra cacti. The family borrowed gold-etched tea glasses in shimmery tints from their Algerian relatives; filled with softly scented lemon candles, they made lovely votives. At a separate kids' area covered with Berber rugs, the food was set on the family's large, round brass trays, which stood just high enough for the tapestry pillow seating.

Rachel loved to dance, and the family hired a dancer to teach everyone the art of belly dancing and other Sephardi dances. Though discreetly clothed in leotard and flowing silk scarves, the belly dancer still elicited some nervous giggles from the kids at first. But she drew them in quickly, and soon the room looked like a hula hoop contest—sans the hoops, of course.

It was a beautiful night, and the Sephardi musicians led the party out onto the beach. Rachel's tutor, who had started a drumming circle at the syna-gogue, brought some drums for the kids, and the bandleader gave out *Miriam's tambourines* and wide streamers for kids to wave as they ran and leaped across the sand. Remembering the shy girl she had been in Paris, afraid to join her mother and aunts in their raucous dancing, Brigitte kicked off her heels and brought Rachel and some of her friends to the older women's circle. "Yuyu," they repeated, and laughing, rotated their hips.

Finally it was time for the candlelighting at the bonfire. Each relative called up took a tiki torch, lit it at the blazing fire, and placed it in one of the special holders provided.

Singing old camp favorites, adults and kids combined graham crackers, chocolate, and marshmallows, and toasted s'mores on the flames, an all-American end to a magical trip through the Diaspora.

MUSIC, DANCING, AND OTHER ENTERTAINMENT

*He caused half-dollars and queens to behave in bizarre ways,
endowed them with sentience and emotions, transformed them into
kinds of weather, raising storms of aces and calling down nickel
lightning from the sky. After Joe finished his act, young Maurice
Hoffman brought over a friend who was having his own bar
mitzvah in two weeks and had determined to impel his
parents to hire Joe for the affair.*
—Michael Chabon, The Amazing Adventures
of Kavalier and Clay

It's not only the jumble of generations, from Great-aunt Sylvia to little Stevie, the neighborhood friend. It's also the gaggle of teenagers, just stepping out of their childhood—the girls still playing with dolls, along with others dolled up in cocktail dresses. He's afraid to talk to girls, that one's had three new girlfriends since September. Then there's the Broadway singer at last week's bar mitzvah and the Willy Wonka and the Chocolate Factory theme at cousin Benjamin's . . .

With multigenerational guest lists, adolescents teeter-tottering into maturity, and peer pressure all around to have a party "just like everyone else's"—whatever that may be—it's no wonder many families think finding a way to entertain everyone will be the most difficult aspect of planning the celebration.

We look for entertainment that is festive and fun, that acknowledges the child's interests as well as the family's good judgment. Take the time to find out exactly what your child wants, at least as a starting point for discussion. Every child is different, and what sounds cool to one may be childish, weird, or worse to another. While we all want our children to be individuals, it's important, especially during adolescence, to be sensitive to a child's desire to conform to what friends are doing at their bar or bat mitzvah. Obviously, this will be more of an issue for some kids than for others, and we are not suggesting that if your child is clamoring for some form of entertainment you feel is inappropriate here, you should just go ahead and make the arrangements anyway. At the end of the day, what is right for your party must be a family decision.

BALANCING JEWISH THEMES AND CONTEMPORARY CULTURE

The reality is that while the bar/bat mitzvah is a timeless tradition, the celebration is rooted firmly in the present, and will, to varying degrees, reflect contemporary culture. Can you draw a line then between appropriate entertainment for a bar/bat mitzvah and entertainment for a milestone secular birthday party? It may be a fine line, but we think so. At special birthday parties, perhaps there is nothing wrong with entertainment like casino games, replete with a roulette wheel, or a beauty pageant that starts with a promenade down the boardwalk and culminates in a crowning title. But at a bar or bat mitzvah, these kinds of over-the-top entertainment hammer home the message: "The Jewish part is over. Now for the real celebration." A bar/bat mitzvah is the first step on the path to Jewish adulthood, a beginning, not an end for the child—a time for a child to demonstrate that he or she is laying a foundation for Judaic values.

We love the continuity that comes with weaving Jewish life into disparate elements of the celebration. But while the entertainment—just like the decor, the food, and so on—need not derive from Jewish traditions, it should be consistent with core Jewish values, including balance and moderation. The goal is not to have guests remark, "Wow, I never saw anything like that" or "That must've cost a fortune," but instead, "There was such a wonderful spirit at that celebration" and "What a great time I had."

In our experience, as the date of the party nears, some families panic that there won't be enough entertainment to keep the kids busy. They want insurance that everyone will be happy. Even those who have decided to draw their inspiration solely from Jewish sources may find themselves bringing in a caricaturist, someone to cornbraid the girls' hair, or other decidedly secular entertainers.

Relax. It is a party after all. And if you have kept your focus on Judaic cultural values and ideals—emphasizing the mitzvah project; connecting to family; manifesting a concern for the environment; including some of the beautiful Jewish traditions, from dancing the hora to blessing the challah; and, most important, maintaining a sense of harmony and proportion—your celebration will certainly have a Jewish flavor.

CONSIDER YOUR CHILD'S GUEST LIST

Before you plan your entertainment, think about the children on your guest list. How many you are inviting, what the boy-girl ratio is, and how well they know each other will greatly influence your entertainment choices. Consider the following:

The number of children. Organized entertainment is not as crucial for smaller groups, who might simply chat and mingle naturally, tell jokes, or play spontaneous games like tag outdoors, and, in general, require less supervision. Hanging out, isn't that what Shabbat is all about? And many low-key activities, like making up humorous or rhyming toasts for the bar/bat mitzvah child; playing Mad Libs or other simple games; or crafts like decorating the chairs to be used in the traditional Ashkenazi chair dance (see chapter 11 "Tradition!"), work best with small groups of children. As a general rule, the more kids you have, the greater the proportion of your budget you will need to devote to entertainment, and the more important it is to structure the entertainment. With nothing to do, large groups of kids left to their own devices are likely to come up with some entertainment of their own: We've seen them playing with candles, dropping things off a mezzanine, and wandering off the premises.

Kid control. As families invite larger numbers of children to bnai mitzvah, DJs and bandleaders have become increasingly important for kid control. An alternative is relying on teenage "moderators"—especially those accustomed to working with large groups of kids at camps and youth centers. We sometimes suggest that celebrants with very large families hire two sets of moderators: one for the bar/bat mitzvah's friends and another for younger siblings and cousins and other little kids.

Boy-girl ratio. Very few of the boys invited to Gabrielle's party ended up coming. As a result, the girls did all the dancing, while the boys gathered in the garden outside. Avoid a similar situation: If the party is not single-sex, make sure there is appropriate entertainment for both boys and girls. If the RSVPs indicate the boy-girl ratio of the party will be radically different from your original expectations, it may be necessary to rethink the entertainment planned.

The Bar/Bat Mitzvah Circuit

Maggie loved the entertainment at her best buddy's September bat mitzvah. The facepainting artists made up the kids with artsy designs and unique decorations, using airbrush techniques, feathers, and rhinestones. Even the boys stood in line to get a cool mask or a sequined eyebrow. But by the time Maggie's celebration rolled around in June, twelve girls in her class had the same idea for their parties. Maggie's mom had to struggle to get the kids to participate.

If most of the kids attend the same bnai mitzvah, take the date of your event into consideration when planning the entertainment. We've learned the hard way that what is novel and exciting at the beginning of the bar/bat mitzvah year may no longer be so at its close.

If you have invited distinct sets of kids who do not know each other—for example, friends from school, camp, and Hebrew school, as well as a large number of cousins— you will need to bring the groups together, whatever entertainment you have chosen. Encourage your child to introduce everyone. Teenage moderators, older cousins, and, of course, bandleaders and DJs can be particularly helpful in introducing the kids through games and other activities.

MUSIC: A JOYFUL NOISE

Music has sounded Jewish revelry throughout the centuries. David and the House of Israel made merry with "songs and lyres and harps and tambourines and castanets and cymbals" (2 Samuel 6:5) as they transported the ark to Jerusalem. Even during the mournful exile in Babylonia, sages declared it was a mitzvah to entertain a bride and groom with music. From medieval Jewish minstrels and wandering singer-poets to haunting Ladino and klezmer melodies, from Mendelssohn to Jolson, from Bernstein to Bob Dylan, folk and popular music traditions have echoed through Jewish celebrations.

Simple Music Suggestions

You could say music was the underlying motif of her bat mitzvah reception. But then music was integral to every celebration in Coryn's family.

As guests arrived at the synagogue in the evening, Coryn's sister Liana and a friend played classical violin duets in the lobby. At sunset, her aunt's clear soprano rang out in the traditional Havdalah melody. Then Coryn's uncle and his bluegrass band began with favorites soft and slow as guests sat down to dinner, gradually picking up the tempo with a sassy, harmonica-driven rhythm and blues set. After dessert, another uncle jumped onstage and joined in, while all the generations swung around on the dance floor. During the second band break, a family friend sang about coming-of-age. She had created the piece—an extra-special bat mitzvah gift—just for Coryn.

Picture a guitarist strumming classic rock as guests walk in; a CD playing lively fusion klezmer-jazz for the candlelighting; or movie tunes creating soft background music on the piano. There are so many ways even the simplest music can set the perfect ambience.

- Hiring an **a cappella singing group** is an excellent way to provide music on Shabbat not only at Orthodox parties, but also at receptions in Conservative synagogues like Matthew's, where playing music is prohibited. The a cappella ensemble his mother Judy found opened with traditional favorites like "Hava Nagilah," "What a Wonderful World," and "As Time Goes By," and during dinner, they walked from table to table, taking requests. But the big surprise came when they launched into a medley of golden oldies—everything from the Beatles to the Temptations. Their rich blend of voices more than made up for the absence of musical instruments, and suddenly everyone was up on the dance floor. You can find a cappella groups at colleges across the country, where they are an increasingly popular phenomenon.
- **Local musicians.** Hire a folksinger, a local music teacher, or a college pianist. Hire an accordion player or a string quartet from a local music school.

- A **solo instrumentalist** can be wonderful: a flutist playing sunny calypso at a late-spring luncheon, a flamenco guitarist performing Ladino melodies like "Boca del Dio" ("From the Mouth of God").
- Take advantage of the excellent **tapes and CDs** available with poignant favorites like "Oyfn Pripechuk" ("In the Oven")—the beautiful nursery song played in *Schindler's List*—to accompany the blessings or candlelighting.
- Inquire if members of a local chorale group or your own **choir** might perform family favorites for a nominal fee.
- If the family plays musical instruments, **form an intergenerational family band** to play a few songs, or ask the bar/bat mitzvah child's or sibling's music group to play.

More Elaborate Music Options

The family had asked their bandleader, Ken, to begin with the hora, so he started the set with some klezmer music. But when the bar mitzvah boy could not be found, Ken deftly segued the band into contemporary dance music. At last the boy appeared, and in a magic moment, Ken wove the familiar, traditional strains into the modern rhythms, and suddenly the band was playing the hora again.

An experienced bandleader can be flexible—reading the crowd, he or she can choose to stretch out a tune or subtly shift into something different. A live band can generate a special energy and excitement that is contagious. On the other hand, DJs play tunes by the original artists who recorded them; this may be particularly important to teens who idolize certain performers, and the DJ's repertoire is limited only by his or her music library. A DJ is usually cheaper than a band (though this may not be the case if the DJ comes with a lot of special equipment, dance "motivators," and so on); and with pre-programmed music, the DJ can keep the music playing seamlessly when on a break. As a compromise for those who can't decide between the two, hire a band and ask the bandleader to program your favorite CDs to play during the band's breaks.

Choosing a Bandleader/DJ

The band at Louise's niece's bat mitzvah had an attitude problem. Maybe they'd done one too many bar mitzvahs that month. Her friend called it "manufactured Judaism," the kind that feels too slick and canned to convey any sense of ruach, or spirit. Maybe it was the hollow way they introduced the family members, cranking it up as if they were celebrities, or intruded on the lovely a cappella Havdalah melody with a brash keyboard accompaniment. But their call to "get done with the candlelighting and on to the REAL partying" was certainly the icing on the cake. Louise would look for a more appropriate band for her son's bar mitzvah.

There's a lot more than music to consider when choosing bandleaders and DJs. They often serve as masters of ceremonies, and even when they don't, they can still exercise considerable control over the crowd by deciding what and when to play. It is essential that you feel comfortable with the musicians you hire and sense that they will be responsive to your family's needs.

Musicians usually book far ahead, so begin looking as early as possible, especially if your reception is scheduled at a time of year that is popular for parties. Some parents enjoy checking out local talent in clubs, bars, and coffeehouses; start going out a year or two before the party, and you might discover a great up-and-coming band.

Many families we know have found bands and DJs through entertainment agencies, which represent scores of musicians and can readily provide a variety of promotional material. Other good sources include friends' parties, word-of-mouth referrals from the synagogue network, bar/bat mitzvah fairs, and ads in local papers.

It's always best to book a band or DJ you've seen perform, but many bands will send you a CD or tape of their music, along with photos. Or request to see them in rehearsal or at a performance. Some bands and DJs will allow you to listen to them at another reception if you remain behind the scenes. Do ask for references and follow up on them.

Here is a checklist to consider when interviewing bandleaders and DJs.

- **Ask about their repertoire or playlist.** Are they flexible enough not only to add favorites, but to delete music you don't want? If you want entertainment to satisfy a variety of ages and tastes, you'll want to make sure they have a wide repertoire or music library. Obviously, this will not be an issue if you've decided to have only kids' music, or if the kids' entertainment will take place in a separate area.
- **Do they have experience with bar/bat mitzvah parties?** If they are unfamiliar with Jewish celebrations, you'll want to fill them in on the traditions. On the other hand, if your family is just learning about simchas yourselves, you may want a more knowledgeable group. Many DJs and bandleaders have a set program:

a drumroll to introduce the family, or a special shtick for candlelighting. Find out what they typically do. Will they accommodate you if you want something different?

- **Ask how they will be dressed.** You may prefer something different from their typical attire. One host provided kooky, colorful hats to a swing band suited up in tuxedos. They instantly became more kid-friendly.

- **Find out about their setup.** DJs with a lot of equipment often have a backdrop; you may want to know what that looks like.

- **Always get a written contract.** The contract should include: (1) the date, the time, and the place of the reception; (2) the arrival time, the time they will begin to play, and the time the program will end; (3) the exact cost of the program, plus any incidental charges, and overtime fees; (4) details on payment schedule—typically, the client pays a deposit on signing the contract, and the balance at the end of the party; (5) any extras included (for example, will the DJ bring special lighting, a sound system or other equipment, and/or favors/giveaways?); (6) any special electrical or other equipment you must provide; (7) the names of band members or the DJ and/or other personnel, and a provision for replacements, should that be necessary; (8) the number and length of the breaks, whether there will be recorded music during the breaks, and a timeline for breaks and the meal (you don't want them to eat right after the guests have finished their dinner—that's when everyone should be on the dance floor); (9) it is customary for the client to provide a meal for performers (if the caterer is charging $75 per person for a prime rib dinner, you may want to arrange for lower-priced meals); and (10) the cancellation and refund policy. You may also want to agree beforehand on tipping (about 10 percent is customary).

Communicating with the Band or DJ

As we explained in chapter 5, "Planning the Festivities," a smoothly run celebration requires good coordination among the party professionals. If possible, the bandleader/DJ and the caterer should sit down together with the host or party planner and go over the party timeline—and it's a good idea to have copies of the party timeline made for everyone involved. Discuss the amount of control you want the DJ or bandleader to have. Are there times you want no music at all? During Havdalah or other blessings? What about during dinner? Is there special music you want played then? Will they take requests?

FROM GENERATION TO GENERATION

For a personal touch, have the band play something from the family's music tradition (anything from a special long-ago lullaby to a family favorite of today).

Ask for your child's input in creating a written song list. Alternatively, you or your child may simply want to specify songs that you particularly do or do *not* want played. There may be songs with objectionable lyrics, you may want to omit line dance songs like the Electric Slide, or cut down on the slow music. Discuss how or if you want the family to be introduced, and how traditional blessings should be handled. One area you might especially want to go over is candlelighting. Bandleader Ken Ulansey plays a medley of Jewish favorites, drumming in between to link each song to the next. See chapter 11, "Tradition!" for more on candlelighting.

Talk to the bandleader/DJ about managing the decibel level. Pay attention to whom you are seating near the speakers. Check the sound system. Synagogues may have rules regarding amplification.

FROM GENERATION TO GENERATION

Continuity embraces not just Judaic traditions, but secular ones as well. Many of today's kids are rediscovering music greats of the past, and we love singing and sharing our favorite oldies with our children. If artists like Bob Dylan, the Beatles, the Stones, and Santana, or musicals like *Grease, Hair,* and others are enjoying a revival among your children and their friends, make sure their music will be played at the celebration. There's nothing like watching adults and kids dancing and mouthing lyrics in the universal language that transcends all generations.

Do-It-Yourself DJ

If you decide to provide your own music, ask a talented older sibling, cousin, or family friend to take charge of the CDs or tapes. Either make up your own playlist for the hora and other events, or ask your appointed DJ to go over his or her own ideas with you beforehand. Some locations may have a sound system available for clients' use. Be sure to test it, or any borrowed equipment, well in advance of the celebration.

Awake and Sing: Suggestions to Involve Your Guests in the Music

Sing-alongs. Kids love to sing. If your bandleader or DJ is amenable, arrange to have kids sing a few songs along with the music. Buy some silly plastic microphones and watch the kids ham it up. Or provide karaoke equipment for guests to perform, either individually or in groups. Musical moms or dads might enjoy singing something special for their child. Ben's grandmother rewrote the lyrics to a family favorite, "The Green, Green Grass of Home," as a paean to her grandson's accomplishments.

Group sings. Nothing creates community like singing together, whether it's around the piano, a campfire, or the holiday table. Even if playing musical instruments is not allowed because of your Sabbath restrictions, everyone can still join in a group sing, and sings are particular fun for those who no longer dance—or don't care to. Choose from pop or traditional songs, rounds from Jewish or family favorites, even camp tunes. Arrange to have printed sheets with the lyrics available. An excellent resource is *Rise Up Singing: The Group Singing Songbook*, edited by Peter Blood (Sing Out! Publications, 1992).

Jamming. Kids (or other guests) might join the band for a number or two, or jam between the band's sets. Hand out tambourines, maracas, bells, cymbals, and/or harmonicas.

Music games. Have your bandleader play Name That Tune, using popular songs, with the kids. In Name That Tune Scavenger Hunt, the band plays less-familiar music, like Motown, show tunes, and fifties rock and roll, and the children must locate a grown-up who can tell them the name of the song.

If your guests cover a range of ages, it's thoughtful to include some music that will appeal to all of them.

Dinner Music

Good conversation is also good entertainment. If the music is loud, it's important to have breaks during dinner so guests can talk. Or provide some low-key music while guests are eating: Ask the band to play soft background music or have a single musician go from table to table playing requests. If you're using a DJ, this is the time for mellower tunes.

MAKE IT A MITZVAH *Save the Music is dedicated to passing on Yiddish and Ladino folk music from generation to generation. Your funds will help them locate old songs and lyrics, and inspire performers to create new versions of them. Contact www.savethemusic.com.*

Promote harmony in the world: Contribute to Neve Shalom/Wahat al-Salam (Oasis of Peace), a village located between Jerusalem and Tel Aviv dedicated to building understanding between Jews and Palestinians. Contact www.nswas.com.

DANCING

Clasping hands, linking arms—dancing is all about connecting. Like Miriam, who grabbed her timbrel and danced with the women of Israel after crossing the Red Sea, we want to hold onto one another as we kick up our heels and celebrate together.

The Hora

Heidi's most-treasured memory of son Eli's bar mitzvah was the crowd of family and friends winding through all the rooms of the historic house they had rented, stomping, kicking, and swirling as they danced the hora.

Nothing brings the generations at a party together like the hora. As soon as the familiar, tantalizingly slow notes sound the beginning of "Hava Nagilah" (the usual accompaniment, and, according to noted Jewish musicologist Yale Strom, "easily the world's most famous Jewish melody"), even those glued to their seats suddenly spill out onto the dance floor. Immediately the pace quickens and the circle widens as more and more join in, serpentining the line first left, then right, spiraling into the center and back again.

Descended from a much slower Romanian peasant dance, also called the hora, this wildly popular folk dance developed during the early part of the twentieth century in Israel, where, according to Fred Berk in *The Jewish Dance*, the democratic nature of the dance "fitted perfectly the pioneer character of those settlers and the social set-up of the kibbutz especially. The tightly closed circle, with linked arms and hands on shoulders of neighbors, was the exact expression of the close human relationship between all the members of the community, all . . . with equal rights and equal value, regardless of sex or of dancing ability." Exuberant and simple, the hora also has great appeal to kids, who always find its high energy a superb release, its easy steps so accessible.

The hora is so well loved, in fact, that we often find the floor gets too crowded to keep it up for long or to accommodate everyone who wants to dance, and inevitably some people are forced to drop out and become spectators. So why not expand and circle around the entire room, rather than limit guests to the dance floor? Because it is always a highlight of the celebration, you might want to have two horas: one to get the party going, and another after dessert or the candlelighting, or to bring the party to a close. By the way, you can call for a hora just about any time during the evening. Just don't leave it for the very end, or the moment may get lost. The bandleader, the DJ (excellent hora medleys are available on CDs), or their "party prompters" can provide guidance, calling out changes in direction, even urging the dancers to branch out and snake around the room.

Remember that some guests will be unfamiliar with the hora. The steps are easily picked up as you go along, but at one party given at the beginning of the bar/bat mitzvah year circuit, when the dance was still new to many of the kids, the family asked a gifted relative to start off in the middle of the circle, demonstrating the movements. It was a huge success: The hora became the defining moment of the bar mitzvah, as kids, Jewish and Gentile, took turns strutting their stuff in the center of the circle, arm-in-arm with a grandma or a great-uncle.

Other Folk Dances

Jonas celebrated his modest autumn bar mitzvah with a fun dance party at a local theater space. Along one wall there were tables set with a variety of homemade pies, freshpressed apple cider, and good hot coffee. The floor was cleared for square dancing, and a hired caller had all the generations do-si-do-ing. For their encore, the fiddlers impro-

vised some klezmer music, and when the caller yelled, "All grab hands," the guests cir-cled for a riotous hora.

If you are unfamiliar with the dances that follow, but would like to include them at your party, you can hire a folk dance instructor. Contact local dance schools, colleges, synagogues, or Jewish Community Centers for recommendations. We've even found detailed dance steps on the Internet.

And there is almost always someone in the crowd knowledgeable enough to lead a simple folk dance. A professional tip from folklorist and dance educator Anna Richman Beresin, Ph.D.—if guests aren't responding to the instructor, "Go pick three of your craziest, wildest friends to join in."

Other Israeli dances. The Israeli repertoire embraces dances from many cultures. Some involve very simple movements. Anna describes Mizrachi line dances as "Stomp, hoot, and shake your shoulders." Just some of the intriguing ones we've danced: S'aee Yonah (Flight of the Dove), in which dancers cross their hands and make wings like birds; Oneg Shabbat, simulating blessing the candles at Shabbat, which Anna has characterized as a "Jewish macarena"; Hora Medora (Dance of the Campfire), especially good for kids, because it doesn't matter what your feet are doing as long as you go in and out of the circle.

Freylekhs. If you've watched the exuberant wedding and bar mitzvah scenes in the grainy old black-and-white films from eastern Europe, chances are the celebrants were dancing *freylekhs*. These were always extremely popular because, though they are group dances, participants literally make up their own steps, improvising at will from certain basic movements. Dancers travel in a circle or in a line formation, moving into the center when they want to show off their fancier steps.

***Sher* (or scissor) dances.** Similar to square dances, these are wonderful even without special dance instruction, because the moves are called out. *Sher* CDs have both music and moves.

Everybody Up on the Dance Floor

Getting the boys and girls to dance together can be a problem, especially if this is an early coed party for most of them. When interviewing a bandleader or a DJ, it's a good idea to ask what he or she would do if the two sexes aren't mixing. Thirteen-year-old Paul says that at coed parties, while he favors a "good combination of fast and slow

---

FROM GENERATION TO GENERATION

Jewish dance instructor Helen Winkler tells this story about one of her students: "Her grandfather, now deceased, used to play *sher* music on the old seventy-eight records. He tried to explain to the family how the *sher* was danced in Russia . . . [After she learned the dance,] the granddaughter finally understood what her grandfather was trying to say. At last she had a dance connection with her grandfather."

---

dances, it's important to have more than one slow dance to give the boys a chance to warm up." Be sure to ask the musicians to be on the lookout for others who aren't getting up to dance. They may be waiting for a change of rhythm.

Here are a few suggestions to get your guests dancing.

- From the Orthodox tradition, but equally nice at any party, is the custom of having the women dance around the bat mitzvah girl or the men around the bar mitzvah boy.
- Who's Got Soul? The bandleader/DJ taps the couples (or solo dancers) on the dance floor who move with the most spirit. During the next dance, those chosen have the dance floor to themselves, while the other guests watch and cheer them on.
- A dance game, like limbo, is especially nice for the kids when they have finished eating and the adults are still working on dinner. Close friends or young relatives might enjoy making up special calypso lyrics about the bar/bat mitzvah child for this dance.

MAKE IT A MITZVAH *The year after your bar/bat mitzvah, join with kids from other synagogues, organizing and hosting a dance marathon at a local JCC to raise money for special needs kids. • Help children with disabilities connect with the joys of movement. Become a buddy for a special-needs soccer, Little League, or wheelchair basketball player. Contact your local office of Mental Health and Mental Retardation (MHMR).*

OTHER CREATIVE ENTERTAINMENT IDEAS

From the time his grandfather let him play with the rooks and knights, Ian was smitten with chess. Quite adept by age seven, in junior high he formed a chess club with his best buddies. So it was kismet when his parents met a young chess master who agreed to work at Ian's bar mitzvah. The kids had a grand time playing short, timed games against him.

Great entertainment need not be expensive or elaborate if it engages your guests, encourages participation, and, best of all, matches your child's interests and personality. Look for that extra bit of color that makes a simple game special fun: Ian's chess master wore a silly, oversize hat and challenged the kids in a quirky chess corner.

Many of the following ideas are intergenerational, and often kids-only entertainment is so much fun that we find adults sneaking over to watch—or join in. You'll find some suggestions below that will work especially well to fill in a lull, during a cocktail hour (if you are having one), or while adults are finishing dinner. In addition to the sources already mentioned on page 173, "Choosing a Bandleader/DJ," inquire at local schools for recommendations regarding entertainers and other entertainment ideas. Don't overlook art and drama schools, and talented relatives and friends.

Entertainers

The best ones—whether they are performing on stage, mingling with everyone, or simply working from a designated corner—not only entertain, but interact with your guests as well.

Storytellers. *Amol iz geven*, "once upon a time," eloquent storytellers dazzled young, old, and those in between with stories from the rich Jewish repertoire. Today Syd Lieberman, Peninnah Schram, Steve Sanfield, and scores of other major players in the current storytelling revival taking place in America connect us once again to the Jewish salts and tricksters, heroes and wise ones, schlemiels and schlimazels that have inspirited our oral tradition for centuries. And if you think storytelling is just for schoolchildren, think again: A gifted teller who vividly brings to life outrageous, funny, and poignant stories speaks to every member of the audience. If traditional stories do not appeal, you may prefer a spinner of multicultural tales or more contemporary stories, or a "facilitator," who later helps listeners shape and tell their own stories.

To find a local storyteller, check newspapers for announcements of storytelling events and ask at local libraries. Or contact the National Storytelling Network in Jonesborough, Tennessee; it publishes the National Storytelling Directory.

> **MAKE IT A MITZVAH** *Support the Shoah Foundation as it raises funds to share the stories of Holocaust survivors (www.vhf.org). • Contact the National Clotheslines Project to organize a display of T-shirts designed by volunteer artists that tell the stories of victims of domestic violence (www.mcbw. org/clothesline.htm).*

Character actors. Remember Bill Cosby's ingenious riff on Noah, "A Hard Rain's Gonna Fall," or Mel Brooks's Moses with his tablets? Talented actors impersonating biblical characters (think Samson and Delilah or David and Goliath) and other traditional types (like the fools of mythical Chelm) can be hilarious as they interact with guests. This is a great way to bring a Torah or Haftarah portion to life.

Street performers: magicians, mimes, impersonators, and jugglers. In ancient times, jugglers entertained revelers in the Temple courtyards on festivals like Sukkot, and they have traditionally delighted guests at bar mitzvahs and weddings. Today there are even special organizations for Jewish jugglers.

Visual artists. Caricaturists or **quick-sketch artists** can draw pictures of guests or their favorite characters. For **scribes and calligraphers**, set up a table where they can use a traditional feather pen and parchment or papyrus (available at well-stocked art supply stores) to transcribe guests' names into beautiful Hebrew characters, encode secret messages, or write out names or sayings in fanciful lettering. Or hire a **handwriting analyst** who creates personality profiles based on writing samples.

Crafty Suggestions

Fabulous new crafts kits appear everyday in local hobby/toy stores and catalogs. Look for crafts that can be completed tableside: no ovens or traipsing through the dance floor for buckets of water required. Designate a crafts area with brightly colored cloths or balloons in a corner of the celebration space or in a separate kids-only room.

Kids can work unassisted on some of the following crafts; others may call for an older teen's help, or more expert guidance from a hired instructor.

Decorating glasses. Kids can adorn glasses to use for Miriam's or Elijah's cups at Passover, Sabbath Kiddush, or other special occasions. Provide two or three stemmed glasses per child, metallic pens specially made for glassware (available at art supply stores), and, optionally, stencils, mosaics or beads, and glitter glue.

Museum crafts. If your celebration is set in a historic house or museum, ask if there are special themed crafts or other activities available for kids. Some possibilities: churning fresh butter; creating Native American dreamcatchers and dream pillows; or making bayberry candles, clove pomanders, origami, or a sachet of sweet herbs for Havdalah.

Miriam's tambourines. Purchase plain tambourines, and provide colorful nail polishes and perhaps some pictures to serve as inspiration. Finished tambourines can be donated to the synagogue or kept as party favors.

Shaker boxes. Purchase simple wooden boxes in the Shaker tradition, glue pens, buttons, and other supplies at a local crafts store. These handsome boxes are appealing to both boys and girls.

You can find more ideas throughout the book, particularly in the "Decor and Lighting" and "Tradition!" chapters.

MAKE IT A MITZVAH *Many nursing-home residents are highly adept knitters and crocheters who long for a proper home for their creations. Invite them to work with you on a project like Warm Up America! making quilts, one square at a time. Contact www.craftyarncouncil.com.*

Ideas for Fun and Games

You Make Me Laugh. This can be a simple, tableside game. The first player has two minutes to make the second player laugh by cracking jokes, making faces—whatever it takes. To make this a team sport, have the competing players come from opposite teams; a team scores each time they "crack up" the player in the hot seat.

Buddy Trivia. Before the party, the family or close friends make up questions about the bar/bat mitzvah child: what his/her favorite movie, song, food, or sport is, and so on. Divide kids into teams and have an older child or an adult ask the questions. Score one point for each correct answer—the first team to score ten points wins.

Foosball, Air Hockey, and Ping-Pong. Tabletop games, available for rent, are sure to attract guests of all ages. Check under "Amusement Devices" in the Yellow Pages and on the Web.

The Great Outdoors

Jake's Torah portion was about the restrictive laws governing the Nazarites. His ice hockey coach adhered to a clean-living philosophy himself, and played a key role in keeping Jake and his teammates in tip-top shape. Since Jake attended a private boys' school up in Maine, and didn't have a lot of female friends, his bar mitzvah celebration comprised family and close friends, and a bunch of thirteen-year-old hockey teammates in jeans and T-shirts. The cool May sun called, and soon the boys were in the backyard shooting hoops. They walked in flushed but happy, in time for the candlelighting at dusk.

For small, casual parties, simple outdoor fun, like soccer, horseshoes, boccie, hayrides, and spontaneous old favorites like Capture the Flag can be wonderful in the right circumstances.

You Ought to Be in Pictures

When Lily's friends entered the party room, the first thing they noticed was fifty beautiful swaying helium balloons, and the little fabric bags attached to them, lined up neatly on the bench. The kids were directed to find the one with their name on it. Inside each bag was an inexpensive Plexiglas frame and a welcome note from Lily with instructions to have a Polaroid picture taken. There were several cameras provided, as well as acrylic paints. Some kids decorated the frames, painting wacky faces on the clear Plexiglas, so that when they inserted their photos, they looked like they had a mustache, horns, a halo, or a spiky do.

Photo booth. For a photo keepsake, set up a booth with old-fashioned hats, like fedoras, babushkas, turbans, or brimmed picture hats. You might include tall, embroidered yarmulkes from central Asia, or poufy velvet ones from France. Don't forget mustaches and beards. Have guests take Polaroids of each other in costume, or hire someone for the job. Guests can mount the photos in an album provided, creating a kooky bar or bat mitzvah scrapbook.

Video game. Kids can videotape the event with some structure and guidance. Have a teen or adult oversee everything. Kids sign in to use the one or two video recorders provided. Have a preset list of assignments: Interview the oldest guest, the bar/bat mitzvah child, and so on; record the hora; and capture the candlelighting. Prepare a list of questions for the novice interviewers to ask, or suggest that they record special wishes for the bar/bat mitzvah.

Food Fun

Noshes can also be entertainment: piling on the toppings at a sundae bar; a stand for dipping ripe fruit in warm melted chocolate or caramel; gaily decorated carts spinning cotton candy in circus colors or seducing everyone with aromas of roasting popcorn and fresh, hot deli pretzels.

Carved fruit is lovely for a Tu B'Shevat party, and carved vegetables are perfect for Sukkot. Look for carvers at Asian restaurants, local culinary schools, or the Caribbean street vendors who sculpt mango fruit flowers. Or ask your caterer.

For more on food as entertainment, see chapter 13, "Celebration Food and Drink."

Entertainment in Holiday Dress

Purim or the whole month of Adar. Use karaoke equipment for story- and joke-telling. Ask guests to come in costumes (Not just kids: The annual Purim Costume Ball at the Jewish Museum of New York is a gala adult affair.). Set up a mask-making table, hire clowns or mimes, and play You Make Me Laugh.

Hanukkah. Spin a giant dreidel. Give out gold-foil wrapped chocolate Hanukkah gelt, little Maccabee candies, and caramels to the winners.

Sukkot. Have kids decorate a sukkah with autumn fruits and vegetables, or strings of popcorn. Or buy tiny play fruits and vegetables (available at toy and hobby stores), or pretty little marzipan autumn produce to hang on a miniature sukkah. Hang up a harvest piñata: Fill a papier-mâché pumpkin (or other fall vegetable) piñata with candy, coins, and tchotchkes for the kids to "harvest" with a decorated baseball bat.

FAVORS AND GIVEAWAYS

Kids adore party favors and giveaways—prizes for contests and the little gifts DJs and bandleaders shower on them. Teens in sparkly head boppers and oversize shoes can really jazz up the dance floor. But whether the favors or giveaways are quality items or cheap throwaways, they can add up in cost. We dislike those that will be tossed away by the end of the night, adding to the mounting burden on our fragile environment. Before you say yes, consider how many you want to have or if you want to have them at all.

Here are just a few that we have enjoyed, but you'll find many more in other chapters, especially "Decor and Lighting" and "Flowers and Centerpieces."

- **Prizes and giveaways on the dance floor.** Funky socks, oversize sunglasses, anything with lights or glow-in-the-dark fun, or gift certificates from local bookstores.
- **Favors.** CDs burned by the bar/bat mitzvah child with a mix of his/her favorite music, decorated T-shirts, mugs, or candy in personalized wrappers (easy to do at home).
- **Sweet treat.** We love to say good-bye with something sweet: a few homemade cookies, a pretty packet of dried fruit and nuts, a mini babka for tomorrow's breakfast.

MAKE IT A MITZVAH *When giving away cool baseball cap favors to your friends, give to Hats of Hope, whose hats bring messages of hope to cancer patients about to lose their hair as they undergo chemotherapy. Contact www.hatsofhope.com.*

For T-shirts, check out the great looking "Human-i-Tees" T-shirts from the Rainforest Alliance. You'll be protecting the rain forest and raising environmental awareness. Contact www.humanitees.com.

Or fold a colorful, computer-generated note at each kid's place setting explaining that instead of buying favors, the bar/bat mitzvah child is sending ten underprivileged kids to a New York Yankees (or other local professional baseball) game.

CELEBRATION FOOD AND DRINK:

PLANNING THE MENU

DURING THE YEAR *leading up to Arielle's bat mitzvah, her family explored the different cuisines of the Diaspora. It was a delicious way to bring to life the history and traditions of the Jews, especially for Arielle's father, a recent convert.*

The Sicilian foods of the Venetian Jews told the tale of Jews who had once prospered on the island, but fled north during the Inquisition when Spain ruled parts of southern Italy. They traced the Bombay Jews' taste for sweet-and-sour dishes to Iraq, from where storied merchant families, like the Sassoons, had originally set sail. They learned why Greek Jewish dishes may have Spanish names and how Shavuot blintzes could owe their origin to the Russian pancakes that evoke the sun at Shrovetide.

For Ari's bat mitzvah, the family decided to showcase the Diaspora foods they had come to love best: pasta with Roman Jewish artichokes, Turkish halibut in rhubarb sauce, a Passover breast of veal stuffed with spinach and fresh herbs from Provence, an Iranian chicken golden with turmeric that was eaten Vietnamese style: little mouthfuls of the meat rolled in fresh green herbs . . . the list went on and on. They discussed their ideas with the local country club where Ari had been playing tennis since she was a toddler. The caterer there was enthusiastic about taking on the project and suggested a buffet-style meal, with a different station for the foods of each Jewish community. They culled from the list, choosing the recipes she could best execute, and refined the menu, adding some surefire standards from her files.

At the caterer's recommendation, the guests would be reunited at a single dessert table featuring all-American favorites, after having been "scattered" at the various food stations. As party favors, guests would receive a booklet of the evening's collected recipes.

Foods inspired by our heritage connect us to our roots and remind us that this is not just any party, but a bar/bat mitzvah celebration. We might serve a clever riff on a Jewish classic, like a knish of garlic-mashed potatoes in a buttery phyllo crust; a classic Moroccan *couscous de cérémonie*, ringed with dates and toasted almonds; or a shot glass of beet-fennel borscht at the vodka bar. Perhaps an allusion to the Torah (grilled quail for the Manna and Quail *parshah*), or something as subtle as a biblical food—figs, barley, pomegranates, fine olive oil—that still locates a dish as Jewish for us.

Today Jewish food is trendy and sophisticated. Wolfgang Puck's seders at the world-class Spago restaurant in Los Angeles feature delicately poached, tarragon-scented gefilte fish. In New York, the elegant Tocqueville restaurant highlights "schmaltz-glazed free-range chicken" on its menu. Sages tell us that after the Temple was destroyed, the table became our altar. Look beyond that rib roast to the world of glorious foods available.

WHAT KIND OF PARTY
ARE YOU HOSTING?

Customarily, every family serves refreshments after the bar/bat mitzvah services to the congregation and invited guests. This might be a simple taste of challah and a sip of wine or grape juice, an elaborate luncheon, or something in between. In addition, you may be continuing the celebration for invited guests at anything from an informal garden lunch at home to a sit-down dinner in a tony hotel. In this chapter, we'll show you how to plan your menus. In the next chapter, we'll talk about setting up and serving the food and drinks, and getting help from a caterer, family, or friends.

PLANNING THE MENU

"My dear'" [a guest tells Marjorie Morningstar at brother Seth's bar
mitzvah], "you may as well resign yourself to not eating for a week.
Lowenstein [the caterer] is fantastic."
—HERMAN WOUK, *MARJORIE MORNINGSTAR*

To many of us, a taste of chopped liver alongside a radish rosette is enough to unleash a Proustian flood of memories, replete with groaning smorgasbords, loosened belts, and rubber chicken.

But those days, we hope, are well behind us. We don't need, as Wouk described in 1955, "a cascade of raspberry soda on a terraced frame of snow, and a Star of David in solid ice bordered by blue neon." For us well-prepared food is magical when it is fresh and seasonal, and we build our elegant bar/bat mitzvah menus on traditional Jewish principles of balance and harmony.

Good menu choices should reflect not just the time of year, but the time of day as well. Portions are smaller at lunch, and food and alcoholic consumption are generally lighter then, too. How you plan to serve the food—sit-down, buffet, or a combination—and the kitchen facilities available will also affect the kind of menu you can best accomplish. (See "Styles of Service," page 229, chapter 14.)

TWINS IN A SUKKAH: DANIEL AND REBECCA'S AUTUMN BNAI MITZVAH

MENU

AT BAR
Blender drinks for kids

Pomegranate martinis for adults

DUMPLINGS AND SAVORIES STATION
Potato kreplach, mushroom tortellini, chicken wontons,
mini-empanadas, samosas

SIT-DOWN LUNCHEON

First Course

Heirloom tomato salad with curly red leaf lettuce
and basil vinaigrette

Za'atar pita toasts, purple basil garnish

Entrée

Wild striped bass with sauce verte

Breast of chicken with herbed panko crumb crust
and rosemary sauce

Grilled lamb chops with lavender

Mushroom risotto cakes

Sukkot pepper cornucopia filled with grilled corn succotash

Dessert

Tiered berry dacquoise

Double chocolate decadence bnai mitzvah cake

Seckel pear almond tart

Caramel lady apples

Coffee and teas

Here are more specific guidelines to consider when composing your menus, alone or with your caterer.

Your Guests' Food Preferences

Of course, you'll want to bear in mind the tastes and culinary idiosyncrasies of your guests. Conservative? Foodies? Hearty eaters? Are they vegetarian, or do they simply avoid red meat? Many people find certain foods politically incorrect; besides veal, Chilean sea bass and other fish considered endangered because of overfishing may be off their lists as well. And parents may come from completely different food traditions: One side may be strictly meat and potatoes, the other tries a different ethnic restaurant every week. Children, too, come in a variety of palates. We will discuss kid-friendly foods in detail later in this chapter (see page 214).

Balance, Moderation, and Harmony

Aim for a variety of flavors and textures. If you are serving cheese and creamy foods, you'll want to offset their richness with cleaner tastes, like vegetables in a vinaigrette, and cut down on heavy soups and sauces. Don't repeat strong flavors, like toasted sesame oil and blue-veined cheeses, in more than one dish. Avoid serving too many foods cooked the same way: a deep-fried appetizer, followed by a fried entrée, or a buffet of braised meats and braised vegetables with no crisp salads to refresh the palate.

Create visual interest with color. Whether you are serving preplated dishes or buffet-style, imagine how the foods will look together on the plate. A sea of brown meats and roasted potatoes may be a feast for the tongue, but it's a bore for the eyes. We like to include something green (usually a side dish or condiment), and, if possible, something red-to-orange: tomatoes, carrot slaw, a garnish of chili peppers. (For more on creating pretty plates and other displays, see "All Dressed Up: Beautiful Buffets, Pretty Platters," page 232, in chapter 14.)

Feed your guests generously, but don't overwhelm them with a tsunami of never-ending food. When planning your menu, take into account the hors d'oeuvre (if any), the balance of light and heavy foods, and the number of courses you are serving.

Choose foods that will work well together, not a mishmash of fighting flavors. You wouldn't be served pasta puttanesca, followed by roast duck enchiladas and curried rice, in a fine restaurant.

A CELEBRATION AT HOME: LINDA'S EARLY SPRING BAT MITZVAH

MENU

BUFFET
Roasted salmon pinwheels brimming with fresh herbs

Tzatziki sauce

Egg barley studded with lentils, mushrooms,
and artichoke hearts

Green lasagne "quattro formaggio"

Leeks and roasted red peppers vinaigrette

Lemon-roasted asparagus

Walnut-cilantro challah in special simcha braid

DESSERT
Magda's homestyle plum torte

Grandma's iced brownies

Coffees, spiced and herbal teas

Food for a Crowd

Gorgeous wheels of cheese, big cuts of meat and loins of tuna, farm-fresh fruits and vegetables purchased by the crate, magnums of wine—some foods are divine in large editions. Others, however, are dreadful when it comes to crowds. Avoid these dishes which are difficult to prepare well in quantity:

- Foods that require precise timing are troublesome to execute. Thin, delicate cuts, like flounder or veal scallops, continue cooking off the heat; if the meal must be delayed because Grandpa Max can't be found for the Kiddush, these foods are even more likely to be overcooked. Look for creative alternatives: tuna seared and served at room temperature, and risotto cakes instead of a risotto, which requires complicated timing.
- Unless there is a well-ventilated professional kitchen equipped with a fryolator, stay away from fried foods during the entrée course. That burnished tangle of shoestring

fries no longer seduces when it is soggy and half cold. Fried hors d'oeuvre (tempura, mozzarella sticks) prepared in smaller quantities are much more doable, or limit them to a pretty garnish, such as crispy leeks.

- Many pastas, especially long, thin, or fresh pastas, often turn gummy when prepared in large batches (though they can be done well at a pasta station). Stick to larger pasta shapes, like butterflies and ziti. Or choose a baked pasta dish, like roasted vegetable lasagne.
- Some foods retain heat poorly. When served in quantity, it's difficult to keep cream and butter sauces (and the foods moistened by them) properly warm. Sauces based on tomato, soup stock, and natural juices are safer bets.
- Predressed green salads made up in large batches will be sodden by the time the meal is served. Either serve the dressing on the side, or request that the salads be dressed just prior to serving.

Stars That Make a Menu Sparkle

Every party may be unique, but after years of creating menus, we've learned three essential ingredients every meal plan should include.

One or more food favorites everyone adores. Forget calorie counts and cholesterol—you're here to party, right? Is there anyone who doesn't love silken mashed potatoes, succulent brisket, or sundae bars? Think updated classics, like chicken sausage and roasted red pepper pizza or pastrami paninis. More surefire crowd-pleasers include perfectly poached whole salmon, a glorious gnocchi, grilled vegetables, golden caramelized onions that would make a sheet of cardboard taste great, and sinfully rich brownies and s'mores.

Family recipe files. We like to serve at least one dish from the family recipe files. Make the meal a culinary photo album with a mini version of Mom's latkes, "Cee-Cee's" cucumber salad, the special antipasto your child always orders at her favorite restaurant.

Our earliest memories are inextricably linked to foods and the people we loved who prepared them—the smell of the mandelbrot baking in Aunt Ida's tiny kitchen, the taste of soup with vegetables from Grampy's garden. For kids, food memories run deep, and it's a special treat to dig into a dish that tastes like home. And let's not forget dessert. Many families have birthday cake traditions: It wouldn't be a celebration without that carrot cake or Gram's coconut layer cake.

The dazzler. Now, this needn't be sushi prepared to order, grilled steaks, or whole

IN A BUTTERFLY GARDEN:
JULIA'S BAT MITZVAH

MENU

BUTLERED HORS D'OEUVRE
Spring rolls, cucumber rolls, figs piped with gorgonzola dolce and
"just-made" guacamole with blue corn chips

LUNCHEON

On the Table

Bruschetta toasts with ramekins of dips
(olive, white bean, carrot)

First Course

Spring sorrel soup with "chai" beet swirl

Assorted breads

Entrée Vegetarian Tasting Plate

French lentil salad with crumbled goat cheese

"Kasha and bowtie": Buckwheat noodles with fennel,
caramelized red onions and parmesan, leek bowtie garnish

Seared Japanese eggplant, fresh basil, and tomato compote

Shitake mushrooms, spring peas, and haricots verts,
atop a grilled portobello

Buffet Dessert

Old-fashioned butter cakes with pastel frostings
ringed with fresh pansies and johnny jump-ups

Vanilla and chocolate ice creams

Coffee and teas

fish right off a fragrant wood fire—though those would definitely fit the bill. But even the same-old same-old can seem spectacular when it is presented in an unexpected way. Think of mugs of steaming carrot soup at a blustery January Kiddush, or creamy polenta served in martini glasses; pyramids of macaroons in rainbow colors, or classic shortbread cookies cut in Hebrew letter shapes.

Any carving station is a dazzler, whether it's simple corned beef or a spice-crusted fillet mignon of tuna. Or try a new take on an old favorite, like fresh-baked challah with toasted walnuts and cilantro. Devise a midrash on a recipe by deconstructing it: Translate Grandma Rebecca's kasha varnishkes into grilled portobellos with kasha, orzo, and roasted garlic. And we love the shabby chic contrast of artichoke *matzo brei* alongside an elegant halibut with *sauce verte*.

FOR EVERYTHING THERE IS A SEASON

From the earliest spring greens and tender young lamb at the seder table to golden pumpkins, quince, and grapes come Rosh Hashanah and Sukkot, Jewish menus have always kept time with the rhythm of the seasons. Here are some of our favorite ways to celebrate the splendors that the change of seasons brings.

Fall

Stuffed cabbage leaves and packed zucchini and eggplant boats, metaphors of the harvest bounty • Wildflower and sage honeys to sweeten vegetables and desserts during the fall holidays • Maple-brined duck breast with peppery cranberry chutney • Woodsy autumn mushrooms: roasted portobellos and sautéed wild mushrooms, folded into pastas and pilafs, covering grilled chicken, or combined with melted jack cheese on thin-crusted pizza. Or a wild mushroom barley soup • Pumpkin and black bean enchiladas • Phyllo "snails" with butternut squash • Autumn salads: spinach leaves, dried cranberries, and crumbled goat cheese, tossed with cider vinaigrette • Caramelized apples, freshly baked in rustic pies • Pear tarte tatin

SEASONAL GARNISHES: Indian corn • Gourds with long goose necks and other fun shapes • Long stems of Brussels sprouts • Little lady apples and persimmons • Pomegranates, whole, cut open to reveal the star of crimson seeds, or a scoop of seeds simply sprinkled onto foods for a burst of color and sweet-tang • Nuts in the shell

Winter

Wild rice pancakes with smoked trout and horseradish cream or grilled mamaliga (Romanian polenta) triangles topped with smoked salmon and chive crème fraîche • Braised short ribs • Chili "cholent" • Smoked chicken salad on endive spears •

Hearty pastas • Latkes, beyond potato to parsnip-pear, Jerusalem artichoke, and cheese • Winter salads: paper-thin slices of roasted gold and crimson beets, arugula, feta, and toasted walnuts; slaws of cabbage, carrots, and fresh ginger, or pink grapefruits combined with avocado, watercress, and cilantro • Challah bread pudding topped with caramelized winter fruits • Roasted chestnuts, alone, in stuffings, or dressing up a brisket

SEASONAL GARNISHES: Clementines • Lemons, limes, and oranges (use scooped-out lemon or orange shells to hold mayonnaise, or any citrus shell for individual servings of ice cream and sorbet) • Savoy cabbages • Pearl onions • Black grapes • Dates and dried fruits • Piles of cinnamon sticks and star anise

Spring

Salads embellished with fresh herbs (chives, basil, tarragon, chervil, and more) or edible flowers (like violets, Johnny-jump-ups, nasturtiums—make sure they are unsprayed) • Garden wraps: spinach, radicchio, and arugula leaves enveloping hors d'oeuvre salads and spreads • Tart tastes to perk up winter-weary palates: rhubarb with poultry, sorrel with fish or in a soup, garnished with floating salmon kreplach made from wonton wrappers • Green and purple artichokes, spring chicken, and fresh dill • Roasted asparagus, fat or pencil thin, drizzled with extra virgin olive oil or dipped in herby mayonnaise • Spring morels • The first sweet strawberries, in an old-fashioned shortcake or a brand-new panna cotta

SEASONAL GARNISHES: French radishes in cotton-candy colors—pink, yellow, lavender • Bunches of baby carrots • Fresh grape leaves to line platters and cheese trays • Blossoms of Bibb lettuce and curly frisée heads • Cherry blossoms, lilacs, and other edible spring flowers • Pots of crocuses or daffodils to set off a saffron-colored rice or pasta

Summer

Dead-ripe tomatoes in gazpacho or topping a bruschetta • Heirloom tomatoes, purple, orange, green, and scarlet, circling a platter of whitefish salad or sliced and simply dressed with a fine vinaigrette and confetti of basil • Light, fat-free salsas, infusing the ripest fruits with a zippy pow: grilled beef enlivened with a chunky one of mango, tomatillo, and tomato; roast salmon with green papaya salsa • Cool mint everywhere: over a rainbow of honey-sweet melon balls splashed with lime, in a tabbouleh or a cucumber-dill salad, crushed in raspberry lemonade or pitchers of juice-sweetened iced tea • Pastel peach, cherry, or strawberry soups to start or end a meal, topped with sorbets in matching or complementary flavors • Blueberry lattice pies, blintzes, or open-faced tarts bursting with fresh peaches, apricots, or plums • Sno-cone machines for kids of all ages to make lemon, raspberry, and coconut ices, as well as frozen margaritas and daiquiris

SEASONAL GARNISHES: Tomatoes of all kinds—little teardrop- and cherry-shaped, plum and green-striped zebras • Bushels of Silver Queen corn • Emerald zucchini with their golden blossoms still attached • Herb flowers: white arugula, purple chives, and bright-blue borage tasting of cucumbers • Bunches of lavender and rose petals • Yellow and pink carved watermelons, housing fruit or glowing votive candles

THE KOSHER QUESTION

In the beginning it was easy. We were vegetarians. When God granted Noah permission to eat meat, kashrut, the dietary regulations that determine what is kosher, or ritually fit to eat, was born. The bulk of the kosher principles, however, was spelled out in the Torah Moses received on Mount Sinai, and further elucidated and codified throughout the centuries.

In brief, the animals Jews were permitted to eat are limited to those that chew their cud and have split hooves, eliminating the pig, the rabbit, and the horse, among others; one may eat all poultry, except birds of prey. To be kosher, these animals must be slaughtered by a ritual slaughterer in accordance with stringent rules. Only certain cuts of the meat may be eaten, and they must be soaked and salted first to remove the blood. Among fish, only those that have both fins and scales are permitted: no shellfish, eels, swordfish, catfish, or sturgeon. In addition, foods containing meat and milk must not be eaten at the same time, so a meal will be designated as either meat or dairy. Neutral (or pareve) foods—those that contain neither meat nor milk products, including fish, eggs, grains, vegetables, and fruit—may be eaten with meat and dairy foods.

Observant Jews, complying with the laws of kashrut, will not eat any food prepared by someone other than those they personally know to be kosher, unless that food has been certified as kosher. This means that a package of cookies must bear a special insignia indicating it has been deemed kosher by a recognized Jewish organization. Kosher restaurants and caterers must hire a *meshgiach,* whose job it is to monitor that all the food has been prepared according to kashrut. Besides the food restrictions we have mentioned, everything must be made and served with cookware and dishes that have only been used for kosher foods, and the cooking and eating utensils used for foods containing meat must have been kept completely separate from those used for dairy foods.

Other Jews may follow only some of the kosher laws, eating only kosher meat, perhaps, or avoiding pork and shellfish. And other Jews do not observe kashrut at all.

For the Kiddush, and any other party held at the synagogue, you will have to comply with the synagogue's kashrut policy. Orthodox, of course, and many Conservative synagogues as well, will be strictly kosher, but even more liberal synagogues usually will have some restrictions, too: for example, no biblically prohibited foods, like pork or shellfish; menus must not mix meat and dairy foods; only kosher meat allowed; or only vegetarian meals permitted. Some may have a list of acceptable caterers, and may not permit foods to be brought in that were prepared at home, requiring, instead, that food be wholly prepared in the synagogue's kitchen.

For celebrations outside of the synagogue, the family must personally address the kosher question. Many people who do not regularly keep kosher choose to incorporate at least some of the most basic precepts in their menus on this day of performing mitzvot, because the mitzvah of following kashrut has been such a defining characteristic of the Jewish people from the beginning of time.

The sample menus and recipes we have included in this book are all kosher and avoid ersatz ingredients, like faux bacon bits and dairy substitutes. Preparing delicious, creative meals that are kosher is certainly challenging, but not impossible, as the welter of sophisticated kosher chefs, caterers, and cookbooks in America and around the world demonstrate.

A final word: If you are not serving a certified kosher meal, be sure to make arrangements with a kosher caterer or restaurant to provide appropriate meals for your observant guests.

THE KIDDUSH/*ONEG*

Noah was an active child who loved to use his hands tossing a basketball or whipping up breakfast. He was having some difficulty with the quiet concentration needed to learn the Hebrew chanting for his Torah portion, and he mentioned his frustration one day after services to Becca, his former nursery school teacher, who was currently teaching at a Hebrew day school. "My Torah portion is totally cool. It's from Emor, about baking all these Sabbath challahs. I've been baking challahs with my mom since I was eight. But I just can't seem to sit down and really work on the chanting."

Becca told Noah that when she had lived on a kibbutz for three years, she'd been responsible for making innumerable Shabbat challahs, and had acquired several unusual recipes for them. "I'll bake those challahs with you for your bar mitzvah and help you with your Hebrew if you play with the twins some afternoons when I need to get some work done," she offered.

So every other week throughout the winter and the following spring, they baked a different challah: infused with saffron, flavored with fruit and nuts, half whole wheat—twelve kinds in all. They would let the fragrant bread cool, then wrap it tightly and put it in the freezer. Becca often spoke Hebrew to her sons on those long afternoons, and gradually, she began sprinkling Hebrew words into her conversations with Noah, too. In the relaxed atmosphere of the kitchen, as they kneaded and punched down the bread dough, he found the elusive words increasingly easier to grasp. And Becca's sons adored him.

Noah's family had been founding members of the synagogue, and it was really important to them to invite the whole congregation to his celebration. In lieu of another reception, they decided to sponsor an extended Kiddush for the regular synagogue attendees, as well as their invited guests. On Friday, they placed the frozen challahs in their collection of woven baskets, and brought them, along with the other food and setups, to the synagogue.

Noah did a fine job that beautiful May Saturday at the service. Whenever he sped up, he imagined the aroma of the baking bread as he slowly inhaled and exhaled, and he was right back on track. Meanwhile, using the detailed instructions Noah's mom had written up, the members of the synagogue co-op set up for the Kiddush. They draped the tables with khaki underliners and generous layers of natural fiber cheesecloth. Nestled in their napkin-lined baskets, the twelve golden loaves, completely thawed by now, were arranged according to her diagram, taken from Emor: "Place them on a pure table be-

NOAH'S KIDDUSH

MENU

Twelve different "choice flour" challahs, ranging from traditional to
cranberry-orange—all baked by Noah.

Mediterranean antipasto featuring slices of roasted eggplant,
zucchini, slivered onions, leeks, peppers,
carrots, and artichokes

Focaccia, mozzarella (smoked, fresh, and marinated)
and a selection of olives

Spring vegetables: Baby carrots, radishes, asparagus, red endive and haricots verts

Tzatziki and toasted sesame dips

Fontina, gorgonzola dolce, and ricotta salata cheeses

Crackers, grapes, and apples

Magda's homestyle plum torte

Rachel's mini cheesecakes

Coffee, tea, and cran-raspberry zinger fruit juice tea

fore God in two rows, six to a row." The bread made a magnificent centerpiece, sur-
rounded by small bundles of wheat and oats, and branches of dried berries.

Noah recited the Motzi. Then he added, "God told Moses to bake twelve loaves out
of choice flour, so that's what I did." He grinned. "But I did leave out the frankincense,"
he added, and began passing out the bread.

The Kiddush, a post-services collation central to American synagogue life, is also called
an *oneg,* meaning "joy" or "delight," referring to the joy of sharing conversation and
community at the informal gathering, the delight of host and guest, of giving and re-
ceiving. After the bar/bat mitzvah ceremony, the Kiddush offers a wonderful way to mingle, allowing members of the congregation and guests to meet and socialize with the
celebrant and his or her family.

The emphasis here is on the congregation—all members of the synagogue are invited. After all, the bar/bat mitzvah is a public celebration of the child joining the com-

ZANDER'S KIDDUSH

MENU

Grandpa Max's oniony egg salad
Tuna and chick pea salad Nicoise with green beans
Black bread and knot rolls
Lemon-roasted asparagus
Garden greens vinaigrette
French lentil salad with crumbled goat cheese
Red bliss potato salad with scallions and Dijon vinaigrette
Apple challah bread pudding
Pecan crescents and brownies
Seasonal fruits
Coffee, tea, and seltzer
Egg creams for kids

munity. The child's first act as a part of this community is akin to a public display of thanks, the family hosting a party celebrating the community's acceptance of its newest member. And these are hungry people—many of whom have skipped breakfast!

For some people, a lovely Kiddush may serve as the entire simcha. For others, it is the prelude to another meal, a luncheon for invited guests directly afterward at the synagogue or another location. Some may be hosting an evening reception for friends and family later on. You may not want to serve an extensive menu at the Kiddush if you are having an elaborate luncheon afterward (unless required by the synagogue—see "Guidelines for Hosting a Kiddush," page 203). On the other hand, if you are hosting a dinner party at night, and you have several out-of-town guests, you may want to serve a light lunch.

We can't emphasize emough how important it is to arrange for help with your Kiddush. Even if you prepare most or all of the food yourself, you will without a doubt need assistance putting it out and removing leftovers. While we discuss getting help in general throughout the book and more specifically in the next chapter, it is absolutely essential for the Kiddush, where you will want to devote your full attention to your child, looking after relatives, greeting everyone, and so on.

Fortunately, many synagogues have set up a system in which volunteers will coordinate or assist you in preparing your *oneg*. While helping with *onegs* is a mitzvah, many committees will still require you to reciprocate in order to keep the system going. If your synagogue does not have a volunteer committee in place, consider starting one for all *onegs*, including regular Saturday Kiddushes when there is no bar or bat mitzvah, baby naming, or other social occasion. You could also get the parents of the bnai mitzvah class together and form a co-op, taking responsibility for each others' Kiddushes. Arrange for help through your network of friends and family members, or hire someone (the synagogue may be able to recommend people) to set up and clean up afterward. If you've engaged a catering service, find out how much of the setup it is willing to take charge of. Often someone from the synagogue will act as "point person," coordinating everything—especially useful when your help is unfamiliar with the synagogue's procedures.

Guidelines for Hosting a Kiddush

- If there is more than one bar/bat mitzvah scheduled for the same date, will you be **sharing the Kiddush?** Make sure to work out the details with the other family if you will be hosting the Kiddush together.

- What is the synagogue policy on **kosher** food? (See "The Kosher Question," page 198.)

- There may be **other food requirements** as well. Some synagogues ask you to provide a somewhat substantial meal for the congregants because socializing after services is an important part of the synagogue culture, and some members, particularly the needy, the elderly, or those living alone, may depend on the Kiddush for their Saturday lunch. Some require you to provide a minimum of two challahs, uncut, in accordance with biblical commandments. And we've heard of synagogues that ask families to serve only white wine and grape juice, to prevent carpet stains!

- **Does the synagogue provide** some or all of the following: wine, grape juice, cups, urns with hot water, coffee, tea, sugar, and serving utensils?

- Approximately **how many** congregants will be expected at the Kiddush? The number who attend services regularly will vary, of course, but the synagogue should be able to give you a ballpark figure.

- **Where** does the Kiddush take place? In a separate room, downstairs, separated from the sanctuary by curtains? It is a good idea to revisit the space ahead of time if you are having anything more elaborate than wine and challah or cake, so that you can plan your preparation details and layout better. Remember, you will be leaving written instructions for someone else to do the actual setting up. If you are unfamiliar with the kitchen, you may want to make arrangements to check it out as well.

- What **help** is available? Is there a Kiddush committee, or custodians or janitors, who can assist you? Is there a fee involved?
- When can **deliveries** be made, and will there be someone available to accept them? When can you arrive to set up? The day before? Can you decorate the space?
- What is the procedure for **putting away foods?** There may be specific policies based on adherence to kashrut or Sabbath observance: For instance, food placed in the synagogue refrigerators may be put into only new containers; food and servingware may not be carried home until after the Sabbath. Plan on donating any nonperishable foods and supplies to the synagogue.

WHAT TO SERVE AT THE KIDDUSH

The only requirement for the Kiddush is that the wine blessing be followed by a *seudah* (meal)—which can be as little as a bit of bread or a cookie. Decide what you want to have: anything from the simplest option—a nosh of wine and challah or a plain, light cake—to a more ambitious menu, equivalent to a full lunch.

If there will be limited seating or none at all, which is the case at most synagogues, choose foods that are easy to eat at stand-up buffets: cut into small portions, so no knife is needed; no drippy sauces. Streamline your menu—having too many choices, particularly if the Kiddush takes place within a short time span, creates anxiety. Focus instead on quality.

In addition to the suggestions that follow and the Kiddush menus in this section, there are many more ideas throughout this chapter and the rest of the book. If you are serving an extensive Kiddush, be sure to look at suggestions for luncheon parties as well.

Ideas for a Simple Kiddush

If serving more than just challah, and wine/grape juice, choose a complementary selection of one or more of the following. (Please note that we prefer pastries and desserts that are not too heavy-duty if the Kiddush is not a full lunch.)

A SIMPLE KIDDUSH

MENU

Citrus cake with fresh fruit compote of pineapple and mango
Pear-cranberry buttermilk noodle kugel
A pyramid of multicolor macaroons:
Raspberry, pistachio, lemon, and chocolate
Coffee, tea, sparkling water, and natural fruit sodas
Mint lemonade for kids

- **Fruits.** Pick-up fruits, like berries, cherries, grapes, or cut-up pineapples and melon, are always pretty, especially on trays interspersed with a few flowers and some mint leaves; or try dried fruit, like apricots, dates (delicious stuffed with a walnut or almond), and raisins, a favorite of the little ones.
- **Pastries.** Offer your guests fresh sticky buns, homemade quick breads, or little corn, blueberry, or maple walnut muffins (these can be made weeks in advance and frozen); pound cake, coffee cake, fresh apple cake, or sponge cakes made of walnuts and almonds; the panoply of North African and Middle Eastern pastries made of kadaif (vermicelli or shredded wheat) and phyllo, of which baklava is only the beginning; rugalach, little hamantaschen, Linzer hearts, or other cookies with a homey feel.
- **Light desserts.** Serve rice puddings and panna cottas when the weather is hot.

Ideas for an Extended Kiddush

- **Mediterranean dishes.** Because so many Sephardi foods are light and refreshing, they are very appealing at an extended Kiddush, like several of the dishes traditionally served at *desayuno*, the meal served after Sephardi Shabbat services. Lots of these have long been standard fare: lentil hummus; eggy *fritadas*, or *eggahs*, the legacy of the Iberian Jews, made with Mediterranean vegetables like spinach, eggplant, and zucchini, often with cheese, which can be prepared and baked ahead, then frozen (see our Swiss Chard Fritada).
- **Do-ahead vegetables and salads.** In addition to the ones we mention, consider tabbouleh, Israeli cucumber salads, North African red pepper and tomato, eggplant

THE ISRAELS' DESAYUNO KIDDUSH

MENU

Spinach-cheese phyllo triangles and stuffed grape leaves

Swiss chard fritada

Sephardi grain salad: Brown lentils, barley,
caramelized onion, and cilantro

Herbed labneh, eggplant caviar, and toasted sesame dip

Cherry tomatoes, fennel, and celery sticks

Pocketless pitas

Roasted beet salad with feta, walnuts, dill and red onion,
walnut oil vinaigrette

"Pepper-Mint" salad with chunks of avocado

Sweets: Apricot squares, baklava, and "alef-bet"
cardamom butter cookies

Grapes, fresh figs, and Medjool dates, fresh mint garnish

Turkish coffee, mint tea, and Bellinis for adults

caviar, and baba ganoush. Hold off on dressing salads until just before serving in order to preserve the fresh taste.

- **Soups.** These include hot, chunky soups or warming broths, served informally in mugs or hot cups, or try a cold fruit soup, based on fresh and dried fruits and a "stock" of brewed tea and fruit juice.

- **Smoked or cured salmon.** Purchased, or made at home for a fraction of the cost, and served in countless ways, including the best-loved, with bagels, bialys, and all the trimmings, this is always a hit.

- **Deviled or hamine eggs.** And many synagogues serve **meat** at Kiddush. Try hearty cholents and other Sabbath stews, or the deli meats that are the standby of so many Jewish parties (jazz up the pastrami and corned beef with smoked chicken or turkey; serve homemade potato salad, fennel and citrus salad, and an assortment of mustards).

- **Sandwiches.** If you are serving little sandwiches, set out all the fixings rather than prepare them ahead. This saves on labor, and assures that the bread won't be

---

SAM'S WINTER KIDDUSH

MENU

Hot soups: Tomato vegetable pistou and curried apple butternut squash

Gravlax with sweet mustard sauce, toasts,
and fresh dill

Wild mushroom strudel

Spinach salad with pecorino, pine nuts, lemon vinaigrette

Cheeses: Farmhouse cheddar, Brin d'Amour,
and Taleggio

Crusty Italian bread

Clementines, dried apricots, and whole walnuts

Linzer squares, chocolate rugelach, and
Rachel's mini cheesecakes

Sparkling water, apple cider, and wine

Coffee and teas

---

soggy by the time your guests begin to eat. Flatbreads look great piled high, and what's more beautiful than a display of excellent artisanal breads and focaccias? We also make gourmet sandwiches of soft tortillas, rolling up smoked turkey, herbed mayo, and frilly baby greens into cones and wrapping them in doilies. For fun, roll the tortilla from both sides, so your wrap resembles a little Torah scroll, and secure with a scallion tie or a pretty ribbon.

What Makes a Kiddush Memorable?

Homemade challahs. These always elicit oohs and aahs. They can be made well in advance and frozen, as Noah did (see page 200). In Larchmont, New York, Fred is known for the buttery-tasting challah he bakes for friends' simchas, like Jonathan's bar mitzvah. Rosalie sprinkles little sugar crystals on top of hers. See our recipe for a challah, plain or flavored with onions, orange-cranberry, or walnut cilantro. Or try a Sabbath bread from Yemen (these are sold frozen all over Israel), or a fragrant Algerian anise loaf.

Great coffee. Prepared with generous amounts of a flavorful blend, coffee is always a good idea after a morning service. Unless you are serving a meat meal, be sure to offer real milk, not nondairy creamers.

Spiffed-up versions of traditional favorites. Substitute chopped fennel for celery and grapefruit juice for lemon in a whitefish salad, and serve it in red and green endive leaves. Add olives to chicken salad and curry to your eggs—or tell your caterer to. Or offer a surprise homemade treat, like strawberry-rhubarb crisp, so easy to make.

Beautifully presented food. We eat with our eyes as well as our mouths, and it's just as important to set an attractive table for the Kiddush as for a bar/bat mitzvah dinner celebration. Take a special cloth from home, fresh flowers, and a vase. Move the table into the sunlight. If you're having a more elaborate Kiddush, arrange savories and desserts on separate tables; even at the simplest Kiddush, separate the beverages from the noshes. Breads always look more enticing on cutting boards or a silver tray. Bring pretty serving pieces and baskets, your good cream-and-sugar set. Pour drinks into pitchers (big plastic bottles of juice, so unattractive, are always difficult for kids to pour). But be sure that any serving pieces you use comply with synagogue kashrut policy. ("Unkosher" baskets may be permitted if they are lined with linen napkins, for instance.) Look for more tips on beautiful buffets throughout the book, especially in chapter 10, "Setting the Table," and "All Dressed Up: Beautiful Buffets, Pretty Platters" (see page 232 in chapter 14).

Setting Up the Kiddush

Whether it's possible to set up the night before will depend on synagogue policy, where the Kiddush will be, and if and where refreshments are served at the Friday night services. Sometimes folding screens can be used to separate the Kiddush from the area where services are held.

Always make arrangements ahead of time, and designate someone to be in charge of setting up. Leave detailed written instructions, easy-to-read Post-its, a diagram—whatever is necessary. Include information on clean up and storage of leftovers. Remind your helpers to keep their voices down, especially if they are working during services.

THE MAIN MEAL, WHETHER LUNCH OR DINNER

In addition to hosting a Kiddush, many families serve a festive meal. This could be anything from a full lunch for the congregation to a gala dinner on Saturday night for family and friends. Whether the meal is lunch or dinner, chances are it will consist of more than one course. This is true not just of receptions with waiter service, but simpler parties as well, where everything is put out on the buffet table at once: appetizers at one end, desserts at the other, and entrées in the middle. But while we focus on each course separately in this section, we emphasize that you should never lose sight of the whole picture. As we've mentioned in "Planning the Menu" (see page 190), look for balance and harmony, not just in the flavors and textures, but in the amount of food you will be serving during the meal as well—especially at an hors d'oeuvre buffet, which can wind up being more substantial than the regular meal itself. As Jon, Lori's husband and co-owner of Peachtree & Ward Catering, explains, "Hors d'oeuvre are usually Act One, but don't forget there are Acts Two and Three to follow. You don't want to give away all of the play in Act One, so guests won't stay through the intermission (main meal). And you do want them to stay. It's a question of pacing."

Pacing a Long Meal

Unlike a restaurant meal, where you typically spend a maximum of two hours, a bar/bat mitzvah reception can run for four hours or more. The purpose of this long party time is to facilitate a cocktail hour for guests to mingle, a candlelighting, perhaps, and/or dancing—not, of course, because your guests are hungrier! There is, after all, only so much that your guests can eat, and serving an excessive amount inevitably leads to waste, and, more often than not, food quality suffers as well.

If you plan to serve food continuously during a long bar/bat mitzvah party, consider adjusting your menu, modifying the portion size and pace of the food you serve. For example, if you are planning a lengthy hors d'oeuvre hour, followed by dinner and dancing late into the night, you might serve smaller portions during the cocktail hour, choose a grazing menu for the sit-down meal, or extend the meal service with two desserts while guests are dancing.

Hors d'Oeuvre (Passed or Served at Stations)

The hors d'oeuvre hour is the time to have fun with your food. Hosts can offer more un-usual treats, spicier tastes, or personal favorites. Guests love the hors d'oeuvre hour, a chance to sample different little bites packed with flavor. It's the kids' favorite, too—a time to eat as much or as little as they want of the kinds of foods they enjoy most.

The French call them *amuses bouches,* savories to amuse/delight the palate. They are not meant to satisfy, but to stimulate the appetite for the main course, so we prefer to serve smaller portions, grazing style. We are not big fans of stations slicing large por-tions of prime rib to order—unless the station is part of a main meal. It's not only too heavy, but wasteful as well. If we do serve prime rib, our chefs slice it thinly and layer it on small toasts with a piquant sauce.

We avoid hors d'oeuvre that are overly filling; sometimes, in lieu of pastry shells, we serve little teases in endive leaves and lettuce cups. We also use demitasse cups (for lit-tle shots of soup) and Asian spoons (for teeny salads; delicate, savory mousses; or po-tentially drippy mouthfuls); foods that are easy to eat, especially when there's no seating.

How long should the hors d'oeuvre stage last? Not so long that guests begin to feel anxious, wondering when the meal will be served, and feel obliged to eat a lot. You don't want guests to eat dinner before they eat dinner.

How many hors d'oeuvre should you serve? Calculate ten to twelve pieces of average-size hors d'oeuvre per guest; half that may suffice at lunch. Of course, people can eat fifteen pieces of sushi and keep on going.

HORS D'OEUVRE IDEAS: Smoked salmon napoleon layered with beet chips and crème fraîche • Tuna-ginger tartare served on Asian spoons • Mini Middle Eastern meatballs • Chickpea latkes drizzled with labne and pomegranate molasses • Pear-gorgonzola pizzettes • Cheese station: a selection of cheeses, paired with great breads (walnut, fig, and olive), along with spanakopita, gougères, little quesadillas, even mini savory cheese blintzes • An assortment of dips: carrot hummus, toasted sesame dip, or eggplant caviar

Appetizers

To choose a first course, consider what will precede it: a long hors d'oeuvre buffet, a nib-ble, or nothing at all. We love salads because they offer so much flexibility. They can be assembled ahead (though they should not be dressed in advance), and made more substantial with a slice of caramelized onion tart or mushroom strudel, especially good when there is no hors d'oeuvre hour. Smoked or cured fish is another great accompaniment to salads: Pastrami-Style Cured Salmon with a cucumber "noodle" salad, or beet blini with smoked trout and garnishes.

The Main Course

How many times at bar/bat mitzvah parties have we seen entrées return to the kitchen untouched? When planning your main course, keep in mind what else is on the menu. If hors d'oeuvre stations are slicing hot pastrami to order, perhaps that rosemary-crusted rib eye is not a good choice after all.

Do serve smaller portions at lunch than at dinner. Although it is usually difficult to trim the portion size at sit-down dinners, you can definitely offer smaller pieces at buffets. Guests like to try different foods at buffet time; and besides, they can always take two pieces or come back for more. The purpose of a buffet is to offer choices, so be sure to include at least two entrée selections on your buffet table. We like to offer options at sit-down dinners, too, whenever possible. At Daniel and Rebecca's sukkah party, guests were given a choice of striped bass, chicken, or lamb chops. Try to balance a meat-heavy meal with a salad in a good vinaigrette or a light fruity dessert.

ENTRÉE IDEAS: Anything grilled outdoors: Provençal lamb chops or spice-crusted tuna (gild the lily: Make smoky aromas even more enticing by adding rosemary, wild fennel or grapevine branches, or cherrywood or fragrant bay leaves to the fire) • Peking-style five-spice chicken with braised scallions • Roasted tilapia fillets sandwiching woodsy mushroom duxelles • Short ribs of beef braised with red wine and white bean ragout • The ever-popular salmon dishes appearing throughout this chapter

IDEAS FOR SIDE DISHES: Rice pilafs studded with grains and spices • Potatoes, bubbling in gratins or in wild mushroom potato kugels • Herb-roasted potatoes in purple and gold • Velvety purées of sweet potato, fennel, or celery root, under roasted fish, poultry, or meat • Roasted kabocha and other orange-fleshed squashes • Braised winter greens • Sugar snap peas, stir-fried or combined with silver and gold corn kernels • Bundles of haricot verts • Red peppers and glossy black-and-white eggplants, straight from the grill

Desserts

It seems we can never have too many desserts. Adults adore kids' desserts—they're often the first ones on line at sundae bars—so even if kids don't understand all the double entendres in the goofy labels for Ben & Jerry's flavored "Cohens" (Simchat t'Oreo, Bernard Malamint, Mi KaMocha, Rashi Road, Mazel Toffe-ee), they're definitely worth putting on the table. Make sure to offer fresh fruit options along with rich selections. Spun sugar cages and meringue make excellent dairy-free nests for intense fruit sorbets. For easy-to-serve ice cream and sorbets for sundae bars, place scoops of ice cream on wax paper and return them to the freezer. When ready to serve, remove them from the freezer and place in large bowls.

Dessert dazzlers include anything hot, mile-high cakes, and anything with devil's food or rainbow colors.

BAR/BAT MITZVAH CAKES

For many families, no special occasion is complete without a luscious, showstopping cake. And, of course, for those planning a traditional candlelighting, a glorious cake is a necessity. We believe that every cake should taste as good as it looks. Not for us those centerfold beauties, meant to be seen and not eaten. To find your celebration cake, ask your caterer, or inquire at pastry shops, local bakeries, and restaurants known for desserts, and be sure to taste a sample creation.

Here are cake ideas that would work for either a candlelighting or a dramatic dessert buffet.

Playful twists on traditional themes. A Torah scroll that is a little less serious (after all, it is a cake!), adorned with piped scrolls and squiggles in royal icing would be a good choice. Or a big chocolate chip cookie Star of David on a brownie base. For a Torah portion about Noah, frosted cookies in animal shapes marching upright across a vanilla sheet cake, on their way to the ark.

Homemade creations. Josh's mom honored a birthday tradition at his bar mitzvah with her topsy-turvy strawberry shortcakes, featuring berries studded all over the sides and on top of the whipped cream layers.

Sheer elegance. Try our Chocolate Marshmallow Cake on page 258, and embellish the Fluffy Mallow Mint Frosting with candied violets and purple and white filigree.

Fun with presentation. Serve a lemon cake set with yellow candles, and surrounded by pyramids of tender lemon squares and penny candy jars filled with lemon suckers. How about a chocolate cake served on chocolate bars, and garnished with Hershey's Kisses? And where does it say that you must stop at one cake for your candlelighting? Or that you must have a cake at all? For Liz's bat mitzvah, we baked thirteen different cakes and pies, each representing a letter in her name. At candlelighting time, when they were laid out side by side on the table, the bright piped letters, set among frosted spring flowers, spelled out E-L-I-Z-A-B-E-T-H A-N-N-A.

The "sweetest" cake we've seen was beautifully sculpted from fresh fruits for a child with juvenile diabetes. Guests watched as the carver created intricate layers of watermelon and pineapple, topped with mango and strawberry blossoms, kiwi leaves, and an "icing" made of coconut curls.

KID-FRIENDLY FOODS

They beheld God and they ate and drank.
—EXODUS 24:11

"Creating wonderful menus, cooking delicious dishes, and asking people to 'Eat! Eat! Eat!' is another good way of feeling close to God."

The words of some food hedonist? Actually, a bat mitzvah girl named Chana said them, commenting on the Torah portion in which Moses and seventy elders are invited to share a meal with God on Mount Sinai. With all the enthusiasm of a bubbly thirteen-year-old, she told the congregation how much she loved her mother's Passover foods, "Chicken and matzo ball soup, boiled chicken, baked chicken, lamb stew sweetened with prunes and other fruit. Mmm . . . And it all started on Mount Sinai."

For Chana, and many children like her, the fabulous food at a bar/bat mitzvah is one of life's special treats. These days particularly, a lot of children grow up eating designer pizzas at home, dining out with their parents on sushi and fine French food, even cooking quite sophisticated dishes on their own. Even the child who would touch nothing but plain white rice at four might be happily twirling strands of homemade pasta at thirteen. Other adolescents may be finicky eaters, uninterested in food when there is music or other entertainment.

Think about the kind of food your child and his or her friends really enjoy eating. Choosing what to serve can be a tricky tango between the foods that picky eaters will

JULIA'S LUNCHEON

KIDS' MENU

Hors d'oeuvre

French fries in paper sacks with cheddar cheese, sour cream-onion,
and other kid-friendly toppings

Antipasto: Roasted peppers, grilled broccoli,
little mozzarella balls, olives, cherry tomatoes,
and deviled eggs

First Course

Caesar salad with butterfly-shaped croutons,
vegetable confetti and borage flower garnish

Entrée

Thin-crusted pizzas: Margherita with fresh basil,
bianca with mushrooms and roasted garlic

like and the all-too-familiar pizza or chicken fingers that shout school cafeteria, not celebration. Another consideration is that special kids' meals are often less expensive, and you certainly don't want to waste money on costlier foods they won't enjoy.

Talk to your child, and find out what he or she wants to serve the kids: a separate kids' menu or a single menu for everyone with some choices that appeal to the kid in all of us.

Making Foods Kid-Friendly

Buffet stations (for hors d'oeuvre or the main meal) with prepared-to-order and do-it-yourself foods make kids feel special. They love deciding what goes into their food, and they are more willing to try something less familiar when they are in charge.

Grab kids' attention with an **engaging presentation**. Decorate a buffet of Asian favorites with oversize Chinese parasols and woks, each filled with a different display vegetable: red peppers, slender purple and white eggplants, and scallions. Kids are sure to crowd around a salad bar offering edible flowers along with the cherry tomatoes.

Many **Jewish dishes** are kid-friendly. Think brisket, kugels, falafels. Several are great

DANIEL AND REBECCA'S LUNCHEON

KIDS' MENU

ASIAN STATION
Sushi favorites
Chinese wonton pizzas stuffed with leeks and scallions
Vegetarian pad Thai
Asian noodle twists with slivers of Peking duck
Beef and chicken satays
Stir-fry of matchstick vegetables

options for the growing number of teenage vegetarians: peach-raspberry blintzes and cheese pirogi, for example. Other ethnic foods are also good bets.

Kids love **munchies**. Include some healthy ones on their tables: baby carrots, pumpkin seeds, wasabi peas, some dried fruits, and nuts. Pickles, too—they love them.

Ideas for Kid-Pleasers

Try these on separate kids' buffets (or table service menus) or mixed among your adult choices.

HORS D'OEUVRE (beyond the ever-popular pigs-in-a-blanket): A pushcart of soft pretzels (or use breadsticks made of pizza dough), flavored with garlic butter, cheese, sesame seeds, coarse salt, or cinnamon sugar, and served with an assortment of dips • A latke bar, offering pancakes made of white and sweet potatoes, as well as other vegetables, with a choice of toppings, even sugar in pretty little shakers (see Sam's menu). Put some toppings in squirt bottles and provide scallion brushes for others, and let children design their own latkes • Guacamole made to order, with lots of different-colored chips, add-ins, and dips

ASIAN STATION: (Many of these would work as hors d'oeuvre as well as for an entrée buffet. If serving these as hors d'oeuvre, offer chopsticks and "Chinese takeout" containers instead of little plates—an excellent way for guests to hold their

SAM'S KIDS' DINNER

MENU

APPETIZER
Mom's green salad with dried cranberries, apples,
and walnuts, and caramelized onion tart

ENTRÉE
Gnocchi with pink tomato sauce
Roasted vegetable lasagne
Sautéed broccoli
Italian bread (with and without garlic butter)

food as they walk around and mingle.) Sesame noodles and Asian noodle nests,
plain or with slivers of meat or poultry, work well served warm or at room temperature • Several bowls of colorful sliced vegetables for stir-fry made to order • Sushi, either an attractive ready-made variety or made to order by a chef in Japanese dress

ITALIAN STATION: Bruschetta (just a fancy word for garlic bread), is always
popular • A pasta bar, serving pastas in different shapes (butterflies, Star of David,
even hand-cut) and a variety of colors (not just green and white, but pink, from
beets; tomato-flavored orange; and mushroom brown). Put out different sauces: rose
(tomato with a touch of cream), pesto, or a terrific marinara to accompany little
meatballs or grilled veal or chicken sausages • For dairy menus, provide chunks of
Parmesan and a hand-grater for freshly grated cheese • Dress up the familiar pizza
with do-it-yourself toppings or serve individual pizzas or giant ones, to make them
look different • Decorate with a mitzvah centerpiece made of stacked tomato sauce
cans, vases of red and white anemones, and spaghetti boxes in attractive piles

MEXICAN STATION: Fajitas, quesadillas, burritos, and empanadas work well
on both meat and dairy menus. Kids love to add toppings of chopped olives,
goopy cheeses, sour cream, and bean dips. Include fresh cilantro and matchstick
jicama slices, and let them experiment with new tastes. Watch the contests: Who
can eat the jalapeño pepper or stand the hottest salsa, just like at Passover, with

the horseradish? • Decorate with hibiscus blossoms or cacti, piles of mangoes and green bananas, a handsome piñata, or Mexican woven fabric

SALADS: At seated meals, it's nice to have a first-course salad for kids to slow down the pace of the meal and encourage conversation. Consider these suggestions for preplated salads or a salad bar. Colorful raw julienne vegetables, like carrots, purple cabbage, red peppers • Slip in lettuces other than iceberg, like baby spinach leaves in a Greek salad • Kids love homemade croutons, like the butterfly-shaped ones we made for Julia • Caesar salad, tossed to order • Antipasto salads: marinated green beans, roasted peppers, pitted olives, mozzarella balls, hard-boiled eggs • Homemade dressings (infinitely better tasting and cheaper, too). Put them in squirt bottles—more fun and less mess—and place them at the salad station or directly on the kids' tables

DESSERTS: Make-your-own bars for sundaes and banana splits • Crepes or Belgian waffles • Homemade "chipwiches" • Fondues • Milkshakes (blizzards), ice cream sodas, and egg creams • Oversize cookies: chocolate chip, peanut butter, black-and-whites • Little cannoli and other miniature pastries • Pastel cupcakes in small sizes • Checkerboard cake for chess lovers • A surprise visit from a Mister Softee truck at an outdoor celebration

BEVERAGES: Feature a special kids' drink: Kids love them and adults will often abandon their own bar for many of these. In addition to the dessert drinks we mention elsewhere, try fruit smoothies, other blender drinks, and lassis (Indian yogurt drinks), club soda with various fruit syrups; coffee frappucinos (made with decaf coffee)—and offer real whipped cream and a variety of syrup flavors

MAKE IT A MITZVAH *Many elderly residents in nursing homes no longer have the pleasure of preparing their own meals. Rather than bring them a plate of cookies or a pot of soup, invite them into the kitchen (with permission and assistance from the home's recreation director, of course), to participate in a little home-style cooking and baking. And sharing stories!*

LENNY, THE FIFTY-TWO-YEAR-OLD
BAR MITZVAH BOY

Old enough to have had four bar mitzvahs, Lenny was passionate about two things: the bar mitzvah he never had and the jazz saxophone. His celebration at age fifty-two combined both.

In the Torah portion *Shemot*, Moses sees God's sign in the flames that would not be consumed. Lenny found an obvious parallel in his own life, and spoke openly to the congregation about his own "burning bushes," events that had crystallized his thinking about Judaism and led him to the bimah.

He had been a rebellious kid. When he wasn't cutting up in his Hebrew classes, he was cutting them altogether. His grandmother, the only observant member of the family, died when he was twelve, and after that his parents gave up pressuring him about the classes he missed. Eventually, he stopped going. By then, he had fallen in love with the sax, and his parents were relieved that he was jamming with friends instead of hanging out on city street corners.

It was only when his two sons were born that he regretted not knowing any Hebrew. "That was burning bush number one," he explained. At his wife's insistence, both boys had a brit, and he had to recite the blessings in transliteration. Burning bush number two came after he and his wife divorced. Lenny would bring the boys to Hebrew school on Sundays, then work in the synagogue soup kitchen until their classes were finished and he could take them home. He signed up for a class in klezmer at the temple and began to explore his Jewishness through Jewish music. He attended services with the boys and engaged them in lively discussions about their *parshahs* as each prepared for his bar mitzvah.

The last burning bush came when, proudly watching them at their bnai mitzvah, he was seized with the desire to finally have his own. He began learning Hebrew—he had forgotten everything—and set the date when his younger son started college.

At the close of his bar mitzvah service, instead of the traditional passing of the Torah from elder to younger generations, Lenny's sons passed the Torah to him, because "It is my sons who have given me wisdom."

Lenny had fun with the Kiddush at the temple. After the wine, there were buttery rugalach, sliced babka, and all the fixings for egg creams: milk, chocolate syrup, and spritzes of seltzer from old-fashioned blue bottles.

Susan and Louise, Lenny's sisters, had volunteered to help, and they decided to have the celebration in the evening so they would have enough time to prepare following the services. For a nominal fee, Lenny rented a reception area at the university where he taught and hired students to help out with the serving and the cleanup.

Because Lenny loved deli, they planned a simple menu of corned beef, turkey, and brisket. But this would not be your bubbe's Sunday night spread. Not with these hosts. There would be new twists on the old favorites and a special emphasis on beautiful but easy-to-do presentations. And they could supplement the home-prepared foods with high-quality purchased ones.

Weeks before, Susan had made a Jewish gravlax, cured with pastrami-style spices instead of smoked; it froze beautifully, and cost a fraction of the price of the store-bought kind. There were rows of shot glasses filled with chilled fennel borscht, and more shot glasses for the flavored vodkas frozen in decorative blocks of ice (see page 243 to learn how to do this). Old-fashioned oak pickle barrels (available at many garden supply stores) kept the microbrewed beers frosty cold, as well as the white wine and water.

The garlicky brisket with fresh gremolata topping and onion-crusted potato puddings stayed warm on heated brick "hot plates." Piles of freshly sliced corned beef glistened on the carving trays, and there were two large roasted turkeys. Big bowls of homemade slaws and apple-walnut salads, as well as a garden of edible vegetable flowers, created bursts of color near the meats and wooden cutting boards, which were heaped with rolls and fans of sliced rye and black bread.

Susan and Louise had set up the space on Friday afternoon. Jazzing up the room, buffet tables covered in inky black cloth ran smack through the center, lengthwise, so hungry guests could help themselves from both sides. Using a large fern as a focal point in the center of the table, Susan and Louise created two serving areas that mirrored each other. The cascading goldenrods and dill flowers set in Lenny's pilsner beer glasses beautifully set off the yellow mustards nestled, like the other condiments, in among the platters of meats. The dining tables were topped with ruffled green-and-white flowering kale in black pots. Black paper plates, white napkins, and sturdy clear plastic cutlery, along with coffee cups in a black-and-white musical note pattern, made up the place settings.

The invitations had requested guests to send a picture of themselves at age thirteen in the RSVP envelope. These were put into cardboard frames inscribed with each guest's name, and set as place cards around the tables. There was a Polaroid at each table for instant snapshot memories.

Continuing the theme, Lenny blew up black-and-white family photos from the 1950s and 1960s as decorations. There was little Lenny in a crew cut and, five years later, with hair down to his shoulders; Mom being hypnotized by a Borscht Belt comedian; and Louise holding up a snake at Camp Echo Lark. These were interspersed with candid shots of Harpo Marx, Woody Allen, and Albert Einstein, as if these famous Jews were also part of the family tree. The zany montage was affixed with spirit gum to the folding screens the university used to mount exhibitions, and set along one wall.

The small band Lenny found through the university played familiar jazz tunes, but when it gracefully segued into a cover of Cannonball Adderley's fusion arrangement of "Fiddler on the Roof," Lenny and some friends who had brought their instruments sat in with them for a few sets. Sheet music with golden oldies and Motown hits was passed around, and the good-natured musicians did their best to accompany the crowd.

While the server cleared up after dinner, Susan and Louise put out their grandmother's old samovar and the desserts: apple and sour cherry strudels and macaroons, filled like Linzer hearts, with raspberry jam. There were Lenny's homemade fortune cookies, too. Well, not exactly homemade. He bought them in Chinatown, carefully extracted the fortunes with a tweezer, and inserted his own—translations of Yiddish *chochma*, or wisdom: "The food is cooked in a pot and the plate gets the honor." "It's good to learn to barber on another's beard." "If I would be like someone else, who would be like me?"

The band had told Lenny it had another gig for later that night, so he had prepared some entertainment of his own. He plugged in the karaoke equipment and invited guests to sing a song from their teenage years or tell a story about themselves at age thirteen: "Fact or fiction. True or tall tale."

His sons began with a rap roast of their dad. The next volunteer had them in stitches with his tale. And then, a wave of déjà vu rolled over guests of a certain age. Seems he had cribbed the ribald fantasies from one Alexander Portnoy . . .

14

GETTING HELP, SERVING, AND SETTING UP

Can there be a banquet without preparations?
—TALMUD, SHABBAT

GETTING HELP

Yes, we do assume you will have help—even though you may have attended to every detail up to now yourself, even though you may be cooking up a storm for the party. You will want to revel in the sight of your child at the bimah, bathed in the glow of the *Ner Tamid* (Eternal Light), not sit there wondering whether after the service you can get the salads done, the brownies iced, set up the buffets, and, by the way, pick up the beverage order before you even start.

CHOOSING A CATERER OR A RESTAURANT

Think about parties where you've loved the food, and the way it was presented. Decide how much you want—and can afford—to have a catering company do. Drop-off caterers will simply deliver the food they have prepared; you will have to arrange to have it set out and served. Other caterers will typically set up, serve, and clean up, too. Even if they don't provide tableware, they may help with rentals—ordering, checking them in, and repacking them for return. Similarly, they may advise you on purchasing wines and liquor when they don't provide them. Full-service caterers may also guide you through other aspects of the celebration, advising on and coordinating design, flowers, and music.

Get recommendations from friends, the synagogue network, and party professionals (DJ or bandleader, florist/decorator, party planner). Your celebration space usually has a list of preferred caterers, and synagogues always have a list of kosher caterers whose kosher supervision they trust. (Please see "The Kosher Question," page 198, for more information on this subject.) Perhaps your favorite restaurant will cater the party. Do check references and ask if it is possible to visit one of their events. Ask to see their photographs if you have not visited one of their catered events. Do they own nice serving pieces, tableware, and displayware? Will they work with you to achieve the look you want?

Price quotes. Request quotes in writing from several caterers, and find out what the quote includes. Will you have to rent tableware, linens, or special equipment like chafing dishes, or are they provided? Are there added fees for servers and kitchen help? What about taxes and gratuities? What is provided, what services are additional, and how charges are calculated and billed will vary considerably from caterer to caterer.

Menus. Ask for sample menus and consider whether the selections suit your personal tastes and style. Can they arrange a tasting? (A tasting may not be possible for lower-budget celebrations, or the caterers may charge you a fee.) What does the food taste like? Is it carefully prepared, well-flavored, and beautifully presented? Do they use fresh or frozen ingredients? Are the recipes cooked in advance or made on-site? Are the chefs open to suggestions, willing to devise creative ideas tailored to your family? Would they prepare Grandma's chocolate babka or try that French chicken you adored at Susan's wedding? If they offer only set menus, are the options appealing to your family? Are there kid-friendly selections and substitutes for those who refrain from eating meat?

Beverage service. If they provide alcoholic beverages, how are they priced: by the bottle, by the glass, per person, or by the hour? If you want to purchase your own (this can be a substantial savings), would they be amenable? Would they charge a corkage fee?

Party staff. Whether you will be delegating most of the responsibilities for the party to your caterers or working side by side with them, it is essential that you feel comfortable with them and sense that they are genuinely interested in your celebration. Is the staff easy to work with, flexible, and responsive to your needs? Do they willingly answer all your questions? Are they organized? Are they knowledgeable about and respectful of Jewish traditions?

Will a manager or someone else you trust from the company be on-site for the length of the party to ensure that the celebration runs smoothly? Will there be adequate waitstaff, cooks, and bartenders (if necessary)? How are labor charges calculated? Overtime?

HOW TO WORK WITH A CATERER OR A RESTAURANT

Selecting the menu. Share your ideas and recipes, the special requests, seasonal foods, and regional specialties you prefer. Mention foods to avoid: nuts, for example, because of allergies, or foods you do not like (perhaps cream sauces, very garlicky dishes, or spicy recipes). Point out the guests who should not be served certain dishes (no prime rib for your vegetarian cousin, for instance). Do listen to their own suggestions about the menu. They know what they do best, the crowd-pleasers, the foods suited to large groups. They will let you know about the newest things they've seen and liked. If you prefer, ask to be introduced to the chef. Voice your concerns about waste. Inquire about leftovers: Will they be wrapped for you to bring home, if you wish, or donated to a needy group?

Guest count. Always provide an accurate guest count. While caterers typically prepare about 10 percent overage, you want to be sure to have ample amounts for your guests. There is nothing worse than finding yourself two servings short of that fantastic chocolate mousse.

Party timeline. Some families want the entire meal served before the serious dancing begins; others prefer a more staggered service. Discuss how long the hors d'oeuvre or buffet will be served, when to begin the Kiddush/Motzi, how to serve dessert and coffee. Create a complete timeline for the party, noting when each event will take place, and review it with the caterers. Make sure the caterers know what time you must vacate the premises (including cleanup) before incurring overtime charges.

Contractual arrangements. Be sure to ask for proof of insurance, and always get a written contract (for drop-off catering, a detailed purchase order is sufficient). The contract should include the date, the time, and the place of the celebration; the price per meal; the cost of children's meals and special meals for entertainers or other hired help, if different from regular meals; the tentative menu and when the final selections must be made; the deadline for the final guest count; the number of servers and other staff; service and gratuity charges; other charges in addition to the food bill (rental charges for equipment and corkage fees, if any); deposit and other payment terms (ask if you can pay by credit card); and cancellation and refund policy. *Note:* If the party is booked more than a year in advance, there may be an inflation rate built into the pricing.

PULLING IT ALL TOGETHER

This section is directed to all families who are "on their own" to some degree; that is, who are not hiring full-service caterers or a party planner. This includes both those who will be ordering all the food from a drop-off catering service, as well as others preparing most of the menu themselves. There will be many loose ends to attend to, such as ordering the beverages, and finding platters to present the foods and chafers to keep them hot. The guidelines and advice here will help you tie up those loose ends and pull your event together. In short, they'll show you how to be your own caterer.

First, read through this and the preceding chapter carefully; you'll find valuable, detailed information on everything from planning the menu to hiring waitstaff and keeping costs down.

The Menu

Above all, you'll need to choose foods that are doable. While it is important to offer choices to your guests, remember that as a rule of thumb, the longer the guest list, the simpler the menu should be. As food lovers, we know how difficult this will be for some of you. But if it takes three days of labor-intensive work to produce your magnificent pistachio-studded turkey galantine, we have to say, "Let it go." Select something less demanding instead, perhaps our slow-roasted salmon that is a breeze to make, yet still gets rave reviews. And you will find a slew of ideas in the section "Seasonal Garnishes," (pages 196–198) and "All Dressed Up: Beautiful Buffets, Pretty Platters" (see page 232) to turn the simple into the spectacular.

Keep in mind that cooking in large quantities can be daunting for the home cook, especially when working in a home kitchen without restaurant-size pots and pans and a real exhaust system.

Do prepare whatever you can ahead of time. Many foods freeze well, including gravlax (see our recipe for Pastrami-Style Cured Salmon, featured in the celebration story, on page 248), stews, casseroles, kugels, pasta sauces, breads, several pastries, and cookies. (*Tip:* To brighten up frozen dishes, add a burst of something fresh—a generous sprinkle of herbs, a touch of minced garlic, a squirt of lemon juice with grated zest— just before the dish is heated through.) Cy, now in his sixties, remembers baking and freezing all summer long in preparation for his autumn bar mitzvah. There are foods, however, such as mayonnaise-based dishes and watery foods like salads, that are woefully unsuitable for freezing, so do check first.

Be sure to test the recipes you will be preparing. Even dishes you have made several times may turn out to be quite different when prepared in quantity; you may have to make adjustments in cooking times, as well as in seasoning. And some of your recipes may not translate at all well when cooked in quantity.

While we're on the subject of cooking, it's time to assess what to prepare and what you can purchase. Even caterers buy some items ready-made—whether fine breads, fresh pasta, or fabulous phyllo hors d'oeuvre from a local Greek bakery. Buying wisely is an art, too—finding the best cheeses or the perfect pastrami. Scout out purveyors early and be sure to taste their products. Balance the cost of an item against the amount of time you save by purchasing it ready-made. Labor-intensive jobs may not prove worth your while, especially when you are preparing in quantity. So instead of spending the better part of a morning cutting up vegetables for crudités, you might prefer to buy them made up and prepare, say, the soup yourself. On the other hand, how could you roast three large turkeys in your oven at the same time? Better to buy the birds cooked and prepare the asparagus and potatoes. Arranging your store-bought foods in baskets and on pretty platters and trays will go a long way toward making them look homemade.

Now Get Organized

We have already mentioned the importance of lists, but when you are catering your own event, good lists—and lots of them—are essential. After you've decided on your menu, begin making preparation lists and food timelines: when to make the do-ahead dishes, when to phone in the cake or liquor order. A few days before you're scheduled to pick up or receive delivery of an order, it's a good idea to call and confirm.

Write up shopping lists—not only for all the food ingredients you will need, as well as ice and the garnishes and decorative accents you want (like herb bunches and edible flowers), but also for the extra cooking equipment (such as percolators or an extra-large roasting pan) that you will need to borrow, buy, or rent. If you'll need tableware and linens, review chapter 10, "Setting the Table," before writing your order. Picture what you will be serving, and make a preliminary diagram of the display. Then take inventory of the platters and serving pieces you own, and make a list of what you will need to borrow or rent. Do you need equipment to keep hot foods hot? See "Keeping Foods Hot" on page 236 for easy alternatives to chafing dishes and hot trays. Go over "Preparing Your Kitchen for a Celebration at Home" on page 88 and set up your space.

As you near the final countdown, you'll need a special timeline that begins two or three days prior to the party, and includes detailed information for the party itself. This timeline will note when food, beverages, tableware, and the like should be picked up, delivered, or transported. Be sure to write in the amount of money (check or cash) due on each order, and remember to have the requisite amount (including tips) readily available for whoever will be accepting delivery or picking up orders. You should also include your preparation and serving schedule for the party: when the lasagne goes into the oven and when it comes out, when the beverages must be chilled, when the hors d'oeuvre should be passed around.

Get Help

Even if you plan to prepare and/or purchase all the food yourself, you will still need help arranging it, serving it, and cleaning up. For professional help with everything from chopping onions to cooking and serving the food, contact cooking schools and domestic agencies (and see "Waitstaff and Other Hired Helpers," page 228). Or enlist the help of family and friends. But no matter whom you are relying on, make sure he or she is not standing around awaiting your instructions. Go over your lists and timelines with him or her, and draw up diagrams showing how you want the food presented, along with any additional explanations necessary.

WAITSTAFF AND OTHER HIRED HELPERS

The last thing Jake and his family wanted at his bar mitzvah was "a lot of formal wait-ers who would fold the napkin every time a guest got up from the table." They chose re-laxed servers in blue jeans and all shades of blue and green T-shirts—child-friendly college students to greet the guests. They decided on several self-serve buffet areas as well.

. . . . .

It was no surprise that the two waiters Liz hired for her daughter's bat mitzvah were out-of-work actors (so many are!). What was unusual was the idea they came up with for serving the food. Assuming the character of avuncular eastern European types, they urged guests to "Eat, eat a bissel something" as they passed the platters of hors d'oeuvre. "Enjoy, you're anyhow too thin," they admonished good-naturedly, bringing second and even third helpings to the tables. "I feel like I'm back at Grossinger's with my parents," one guest laughed.

If you will be hiring your own staff for the celebration, give some thought to the tone of service you prefer: formal but courteous, or casual and friendly. Look for hired helpers in the Yellow Pages under "Bartending Service," "Party Planning Service," and "Maids' and Butlers' Service," or at local colleges. Inquire at restaurants whether any of their staff would be available for hire. Erica loved the black-tie waiters at an upscale French restau-rant, and found they didn't work a lunch shift Saturday afternoons. Hiring staff from companies committed to minority- and gender-based diversity may be an important con-sideration for you.

How many servers will you need? That is the paramount question, of course. Here are some very general guidelines, since much will depend on the menu and style of service you have chosen (placing platters on the table, family style, may require fewer waiters than preplated service, for example). The higher ratios here reflect more formal service.

- Figure one server to every fifteen to twenty guests for a sit-down meal; one for every twenty-five guests for buffet service, and more if you are having carving stations or other food prepared to order.

- If you are having an hors d'oeuvre hour, you'll need a server for every forty to fifty guests with stationary displays, and more if platters and trays will be passed.
- A full bar requires one bartender for every fifty to seventy-five guests, but bartenders can handle more guests at a wine bar or one without mixed drinks. If you are serving drinks made to order for the kids, however, count on having more.
- Find out if the bartenders you are hiring are flexible enough to switch to serving food after the hors d'oeuvre hour, and whether the waitstaff will complete the cleanup.

While you may be tempted to skimp on staff to cut expenses, we have found that nothing bursts that lovely festive bubble more quickly than guests grumbling about slow service, and waiters who are stressed out and overwhelmed. On the other hand, you may wish to create a more home-style ambience, with more self-service for your guests and a more "invisible" staff presence.

We often hire special waiters whose job is to serve just the kids, especially when we have a separate kids' menu. They invariably establish a great rapport during the meal. If you are hiring younger help, like students, make sure you have at least one professional on hand to supervise them. Meet with the supervisor ahead of time to go over his or her responsibilities and your expectations.

Your written contract should include the date, time, and place of the event; the hours needed (earlier, to help set up; later, to clean up); the base pay rate, overtime rate, and gratuity charges. And don't forget to discuss the attire of the waitstaff. Do you want them in bistro aprons? Black tie? Simple white shirts and black trousers?

STYLES OF SERVICE: SIT-DOWN, BUFFET, AND COMBINATIONS

Sally wanted to offer her guests a choice of entrée selections, and her tastes ran to a more informal style of service, like a buffet. On the other hand, she could picture her guests comfortably sitting and chatting at the outdoor tables, not jumping up to serve themselves. She decided on a seated lunch, served family style: waiters bringing to the table wooden platters piled with different foods hot off the grill for guests to choose.

A CELEBRATION OF HANUKKAH AND THE NEW MOON: SAM'S BAR MITZVAH

MENU

POTATO STATION
Hanukkah latkes: Chickpea, Mom's traditional, and parsnip-pear
Country smashed potatoes: Chive, Yukon Gold, and truffled
Smoked salmon, caviar, goat cheese, applesauce, and other fun toppings

SHEPHERD'S FARM TABLE
Different wine selections, sheep's milk cheeses, breads, figs, and grapes

DINNER

Seated First Course

"Stacked" blood orange salad with crunchy shaved celery and
fennel, toasted walnuts, citrus vinaigrette

BUFFET
Slow-roasted spice oil salmon

Smoked tomato compote and coriander raita

Seared Ahi tuna loin with sesame glaze and scallion brushes

Baked kabocha squash

Toasted orzo with fennel and red onion

Chickpea salad Niçoise

Jon's spinach with garlic, olive oil, and currants

Rustic breads

DESSERT BUFFET
Chocolate Torah log cake with whipped cream and cocoa

Apple tart tatin

Hanukkah fritters with cinnamon-sugar dust

Little "pickups": Pistachio macaroons, carrot cakes,
raspberry tarts, lemon squares, blondies, Rachel's mini cheesecakes,
and chocolate-dipped strawberries

Butlered mini ice cream cones

Coffee and teas

When it comes to service, most of us tend to think in black and white: It's either sit-down or buffet. But these styles are merely end points on the spectrum. There are many permutations of seated and buffet service, combining the best elements of each.

Combining Buffet and Sit-down Service

Our most popular service style for bnai mitzvah calls for serving one or more courses seated and the other ones buffet style. At Sam's bar mitzvah, after standing during the hors d'oeuvre buffet and Havdalah ceremony that followed, guests came downstairs for the seated first course. They felt relaxed and cosseted when served the beautifully presented appetizer at the table. Entrées and later desserts were served buffet style, affording guests not only a choice of selections, but a chance to mingle as well. Although you (or a bandleader or DJ) may need to direct your guests, this method allows you to orchestrate the evening more easily. Having guests seated for a first course makes it easier to gather their attention for a Motzi or a toast. Since guests will have already eaten their appetizers, you can invite them to the buffets a few at a time, and avoid long lines there. Calling guests to a dessert buffet gets them up on their feet, ready to dance or chat with different guests, and focuses their attention on your pretty dessert display. Another good option is a buffet with servers not only to serve guests, but also to carve, or even prepare certain foods to order (omelettes or blintzes at lunch, stir-fries at dinner).

Both sit-down and buffet service offer distinct advantages and disadvantages. The discussion that follows should help you decide which you prefer, or whether you'd like a combination of both.

SIT-DOWN SERVICE

- **Advantages.** Some hosts dislike the idea of waiting in line for their food, and they want their guests to feel indulged with waiter service. Also, standing on line may be difficult for elderly or disabled guests. And, serving preplated meals allows you to control how the plate will look as well as how much food is served. As a result, there is considerably less waste with this style.
- **Disadvantages.** You may need additional servers. And unless the food is presented family style, your guests will have fewer choices. (When offering entrée options, servers will typically take orders at the table from the guests, or the hosts may send a menu selection card with the invitation.) Offering fewer selections may mean cutting down on or eliminating special or unusual choices in favor of the

foods likely to please most of the guests. Also, some families may prefer a more casual style of service, particularly when there are large numbers of children.

BUFFET SERVICE

- **Advantages.** As mentioned above, you'll be able to provide more choices, the chance to sample new foods, and the opportunity for your guests to mix. Buffet service is also the best choice for self-catered parties, since you can have all the food in place before your guests arrive. In addition, depending on whether you have people serving at the buffet, you may require less help. (But even without servers, you will need helpers to replenish platters and keep the tables and buffets neat.)
- **Disadvantages.** There will be more waste, since people usually take more than they can eat at a buffet, and unless you have servers, it will not be possible for you to control portion sizes. And since buffets look best when they are generously appointed, there are bound to be a lot of leftovers. Also, as mentioned earlier, standing on buffet lines can be hard on elderly and disabled guests.

To cut down on waiting at the buffet table, make sure to have at least one line for every fifty people; also, it's best to arrange your tables in mirror images—that is, with doubles of every item you are serving, each arranged at opposite ends of the table. (For more on setting up buffet tables, see "All Dressed Up: Beautiful Buffets, Pretty Platters," below.) And be sure to leave plenty of space around the buffet for guests entering and leaving the line.

ALL DRESSED UP: BEAUTIFUL BUFFETS, PRETTY PLATTERS

Of all the caterers' tricks, how to create visually arresting displays is the one we are most often asked about. There's something mysterious going on when plain old egg salad suddenly seems fresh and alluring, and a chocolate marshmallow cake looks black-tie.

So here we share our secrets.

But first, give some thought to the surrounding decor. In a well-appointed space, you may need nothing more than handsome cloths and servingware, along with attractively garnished platters. Other party spaces cry out for even more pizzazz. You'll find ideas to cover both here.

A TIME TO DANCE:
RACHEL'S JUNE BAT MITZVAH

MENU

OASIS BAR
Hand-squeezed lemonade for the kids and Margaritas for adults

MOROCCAN SAVORY PASTRIES
Cod and beef phyllo "cigares," mini bistillas, Middle Eastern meatballs,
eggplant-almond spread, and sesame wands

FOOD MARKETS

"MANNA" STATION
Lamb chops rubbed with dried thyme and sesame seeds

Tagines: Chicken with preserved lemon and olives

Melted vegetables with fresh cilantro

Couscous pyramids with dried fruits, nuts, and spices

"Pepper-mint" salad

Spring greens with pomegranate vinaigrette

"QUAIL" STATION
Grilled tuna loin with charmoula vinaigrette

Grilled quail with star anise and paprika

Spice-oil roasted carrots

Saffron rice cakes

Orange salad with red onion, cinnamon, and cilantro

Warm sesame pitas

DESSERT BUFFET
"Succès" bat mitzvah cake, with nut meringue
and coconut filling

Chocolate fondue with exotic fruits, pineapple platters,
and minted melon balls

Special display of fragrant spices and chocolate slabs

Passion fruit, mango, and raspberry sorbets in orange shells

Citrus cake

Mezze sweet table: Baklava, almond dates, apricot balls,
and praline macaroons

Moroccan coffee, mint and regular teas

Decorating the Buffet Table

Buffet tables are one of the major design elements in the room, and the attention you lavish on them will give you more bang for the buck than any decorations on the dining tables. Think bigger arrangements, and bolder color and design statements, but always make sure buffet decorations do not interfere with the food or the guests' ability to serve themselves. Candles and vases should be out of easy reach. In addition to the following ideas, you'll find many others throughout the book, especially in chapter 9, "Flowers and Centerpieces" (particularly the section on Practical Matters for Mitzvah Centerpieces, on page 125), and chapter 10, "Setting the Table."

Create Drama: Select something showstopping and highlight it. Play up a challah display with sheaves of wheat; surround a gorgeous platter of baby lamb chops with potted rosemary plants; or use a high-topped table for the bar/bat mitzvah cake. • Ice sculptures need not be overwrought. Steven's dressy reception one midwinter evening was pure theater: simple but dramatically lit moon and star ice shapes on buffets topped with sapphire-blue linens and giant clear-glass platters. • Transform a chandelier above a buffet table into an old-fashioned Sabbath lamp, festooning it with delicate sprays of orchids and greens. On the buffet table, arrange a white cloth, elegant serving vessels, and a garland of greens. • Make a mitzvah centerpiece for a soup kitchen of stockpots chockablock with carrot tops, celery, and other market vegetables

Set the Stage with Props and Heirlooms: You, your caterer, or your florist may have intriguing objects for the buffets. We have borrowed countless objects from personal collections: figurines, a metal gong, a wooden ram (for the *parshah* on sacrificing Isaac), decorative trays, even heirlooms like Aunt Gertie's candlesticks. We filled the tiers on an old iron stand with pillar candles and scented herbs. • One caterer, enchanted by Nora's description of Lot's wife and why she became a pillar of salt, circled the (salt-cured) gravlax with tall glass vases brimming with kosher salt crystals.

Tell the Food Story: Find someone to handletter the menu or print it up yourself, and display it in a pretty frame. • Use historical pictures of bagel peddlers and Orchard Street pushcarts, or seders of long ago.

Play with Color: Contrast dining tables in monochrome with a carnival of color-ful patterned cloths, bright flowers, and mixed potteryware. • To create a cool, mini-malist look at a bar, pair crisp white linens and potted white amaryllis with stemware and bowls for ice in cobalt. • Decorate an elegant springtime table with lavender cloths and bunches of dried lavender tied with deep purple ribbon set between silver serving vessels. • To play up a dessert table of rich browns and mocha colors, cover with a tea-stained crochet cloth and garnish with slabs of chocolate and piles of cin-namon sticks; set off fudgy cakes with powdered sugar stencils. • Evoke colorful bibli-cal themes. Make each buffet table a different color as an interpretation of the four seasons in Ecclesiastes.

Arranging Food on the Buffet Table

When designing your table, it's a good idea to take a moment to step back ten feet and imagine that you are a guest about to serve yourself. So, picture a neat row of platters, placed side by side directly on the buffet table. Ho hum. Now imagine the same platters arranged in groups, displayed at different levels so that the food is more easily visible, and diners can see from a distance what is available and what they want to choose. By using repetition, color, and variations in height, you can create patterns that catch the eye and move it down the table.

When arranging food on the buffet table, keep these guidelines in mind.

- **Aim for symmetry,** especially when creating serving areas that "mirror each other." It lends a formality and readability to the buffet. Group like items together.
- **Use larger platters whenever possible.** Too many small serving pieces make for a chaotic buffet. If you don't have larger platters, group smaller dishes together. Place small bowls of condiments and spices on trays or mirrors, not directly on the table. We nestle the accoutrements for smoked salmon (chopped onions and chives, capers) in a tray covered with red-orange lentils to mirror the color of the salmon.
- **Coordinate serving vessels.** Avoid the "everything but the kitchen sink" approach when selecting platters; instead, choose just two types (copper with wood or white with silver)—or three, if the third lends a little oomph, like a decorative pottery dish.
- **Vary heights.** Starting with a tiered stand, a pedestal, or a tall vase as a focal point, create a sense of movement in the display by using servingware in a variety of

heights: flat platters, deep bowls, and baskets. (A caterer's trick: Raise the basket up a bit with a small box hidden underneath.) You can use cake plates and pedestals to make raised displays. Or create your own tiered display: Place one tray on top of another, using spacers (upside-down stemmed glasses work well) in between, secured with Stickum.

- **Use color effectively.** Set a platter of sautéed carrots across the table from roasted salmon, repeating the orangey color. Arrange vivid grilled red peppers next to a pale pasta dish.
- **Use labels** on special foods or ingredients that are not easily identifiable. Tent cards call attention to Aunt Sadie's schnecken or Adrienne's phyllo squares. It's fun to name-drop once in a while.

Keeping Foods Hot

Besides chafing dishes, there are many ways to serve food hot—without resorting to your mom's old warming tray. To improvise a makeshift burner, place a can of sterno on a saucer and, using bricks (purchased at a home supply store), build an open square around it, just wide and high enough to support a big cast-iron skillet above the sterno flame. Or heat bricks in the oven to make your own "hot plates" for kugels, lasagnes, and pizzas. (Be sure to protect the table with cloth napkins or trivets.) Some pans are handsome enough, and retain their heat well enough, to be used straight from the oven or stove, such as casseroles, copper pots, cast-iron pans, and woks, and they can be set on heated bricks, if necessary, to maintain their heat for extended periods. To keep the soups at Sam's Kiddush hot, we warmed them in our heavy Le Creuset Dutch ovens until they were steaming. We loved the casual look of serving directly from the red-and-blue pots, as we would have done at our own home.

Arranging the Food in Serving Dishes

Create a Sense of Plenty

Heap platters up more than you are accustomed to doing; better to have one full platter than two half-empty ones. When serving sliced meats and fish, do not cut them all at once. Just as you would present a wedge of cheese on a cheese platter along with diced and sliced cheeses, leave a chunk of meat uncut—or buy an extra portion—and place it alongside the presliced items. This not only makes for a more attractive presentation, but even meat from the corner deli will look homemade. Let an upended basket spill crusty loaves of bread onto the table.

Get Playful

The same old foods somehow taste better when presented a little differently. Serve porcini broth in espresso cups or hors d'oeuvre on Asian spoons. Make pickle flowers: Fashion spears of dills and half-sours in endive leaves, layered like daisy petals around a lettuce cup filled with black olives. Or create blooms of frilly scallion brushes.

Versatile salmon can be presented in a bevy of ways. Arrange smoked or cured salmon, rolled or in rosettes (roll a strip of salmon around your finger, stand the roll upright, and curve the "petals" downward with your fingers), in diagonal stripes across a tray, alternating with cucumber rounds or toast points. For a very modern look, roll salmon strips and pack them tightly on a square tray, like candies in a box, with all the fixings on the side. For a more elaborate presentation, arrange rosettes of salmon on cucumber rounds. Squirt on a little sauce (chive crème fraîche or mustard, depending on what kind of salmon it is—smoked or cured), and sprinkle with a tiny dice of onion. These are easy to pick up and good for portion control.

Garnishes

A garnish is often most effective when it helps the guest "read" a dish. Call attention to the "roots" of a potato gratin with a little basket of mixed potatoes, including white, red, and even purple Peruvian potatoes, if you can get them. Globe artichokes on their long stems—sometimes available at farmers' markets and specialty florists—would look glorious in an amethyst vase behind a bowl of pasta tossed with artichokes and mushrooms. At Lenny's party (see page 218), his sisters arranged bunches of white-and-

LENNY, THE FIFTY-TWO-YEAR-OLD
BAR MITZVAH BOY

MENU

VODKA BAR
Pastrami-style cured salmon
Borscht with fennel, served in shot glasses

BUFFET
Platters of hand-sliced meats:
Corned beef and roasted turkey, served room temperature
Hot braised brisket with thirty-six cloves of garlic and Jerusalem artichoke purée

Onion-crusted sweet potato kugel

Bibb, apple, and walnut salad

Cider vinaigrette

Slaws: Broccoli-ginger, carrot-red onion, and
celery root-caraway

Olive, mustards, and pickles

Sour corn rye, Russian black, and challah knots

DESSERT
Apple and sour cherry strudels

Raspberry macaroons and chocolate-swirl cookies

Espresso sorbet

Coffee and tea

purple garlic near the brisket, and clustered baskets of Granny Smith apples and red-tipped lettuces (resembling blossoms) around an apple-walnut salad.

Add a jolt of green to platters, but don't garnish with a field of parsley. We like to use herbs in bunches—much more striking than a few sprigs—that we have used in the recipe or that complement the flavors in it. Instead of using just the lettuce leaves to garnish trays, leave room for an attractive small whole or half head.

Fruits and edible flowers add color and drama. (Again, make sure the flowers are unsprayed.) Picture violets dotting a platter of creamy white polenta, nasturtiums setting off the apricots in a brisket with dried fruits, magenta blossoms cut from inexpensive sprays of orchids encircling a white chocolate cheesecake. Bunches of grapes—black, red, or green—are great cascading from a cut-glass footed pedestal or placed directly on the table.

Large patterns make eye-catching displays. Add snap to a big platter of smoked fish, even a simple one of tuna salad: Ring the perimeter of the platter with alternating slices of lemon and cucumbers, using radish, cherry tomato, or black olive spacers for accent.

Paint with sauces. Fill plastic squirt bottles (the kind sold for mustard and ketchup) with sauces like pesto or chocolate glaze, and pipe swirls or dots around a platter's edge.

Plates, Cutlery, and Napkins on the Buffet

Stack plates in two or three piles near the beginning of the buffet line (if necessary, store extras in a crate under the table). Place napkins and cutlery at the end of the buffet, so guests don't have to carry them while moving through the line.

You can roll flatware inside cloth napkins, or the napkins can be folded and stacked on the table or in a basket. If the menu requires forks only, you can fan them out or place them on their side on a napkin-covered plate. Paper napkins are unattractive when rolled and unpleasant for guests to use after they have been unrolled. We usually fan them out on the buffet table.

If there is seating for all, we usually prefer to preset the tables with napkins and flatware, along with stemware, water pitchers, and wine.

BEVERAGE AND BAR SERVICE

Alex's family had sponsored a gracious Kiddush for the congregation after services. They wanted a more intimate party for family and friends, something a little different, that would reflect their cosmopolitan tastes. But with two kids already in college, they needed above all to be budget conscious. They decided on an after-dinner celebration; the invitations indicated this was a dessert, wine, and cheese party, and the time was set for 8:30 P.M.

That midwinter Saturday evening, the tables in their living and dining rooms were covered with burgundy and purple cloths, with a velvet topper on the dessert buffet. There were burgundy-colored candles and, as centerpieces, pots of purple-and-white African violets and sugared black grapes nestled around family photographs in silver frames.

The menu featured a selection of cheeses and fruits, chocolate and caramel fruit fondue, and a warm challah bread pudding with drifts of fresh whipped cream. Avid wine collectors, Alex's parents set up a wine bar for the adults, highlighting the wines they had put down the year she was born. On the opposite side of the room, a desk camouflaged by a colorful fruit-print fabric served as a lavish fruit smoothie bar for the kids.

Diagrams for grapevine dances had been painted with poster paint on roller sheets (plain brown wrapping paper sold by the yard) and placed on the floor of the den.

The celebration began with Havdalah. As Alex's father sang the wine blessing, he poured the wine into the family Kiddush cup, holding it above a silver bowl. He continued pouring until the cup overflowed into the bowl, then he made a special blessing about the joy of the bat mitzvah and her family, symbolized by this "cup that runneth over." ("Fruits of the vine" refers to precious offspring, too!) The Kiddush cup was passed around to all the family members, who each took a sip.

There are lots of beverage-service options to consider besides full bar service, a wine bar, or just soft drinks. You can offer your guests a vodka bar (see page 243) or a bar devoted to another single type of alcohol, like tequila or Scotch; a diverse selection of exotic beers or local microbrews; or a single specialty drink, like margaritas. We often feature a seasonal quaff at parties: pomegranate or green apple martinis or sake for fall or winter; daiquiris, gin and tonics, sea breezes, or Bellinis during spring and summer.

Remember, gracious hosts are solicitous of their guests. If your bar is limited to vodka, and you know Uncle Morty drinks only slivovitz, consider buying him a special bottle.

Purchasing Wines and Liquors

Good wine makes a real difference, and needn't cost a fortune. If you're not knowledge-able about wines, get advice from someone you trust: a reputable wine store, your caterer, or an oenophile brother-in-law.

Most people switch from cocktails to wine during dinner, and it's nice to provide a selection of wines. If you are serving kosher wines, check out the many excellent ones available today in all price ranges: Bordeaux, including Margaux, Saint Emilion, and Pomerol; whites from Alsace and the Loire; Nebbiolo from Italy; and other fine wines from California, Chile, and Australia. Consider local wines, wines from Israel, or wines from regions with a special family connection: Brahm's grandmother bought New Zealand Shiraz to honor relatives arriving from that country for his bar mitzvah in Philadelphia. And since you are serving large numbers of people, this is the perfect time for festive magnums of wine.

In chapter 15, we offer guidelines for stocking a full bar with the caveat that these are merely suggestions—preferences and levels of alcohol consumption vary consider-ably from group to group. Much will depend on what is on your menu, the time of day, even where you live (different regions of the country have decidedly different drinking habits). Follow your intuition in making adjustments to this list, and adjust proportion-ately to your number of guests.

You will also find suggested guidelines for purchasing sodas and mixers in chapter 15. Don't forget fresh lemons and limes; fresh-squeezed juices are an especially nice touch.

When Beverage Service Is Included

Restaurants, hotels, country clubs, and other places where beverages are provided will vary in how they calculate your liquor bill. Some will charge a set fee by the hour (this may decrease as the party goes on—for example, $20 per hour for the first hour, $10 per hour for the second); some charge by consumption (a fee for every drink and every soda ordered). Wines drunk at dinner are generally billed by consumption per bottle.

If you prefer higher-quality premium brands, you may need to request them spe-cially. If wine is important to you, ask to taste the standard offerings. If you are unhappy with them, if they are unpleasant or characterless, ask if you can order your own, and check whether you will be charged a corkage fee.

Serving Savvy

Set up the bar in a convenient area easily visible from the room entrance, with enough space to accommodate your guests. Avoid locating it near the kitchen, the bathroom, and other doorways where it is likely to cause a traffic jam. Cover the bar with a pretty cloth. Make a simple bar look top-shelf by stacking glassware in two or three layers, using plastic platters or silver trays between the tiers. You can invert the middle layer of glassware to make the stack sturdier. Not only attractive, this arrangement also saves room on top of the bar. Near the glasses, but out of the bartender's way, place some flowers arching over in a simple glass vase or fill a clear bowl with limes and lemons to pick up the crystal sparkle. More dazzlers that Brian Kappra from Evantine Design taught us: Use colored glassware or sprinkle flower petals in one or two contrasting colors under the glasses.

Remember to have the following items available: corkscrews and bottle openers, a small knife, ice bucket and tongs, beverage napkins (patterned ones are fun), stirrers, shot glasses, a large trash can, and a separate can for recyclable bottles and cans. If you want to cut down on glassware, we recommend an all-purpose twelve-ounce stemmed glass.

Let bartenders know if you prefer a lighter pour. And always make sure that bartenders and servers are vigilant about not serving alcohol to kids. Kids will be kids, asking bartenders for a drink while joking, "Well, today I am a man (or woman)," sneaking glasses off the butlered trays, or fooling around to amuse their friends.

Some bartenders will put out plates for tips. Many hosts find this inappropriate; make sure to mention if you object. We prefer to tell bartenders that they will be tipped by the hosts, and to refuse tips from the guests, with a "Thank you, but we've been taken care of."

To take the crush off the bar:

- Have servers pass trays of wine, champagne, a seasonal drink, or sparkling water.
- Set up a separate wine table, either tended or self-serve, with opened bottles or trays of wine already poured. (Don't preopen a lot of bottles—you won't be able to return them.)
- Place opened bottles and glasses on dining tables preset for the seated meal.

Cost-cutting Ideas

Which is less expensive: a full bar or simply serving wines and beers? That depends on the kind of wines you serve. However, limiting yourself to wines and beers may cut down on or eliminate the need for bartenders.

You can save money by taking these simple steps.

• Buy wines by the case, and purchase mixed cases.
• Trim costs by purchasing liquor (mixers and soft drinks, too) through a discount warehouse or superstore, or wholesale through your caterer.
• Ask your liquor/wine merchant if you can return unopened bottles for credit (if not, be sure to buy brands and wines you like).
• Serve fewer choices.
• Avoid champagne toasts or specialty drinks.

The Kids' Bar

We always set up a separate beverage bar for the kids. It keeps them away from the alcohol, cuts down on crowds around the bar, and makes it easier to serve a special kids' drink, like virgin piña coladas or strawberry lemonade.

Stock the bar with fruit juices or sparkling ciders, sparkling and still water. If you object to serving sodas to kids, look into the excellent fruit juice sodas that are available. Make kids' drinks special by adding sliced lemons, limes, or mint to the beverage pitchers. Or freeze berries, mint leaves, or citrus slivers in the ice cubes. We suggest an all-purpose highball glass for kids' drinks.

The Big Chill

To chill wines, beers, and sodas quickly, without refrigerating them, put them in a big tub (a large planter, a clean trash can lined with plastic, or even your bathtub!) filled with ice and cold water.

To keep pitchers of iced tea or fruit drinks cold but not watered down by melted ice, remove the dividers from several ice cube trays and freeze tea, lemonade, or juice in the trays. Use these large, flavored blocks of ice instead of plain ice cubes.

Create a decorative block of ice to hold bottles of vodkas and other beverages, as Lenny's sisters did (see page 219). Rinse out a half-gallon juice carton and cut the top off. Set a fifth of vodka into the container, and arrange some small fresh flowers (violets,

freesia blossoms, Johnny-jump-ups) or thin slices of lemon or lime around the perimeter. Fill the carton about one-third full with cold water and place it in a freezer until almost solid. Repeat once or twice with additional flowers or citrus and water, until the
water reaches halfway up the neck. Freeze until solid. To serve, just cut away the carton,
and place the block on a tray lined with cloth napkins; hold by the unfrozen part of the
neck to pour. You can use different garnishes to coordinate with various vodka flavors:
for example, whole cranberries or orange slices.

WHEN YOU NEED LESS-EXPENSIVE
CHOICES

*Lynn's family provided a savory Kiddush of soups and salads at the synagogue, and
later welcomed invited guests to their home for afternoon tea. She set out little sandwiches made of challah knot rolls and specialty breads cut in fanciful shapes. There
were delicate scones with fresh cream and preserves, and an array of desserts, including fruit-studded noodle puddings, homemade babkas and cookies. Guests poured
spiced tea from Grandma's samovars and herbal selections from pretty teapots.*

More formal receptions are always costlier. Be sure to check out our other ideas for fun,
casual, but stylish parties, including lighter meals, luncheons, and dessert, wine, and
cheese parties. If you won't be serving a meal, make sure your invitation is clearly
worded, so guests do not expect lunch or dinner: for example, "Join us for desserts
at . . ."

   Besides the obvious—cutting the guest list and avoiding expensive menu items—
there are lots of other ways to trim food costs.

- **Type of meal.** Serving luncheon is usually a less expensive alternative than
  providing dinner. Lunch is a lighter meal; you can skip the expense of an extended
  hors d'oeuvre hour, and cut down on alcohol or eliminate it completely. And you
  can avoid serving both a Kiddush and a luncheon by combining the two. (See the
  "Kiddush/Oneg" section on page 200.)
- **Simplify the menu.** Do you really need ten or twelve varieties of hors d'oeuvre?
  Keep costs and waste down by offering fewer options and stick to safe choices

likely to appeal to everyone. **Room-temperature foods** save on labor and special equipment, like chafing dishes and portable ovens. **Seasonal foods** not only cost less, they also look and taste better. High-quality strawberries, asparagus, and melons are much more affordable in season.

- **Caterers/restaurants.** If you're working with a caterer, ask if you can supplement the menu with home-prepared or purchased food. Ellen's aunt, known for her oniony brisket, brought two for the buffet table. Beth's mother, who lives in Bombay now, bought samosas at an Indian restaurant in Philadelphia to round out the hors d'oeuvre at her grandson's party. Restaurants and caterers may be willing to negotiate pricing on parties held at less-popular times: weekdays, Thanksgiving, or the dead of winter. Investigate catering companies in nearby suburbs outside your city; they may be less costly and eager to expand into new areas. Ask your caterer to suggest ways to trim costs. Caterers are quite used to such requests, and are likely to come up with several money-saving strategies.

MAKE IT A MITZVAH *Heifer International fights hunger with gifts of farm animals to villages worldwide. Help struggling children and families become self-reliant: Give a llama, geese, a swarm of bees, or encourage your class to donate a gift ark of animals in pairs. Contact www.catalog.heifer.org.*

15

RECIPES AND PLANNING TOOLS

SURE-FIRE BAR/BAT MITZVAH RECIPES

We have calculated portions here based on standard meal-size servings, Typically, however, at a bar/bat mitzvah, you will be serving several courses and/or offering a number of choices in each menu category in buffet service. For more accurate figures for your particular simcha, use the guidelines in "Portion Sizes," on page 271, which are based on the total amount of food you are serving.

Pastrami-Style Cured Salmon

YIELD: ABOUT 12 TO 15 SERVINGS

One whole side of fresh salmon fillet (approximately 2–2^1/2 pounds),
    cleaned but skin left on
1 cup packed brown sugar
1 cup kosher salt
^{1}/4 cup molasses
2 tablespoons whole black peppercorns
1 tablespoon mustard seeds
1 tablespoon ground coriander
1 tablespoon juniper berries
1 tablespoon ground allspice
1 tablespoon cumin seeds
4 to 6 garlic cloves, coarsely chopped
1 teaspoon Colman's dry mustard
2 bay leaves, crushed
1 bunch fresh dill sprigs
^{1}/2 cup brandy (optional)

Cut salmon in half, lengthwise. Using a needle-nose pliers or tweezers, remove any remaining pin bones. Line a pan with plastic wrap, making sure that the wrap hangs generously over sides of pan. Place one half of the salmon, skin side down, in the pan. In a bowl, combine the brown sugar, salt, and molasses, and spread evenly on the salmon flesh.

In a small bowl, combine all other ingredients except the brandy and press the mixture onto the salt/sugar layer. If using brandy, pour it over the seasonings. Place the reserved salmon half evenly over the seasoned piece, flesh to flesh, skin-side up. Wrap the plastic wrap over the sides and ends of the salmon to create a tight package.

Place another pan or large plate on top of the salmon, weigh it down with a few cans, and refrigerate. Remove the salmon after 24 hours, drain the accumulated liquid, and discard it. Rewrap the salmon and flip it over so the bottom piece is now on top. Remember to replace the weights after turning fish. Let the salmon cure for a total of 3 days, draining and flipping it each day. Once the salmon is fully cured (its flesh should be opaque), carefully scrape off herbs and spices and discard them. When ready to serve, use a very sharp knife to slice the salmon as thinly as possible on a shallow angle, making sure not to slice through the skin but guiding the knife just above it, parallel to the cutting surface.

SERVING IDEAS: Serve with fresh lemons, chopped onions, capers, and thin pumpernickel for an hors d'oeuvre or starter; or cream cheese, sliced tomatoes, scallions, bagels, and bialys for brunch, lunch, or morning Kiddush. (See "All Dressed Up: Beautiful Buffets, Pretty Platters," on page 232 for ideas on decorating and garnishing salmon platters.)

COOK'S NOTE: You can freeze securely wrapped cured salmon up to 2 months. Defrost overnight in the refrigerator.

"Pepper-Mint" Salad

YIELD: 10 SERVINGS

4 cups seeded and diced plum tomatoes

3 cups peeled, seeded, and diced cucumber

1 1/2 cups seeded and diced green bell pepper

1 cup seeded and diced yellow bell pepper

1 cup finely diced red onion

1/2 cup chopped fresh mint

1/3 cup chopped fresh dill

1 teaspoon ground cayenne

1 tablespoon ground sumac (available at Middle Eastern and well-
   stocked specialty stores)

FOR THE VINAIGRETTE

2 shallots, minced

1/4 cup fresh lemon juice

2/3 cup extra virgin olive oil

salt and freshly ground pepper

In a large mixing bowl, combine all ingredients except the vinaigrette. In a separate mixing bowl, whisk together the vinaigrette ingredients, and pour over the salad. Toss thoroughly. Adjust seasoning.

SERVING IDEAS: This may be served alone or with your choice of greens. For a dressier presentation, pack the salad into a 4-ounce custard cup, and invert onto the plate.

COOK'S NOTE: For extra crunch, we recommend romaine and frisée. To transform this salad into a slightly more filling grain salad, add 3 cups of toasted and cooked Israeli couscous. Also lovely with cubes of avocado added.

French Lentil Salad

YIELD: 8 SERVINGS

1 tablespoon plus 1 cup extra virgin olive oil

6 garlic cloves, minced

2 cups lentils (preferably French green), rinsed and picked over

$^1/_2$ red bell pepper, diced

$^1/_2$ yellow bell pepper, diced

1 small red onion, diced

4 fresh plum tomatoes, diced

$^1/_2$ tablespoon anise seed*

$^1/_2$ tablespoon ground coriander*

$^1/_2$ tablespoon ground cinnamon*

1 tablespoon ground cumin*

1 shallot, minced

1 tablespoon Dijon mustard

$^1/_2$ cup red wine vinegar

salt and freshly ground pepper

$^1/_2$ cup julienned mint leaves

crumbled goat or feta cheese (optional)

*Preferably freshly toasted and ground

Put lentils in a large saucepan and cover with water by 2 inches. Bring to a boil and reduce heat to low. Simmer for 30 minutes or until tender. Drain and cool.

Coat the bottom of a small sauté pan with 1 tablespoon of the oil and place over medium heat. Add garlic and sauté until fragrant. Remove from heat and let cool.

In a mixing bowl, combine lentils, garlic, red and yellow pepper, onion, tomatoes, and toasted spices.

In another bowl, whisk together the shallot, mustard, vinegar, and the remaining 1 cup of oil, and pour over lentil salad. Mix thoroughly and season salad with salt and pepper. Sprinkle mint and cheese, if using, over the top for garnish.

Slow-Roasted Spice-Oil Salmon

YIELD: ABOUT 6 SERVINGS

I cup extra virgin olive oil, plus additional oil for coating pan

1 1/2 tablespoons curry powder

2 tablespoons ground coriander*

2 tablespoons ground cumin*

2 tablespoons ground cardamom*

2 tablespoons ground anise*

I tablespoon ground turmeric

1 1/2 tablespoons honey

I whole side fresh salmon fillet (not salmon steak), approximately
    2–2 1/2 pounds, boneless and skinless

salt and freshly ground pepper

smoked tomato compote (recipe follows)

*Preferably freshly toasted and ground

Two hours before you'd like to cook the salmon, prepare spice oil. Combine all ingredients except salmon, salt, and pepper in a small saucepan and gently heat over low flame for 15 minutes. Remove from heat and let stand at room temperature until ready to use. The longer it sits, the more flavorful it will be.

Preheat oven to 325 degrees.

Season salmon with salt and pepper, and brush liberally with spice oil. Place in shallow baking dish lightly coated with olive oil. Cook 15 to 20 minutes, or until salmon reaches internal temperature of 125 degrees on an instant-read meat thermometer for medium-rare (salmon will still be translucent in the center); for fish that is cooked through, the temperature should read about 135 degrees, and the fish should be opaque in the center. Check frequently after 12 minutes, because fish can quickly overcook.

Serve warm or at room temperature. If serving warm, serve immediately; otherwise, salmon can be prepared a day in advance and refrigerated, but be sure to bring it to room temperature before serving.

SERVING IDEAS: Drizzle salmon again with spice oil before serving. Accompany with Smoked Tomato Compote (see page 254). It is also delicious drizzled with tzatziki, a garlicky Greek yogurt and cucumber sauce. Garnish with some of the following: whole star anise, fennel fronds, cilantro, lime rounds, and cherry tomatoes. Or surround with our French Lentil Salad (see page 251).

Swiss Chard Fritada

YIELD: ABOUT 8 TO 10 SERVINGS

3 tablespoons unsalted butter

2 pounds Swiss chard, cleaned, stems cut into $^1/_2$-inch pieces, leaves
coarsely chopped

3 medium leeks (about $1^1/_2$ pounds), trimmed, washed free of sand,
white and pale green parts thinly sliced

1 tablespoon chopped garlic

salt and freshly ground pepper

8 ounces feta cheese

1 7.5-ounce package farmer cheese

4 tablespoons freshly grated Parmesan cheese

4 large eggs

1 cup coarsely chopped fresh dill

1 cup coarsely chopped fresh mint

olive oil for greasing pan, plus extra virgin olive oil for drizzling

Melt butter in a 12-inch heavy skillet over medium heat. Stir in chard stems and leeks, and saute 2 to 3 minutes. Add garlic, a little salt (feta will be salty, so be careful with the salt shaker), and pepper to taste. Cover pan and cook over low heat, stirring occasionally, until the vegetables are tender, about 15 minutes. Uncover, stir in chopped chard leaves (a few handfuls at a time, if necessary). Cover the pan, and cook over moderately high heat until the leaves are wilted. Let cool, then squeeze out as much liquid as possible from the mixture, and set aside.

Preheat oven to 350 degrees.

In a food processor, blend the feta, farmer cheese, and 2 tablespoons of Parmesan until smooth. Add eggs, pulsing after each addition until blended. Transfer mixture to a large bowl. In the food processor, briefly pulse the cooled, drained chard and leeks, the dill, and the mint, until chopped fine, then transfer to the mixture in the bowl.

Generously grease a 13-by-9-inch glass baking dish, pour the batter in, and smooth the top. Drizzle about 1/2 tablespoon of oil over all, and sprinkle with remaining 2 tablespoons of Parmesan.

Bake about 40 minutes, or until light golden, and edges are starting to pull away from sides of pan. It will feel slightly firm, but the fritada will not set until it has cooled at least 30 minutes.

Serve warm or room temperature, cut into squares.

COOK'S NOTE: Labneh, a rich, thick Middle Eastern yogurt, is wonderful with this fritada. Serve labneh plain or flavored with chopped scallions, mint, cilantro, or other fresh herbs. Or substitute drained sheep's or cow's milk yogurt.

Smoked Tomato Compote

2 tablespoons extra virgin olive oil

6 to 8 fresh plum tomatoes, diced

2 to 3 shallots, thinly sliced

1 tablespoon fresh chopped garlic

1 tablespoon ground coriander, preferably freshly toasted and ground

1^1/$_2$–2 teaspoons smoked paprika (available at specialty stores and some
   well-stocked supermarkets)

salt and freshly ground pepper to taste

Coat bottom of a sauté pan with oil and place over medium heat. Add all of the ingredients, and cook until tomatoes are softened and the liquid has thickened to a saucelike consistency. Adjust salt and pepper to taste. May be served hot, cold, or at room temperature.

COOK'S NOTE: Use to enhance grilled or poached fish, pasta, or polenta. As a variation, omit smoked paprika and add some or all of the following: chopped basil, chopped olives, capers, fresh or dried hot chile pepper.

Walnut Cilantro Challah (and Variations)

YIELD: 2 AVERAGE LOAVES OR 1 LARGE SIMCHA LOAF

1 package or 2^1/$_4$ teaspoons active dry yeast

1 tablespoon honey

^{1}/$_2$ cup warm water, plus 1^1/$_2$ cups water

3 large eggs

6 tablespoons vegetable oil, plus additional oil for greasing bowl

2 tablespoons walnut oil

5^1/$_2$ cups unbleached bread flour, plus additional flour for kneading

^{1}/$_2$ cup whole wheat flour

1 heaping tablespoon salt

1 cup walnuts, lightly toasted and roughly chopped

^{1}/$_2$ cup chopped fresh cilantro or chives

egg wash: 1 large egg plus one yolk, beaten

In a small bowl, stir together yeast, honey, and ^{1}/$_2$ cup warm water (about 105 to 115 degrees) until yeast is activated and mixture starts to get bubbly, about 5 minutes. In a medium bowl, beat eggs, then beat in 1^1/$_2$ cups water and both oils.

Stir together both flours and salt in a very large mixing bowl. Make a well in the flour and pour in yeast and egg mixtures. Mix with a wooden spoon or on low speed with a beater until thoroughly combined and dough forms a cohesive mass.

Turn out onto a floured board and knead until dough is smooth, elastic, and no longer sticks to your hands, 5 to 8 minutes, adding more flour as needed. Fold in walnuts and cilantro, kneading until well incorporated. Put dough in a well-oiled bowl (turn dough over once to coat both sides) and cover with plastic wrap. Let rise in warm, draft-free area until at least doubled in size, approximately 3 hours.

Punch dough down and divide into two equal balls. Separate one ball into three equal pieces and roll pieces into identical long ropes. Braid the ropes: start braid in the middle, then turn it around and braid the other side. Turn the ends under and press down to keep them joined together. Repeat with the second ball. Alternatively, make one large Simcha Loaf, following instructions below.

Transfer to a baking sheet lined with parchment paper. Brush with egg wash (three times for really shiny top). Preheat oven to 350 degrees. Cover dough with plastic wrap and let rise 30 minutes. Bake about 40 minutes or until loaves are golden brown and sound hollow when tapped on bottom. Transfer to rack and let cool.

To make a Simcha Loaf, an attractively shaped challah that breaks off easily much like Parker House rolls, divide the dough in half. Form 12 small balls out of one of the halves and place them on parchment-lined baking sheets in 2 rows of 6 balls each. The balls should be touching so that they will all join together when they rise. Make a slight indentation down the middle of the row to hold the braid that will go on top. With the remaining half of the dough, form 3 long ropes and braid as before. The finished braid should be equal to the length of the 6 balls. Place the braid on top of the indentation in the center of the loaf. Brush with egg wash, let rise, and proceed as directed, baking an extra 10 minutes.

Variations:

Substitute the following for the walnuts and herbs, and prepare as above.

Cranberry-orange: 1 cup chopped dried cranberries and grated zest of three oranges

Onion-poppy: 2 cups onions (diced, lightly sautéed in oil, and well-seasoned with salt and freshly ground pepper) and 1/2 cup poppy seeds

COOK'S NOTE: The walnut challah is especially delicious toasted. To make a sandwich bread for toasting, omit braiding and shape dough into traditional loaves.

Lori developed this challah based on her friend Elissa Goldberg's excellent recipe.

Rachel's Mini Cheesecakes

YIELD: 24 MUFFIN-SIZE CAKES

Vegetable oil spray

1 9-ounce package of chocolate wafers or gingersnap cookies

9 tablespoons unsalted butter, melted

2 pounds cream cheese, softened

1 1/2 cups granulated sugar

2 large eggs

1/2 cup mascarpone cheese (available at many well-stocked supermar-
     kets or gourmet shops)

2 vanilla beans, split lengthwise

Preheat oven to 350 degrees.

Generously coat two standard 12-muffin pans with oil spray. Place a sheet of plastic wrap over each muffin pan, and mold the wrap with your fingers so that each muffin cup is entirely lined with it. (The spray will help the plastic wrap "hug" the muffin cups.)

In a food processor, pulse the cookies until they become fine crumbs. In a small bowl, stir together the crumbs and melted butter. Spoon 2 tablespoons of crumbs into each lined muffin cup. Using fingers or the back of a teaspoon, press crumbs into the bottom to make crust smooth and even.

In a medium mixing bowl, beat cream cheese and sugar on medium speed until light and fluffy. Slowly beat in eggs, one at a time. Scrape down sides of bowl and beat in mascarpone. Continue beating until well incorporated. Scrape the seeds from the vanilla beans, and stir in.

Using a large spoon or an ice cream scoop, fill muffin cups until just full, and smooth tops. Place pans on a baking sheet and bake for 15 minutes, rotating pans halfway through baking time. Cheesecakes are done when lightly brown on the edges, jiggly, but not wet in the centers. Do not overbake. If cracks form on the tops, cheesecakes are overbaked and it will be difficult to unmold them.

Remove pans from oven and let cool on rack. When cool enough to touch, place pans in refrigerator at least 1 hour. To unmold, lift the plastic wrap from each muffin tin and the cheesecake should peel off easily from the wrap.

Serve plain, or top with your favorite fruit or fresh whipped cream.

Citrus Cake

YIELD: TWO 9-INCH ROUND CAKES

Juice and finely grated zest of 1 medium orange and 1 medium lemon
(in all, you should have $1/2$ cup of juice and 1 teaspoon zest)
$1^1/_4$ cups granulated sugar, divided
2 tablespoons finely grated carrots
$1/2$ cup dried cherries, chopped
5 large eggs, separated, plus 2 egg whites
1 cup unbleached all-purpose flour, sifted
$1/2$ teaspoon salt
$1/2$ cup plus 2 tablespoons extra-virgin olive oil (choose a fruity,
buttery-tasting oil)
Vegetable oil spray

Preheat oven to 375 degrees.

Bring juice, zest, and 1/2 of the sugar to a boil in a small, heavy saucepan. Remove the pan from the stove, and stir in the carrots and cherries, and let the mixture cool.

In a large bowl, beat the yolks with $1/2$ cup of the sugar over medium-high speed until pale and creamy, and ribbons form when beaters are lifted.

In a small bowl, stir together flour and salt, and add slowly to egg mixture, beating until well combined. Continue beating while slowly adding carrot-citrus mixture and then olive oil.

In a clean bowl, beat the egg whites on medium speed until soft peaks form. Add the remaining $1/4$ cup of sugar, and continue beating until peaks are stiff, but not dry. Carefully fold into the batter.

Coat bottom and sides of two 9-inch round cake pans with vegetable oil spray and line them with parchment paper. Spoon batter into pan. Bake for 20 minutes, then decrease temperature to 325 degrees. Bake 20 minutes more, or until a toothpick inserted in the center comes out clean. Turn off oven, cover loaves with greased parchment paper (greased side down), and allow cake to rest in the closed, warm oven 10 minutes. The cake will sink a bit as it cools. Remove cake from oven and cool on rack. To unmold, run a knife along sides of pans and invert onto a platter.

SERVING IDEAS: Serve with fresh fruit or compote. If serving cake plain, you can dust it with powdered sugar while still warm, if desired. The cake has a lovely texture when cubed and toasted, and is especially nice for dipping into chocolate or caramel fondue. Arrange cubes on a serving platter, and poke a long skewer, porcupine style, into each.

COOK'S NOTE: This was inspired by the olive oil cake in Alice Waters' *Chez Panisse Menu Cookbook*. You'd never guess it is dairy-free, in accord with the dietary laws for meat meals.

Chocolate Marshmallow Bar/Bat Mitzvah Cake

YIELD: ABOUT 12 SERVINGS

Vegetable oil spray
2 cups granulated sugar
1 3/4 cups all-purpose flour
3/4 cup excellent-quality cocoa powder
1 1/2 teaspoons baking soda
1 1/2 teaspoons baking powder
1 teaspoon salt
2 large eggs
1 cup buttermilk
1/2 cup vegetable oil
1 teaspoon vanilla extract
1 cup freshly made strong peppermint tea

Preheat oven to 350 degrees. Generously coat two 9-inch round or square pans with vegetable spray. Line bottoms of the pans with parchment paper, and spray the tops of the paper.

In a large bowl, stir together the sugar, flour, cocoa, baking soda, baking powder, and salt. In a separate bowl, mix together the eggs, buttermilk, oil, and vanilla extract. While beating on low speed, gradually add this mixture to the dry ingredients. Beat for 2 minutes on medium speed. When well mixed, stir in tea. Divide batter between pans. (Batter will be runny.)

Bake 35 to 40 minutes, or until a toothpick inserted in the center comes out clean. Cool cakes on wire rack 15 to 20 minutes, then turn out and remove pans to finish cooling.

To assemble, place one cake on a cardboard bottom cut to the exact size of the cake. Place on a cooling rack with a tray underneath to catch spills. Spread a layer of Fluffy Mallow Mint Frosting (recipe follows) on top of cake only, about 1/4-inch thick. Place second cake on top of the first, and generously spread more frosting over top and sides of cake. Spread Ganache (recipe follows) over this, generously covering top and sides. Decorate cake, if desired, using Fluffy Mallow Mint Frosting or whipped Ganache for rosettes, writing, and so on. Garnish with sprigs of fresh mint before serving.

Variation:

For fans of coffee and cinnamon flavors, add 1/4 teaspoon cinnamon to dry ingredients and substitute coffee for mint tea in cake recipe. Omit mint extract from the Mallow Fluffy Mint Frosting.

For a white exterior, start with the Ganache, and top cake with the Fluffy Mallow Mint Frosting. Use whipped Ganache to decorate.

For an easy version, perfect for a kids' party, bake the cake in 2 brownie pans. After cakes have cooled, frost with Fluffy Mallow Mint Frosting or mini marshmallows and Ganache, and warm in oven until gooey and delicious.

FLUFFY MALLOW MINT FROSTING

YIELD: ABOUT 3 CUPS

I cup granulated sugar
I tablespoon corn syrup
$^1/_2$ cup water
3 large egg whites, at room temperature
A few drops of mint extract (to taste; a little goes a long way)

In a heavy-bottomed saucepan, combine sugar, corn syrup, and water. Cook over medium-high heat, stirring occasionally to dissolve sugar. Use a pastry brush dipped in water to frequently wash down any sugar crystals from sides of pan. Stop stirring as soon as mixture begins to boil. Cook until syrup reaches 235 degrees on a candy thermometer (soft ball stage).

Meanwhile, whip egg whites in a bowl until they form stiff peaks. When syrup reaches 235 degrees, remove pan from heat, and with the mixer on medium speed, slowly pour hot syrup in a steady stream down the side of the bowl. When all the syrup is incorporated, turn mixer to medium-high, and continue beating until frosting is cool to the touch, about 5 to 7 minutes. Beat in mint extract. Use immediately.

DARK CHOCOLATE GANACHE

YIELD: ABOUT 1$^3/_4$ CUPS

$^1/_2$ pound dark chocolate (half bittersweet, half semisweet, or according
    to preference), chopped
I cup heavy cream

Put chocolate pieces in heat-proof bowl. Heat cream to boiling in saucepan. Remove from heat and pour over chocolate. Stir until chocolate is melted and smooth. Let cool completely before using. Thoroughly chill any ganache that you will be whipping for rosettes and other decorations.

PLANNING TOOLS

Budgets

GENERAL BUDGET CHECKLIST (INCLUDING A RANGE OF EXPECTED COSTS)	
Synagogue donation	$250 to $500
Program	$0 to $75
Tallit	$30 to $150
Kippot (by the dozen)	$18 to $24
Attire	Varies
Invitations	$100 to $800
Photography/videography	$500 to $5,000
Location	$0 to $3,000
Catering packages (food, rental, staff, bar setup and taxes)	
Lunch or dinner	$60 to $100 per person
Kiddush packages	$25 to $60 per person
Lunch or dinner menu (food only)	$25 to $60 per person
Kiddush menu (food only)	$15 to $35 per person
Rental (tables, chairs, tableware, linens, etc.)	$12 to $30 per person
Tablecloths	$10 to $45 each
Servers' rates	$10 to $30 per hour
Florists	
per centerpiece	$35 to $150
per larger arrangement	$75 to $400
Music	
DJ packages	$500 to $5,000
Bands	$1,000 to $6,000
Full bar	$6 to $30 per person
Wines, per bottle	$15 to $45
Tzedakah (charity contribution)	3% to 5% of total cost

Sample Budgets

In each of the following budgets, the families spend additional money for their charitable contribution, not included here.

LINDA'S BAT MITZVAH: A CELEBRATION AT HOME (24 GUESTS)

Synagogue donation	$100
Program	0
Tallit—gift	0
Attire	$75
Invitations	$60
Photography	$100
Location—gift to friend who loaned house	$50
Tables and chairs	$75
Food	$400
Fabric for cloths	$40
Candles and ficus trees	$70
Service	0
Florist	0
Music	0
Beverages	$30
TOTAL	$1,000 or $41.67 per person

NOAH'S EXTENDED KIDDUSH (100 GUESTS)

Synagogue donation	$150
Program	$15
Tallit	$40
Kippot crocheted by friend	$30
Attire	$75
Invitations	$100
Photography	$200
Catering package @ $35 per person	$3,500
Florist	0
Beverages	$50
Nighttime kids party	
DJ and pizza	$600
TOTAL	$4,760 or $47.60 per person

DANIEL AND REBECCA'S BNAI MITVAH: TWINS IN A SUKKAH
(220 GUESTS)

Synagogue donation	$100
Tallit—a gift	0
Program (provided by synagogue)	0
Kippot	$144
Attire	$500
Invitations	$300
Photography/videography	$1,400
Location	0
Catering: dinner menu package	
$70 per person x 150 adult	$10,500
$45 per person x 70 kids	$3,150
Bar and wine	
$10 per person x 150 adults	$1,500
$4 per person x 70 kids	$280
Flowers (centerpieces)	
15 adult tables @ $50	$750
7 kid tables @ $25	$175
Decoration of room	$1,200
Pumpkins and gourds	$75
DJ	$3,000
Hayride	$200
T-shirts	$300
TOTAL	$23,574 or $107.15 per person

RACHEL'S BAT MITZVAH: A TIME TO DANCE (150 GUESTS)

Synagogue donation	$150
Program	$50
Tallit	$80
Attire	$360
Invitations	$450
Photography	$1,500
Location Country Club	$2,000
Catering dinner menu package	
$125 per person x 100 adults	$12,500
$50 per person x 50 kids	$2,500
Bar and wine package	
$25 per person x 100 adults	$2,500
$10 per person x 50 kids	$2,500
Flowers	
15 tables @ $75 each	$1,125
3 large @ $150 each	$450
Band	$1,800
Belly dancer	$200
Market decorations	$650
Tiki torches	$50
TOTAL	$26,865 or $179.10 per person

SAM'S BAR MITZVAH HANUKKAH CELEBRATION (150 GUESTS)

Tallit	$40
Program	$25
Kippot	$108
Attire	$300
Invitations	$200
Photography by a friend	0
Location	0
Catering dinner menu package	
$75 per person x 125 adults	$9,375
$50 per person x 25 kids	$1,250
Bar and wine	
$10 per person x 125 adults	$1,250
Bar setups $2.50 per person	$375
Flowers	
Greens and candles on tables	$300
1 large arrangement	$250
Lighting	$1,000
Band (barter)	0
Accordionist	$50
Character actors	$400
Menorahs, dreidel games, etc.	$150
TOTAL	$15,073 or $100.49 per person

JULIA'S BAT MITZVAH: IN A BUTTERFLY GARDEN (125 GUESTS)

Synagogue donation	$200
Program	$75
Tallit	$150
Kippot	$120
Attire	$750
Invitations	$650
Photography	$2,000
Location: tent	$2,500
Food	
$40 per person x 100 adults	$4,000
$30 per person x 25 kids	$750
Rentals: tables, linens, chairs, tableware, dance floor	
@ $22.50 per person	$2,812.50
Service staff, 7-hour shift	
14 @ $22 per hour	$2,156
1 @ $30 per hour	$210
Flowers bought at nursery	$350
Table netting and petals	$100
Gardening services	$250
Klezmer band	$2,200
Wine and liquor	$1,000
Bar setups @ $4 per person	$500
Butterflies	$150
TOTAL	$20,923.50 or $167.39 per person

ZANDER'S BAR MITZVAH SYNAGOGUE LUNCHEON (175 GUESTS)

Synagogue donation	$150
Kippot	$125
Tallit—heirloom	0
Attire	$300
Program (homemade)	0
Invitation (homemade)	$90
Photography—synagogue member	$200
Location (including custodial fee)	$200
Food	
Caterer @ $20 per person	$3,500
Extra takeout foods to supplement	$500
(antipasto trays, breads, cookies)	
Cake	$125
Rental linens, china, tableware	$1,750
Wine and beer	$1,200
Beverages and setups	$200
Service staff	
10 servers, 2 cooks @ $126 each	$1,512
Flowers (arranged by friends)	$350
Favors for kids	$100
DJ	$1,500
Simple Kiddush	$250
TOTAL	$12,052 or $68.86 per person

Sample Long-Term Preparation Timeline
(Based on Daniel and Rebecca's Bnai Mitzvah, "Twins in a Sukkah")

Everyone's party planning path will be different: Some people will book a bandleader three years in advance, others just three months before. Nevertheless, here is a long-term preparation timeline based on Daniel and Rebecca's bnai mitzvah, "Twins in a Sukkah," to guide you in assembling yours. Please refer to pertinent sections in the book for specific details regarding each line item (getting the date, family talk, etc.).

KINDERGARTEN	Start Hebrew School
THREE YEARS BEFORE	Twins' Hebrew School forms bar/bat mitzvah co-op Do research, discuss matters with rabbi Set bnai mitzvah date Reserve synagogue for reception
TWO YEARS BEFORE	Contact caterers, compile quotes Contact DJs, compile quotes
ONE YEAR BEFORE	Meet with bar/bat mitzvah class and rabbi Make contact with tutor Family talk Start mitzvah projects Start attending Shabbat services on regular basis Confirm catering and DJ arrangements Contact florists/decorators, compile quotes
NINE MONTHS BEFORE	Start weekly tutoring Start composing guest list to get sense of count Create budget and start organizational notebook Meet with cantor Contact photographers/videographers, compile quotes Confirm florist/decorator, choose cloths and room decor
SIX MONTHS BEFORE	Meet with rabbi Revise budget, discuss tzedakah

	Visit stationery stores for invitation ideas
	Confirm with photographer and DJ, refine details
	Reserve hotel rooms for out-of-town guests
	Make plans for Sunday supper preceding bnai mitzvah
	Hire party helper
	Contact orchard about hayride
TWO TO FOUR MONTHS BEFORE	Confirm invitations, compile addresses and directions
	Shop for attire
	Work on program book, assign aliyot, get Hebrew names
	Order T-shirts for kids/gift baskets for out-of-town guests
	Order kippot and choose tallitot
	Order willow branches
	Order bar/bat mitzvah cakes
	Finalize menu and catering details
	Get recipe from Aunt Sarah for fried potato kreplach
	Review photos for sign-in board
	Mail invitations
ONE MONTH BEFORE	Assist twins with *dvar Torah* and rehearsing of Hebrew
	Purchase sundries such as candies, soaps, guest towels
	Purchase items for Rebecca's gleaning areas
	Purchase liquor and wine
	Order challah
	Buy paper goods for Sunday supper
	Review and confirm all details with party professionals
	Review party timeline
	Contact bar/bat mitzvah class co-op and coordinate help
	Confirm special honors, firm up program book
	Contact friends to assist the week of and day of
	Ask cousins to decorate chairs for chair dance
	Visit tailor
TWO WEEKS BEFORE	Rehearse with twins at home
	Confirm final counts
	Create seating chart; write up placecards
	Pick up ordered items such as kippot, program books, etc.

	Go lady apple picking with twins
	Collect pumpkins, grasses and gourds for sukkah
	Rosh Hodesh ritual for Rebecca
	Think about parental blessing
	Compose candlelighting poems with kids for *Ushpizin*
ONE WEEK BEFORE	Dress rehearsal
	Help to decorate sukkah
	Tefillin ritual for Daniel
	Last-minute errands, haircuts, seating changes, etc.
	Contact party professionals for last-minute details
	Make checklist of what to bring on the big day
	Keep calm
	Compose parental blessing and any other toasts

DANIEL AND REBECCA'S BNAI MITZVAH ("TWINS IN A SUKKAH") PARTY TIMELINE

12:30	Service ends
	Guests enter reception space
	Motzi and Kiddush in sukkah
	Special drinks and butlered hors d'oeuvre are served
12:45	Hors d'oeuvre station opens
1:30	Guests called to their seats
1:45	Guests fully seated
	Wine service
	Entrée orders taken for adults
	DJ leads kids in dancing/games
1:55	Toast by Uncle Melvin
	Dancing for kids and adults
2:00	First course for adults
	Kids' buffet opens
2:20	Dancing for adults
	Adults' first course cleared
	Tempo increases as kids join in after they finish eating
	Hora and chair dance
2:50	Kids depart for hayride
	Entrée served to adults
3:10	Entrée cleared, dancing for adults
	Coffee service at tables
3:30	Kids return from hayride
	Apple dipping
	Dessert buffet opens
3:45	Guests eat dessert
	More dancing, winding down
4:15	Departures, well-wishes, kisses and hugs
	Band plays one last tune for lingering friends
	Family gathers in sukkah
5:00	*Ushpizin* candlelighting to end the day

PORTION SIZES

These are very general guidelines to help you figure out how much food to serve your guests. Please make adjustments for your guests' preferences and style of eating, and the hors d'oeuvre (if any) on the menu, as well as for the time of day you are serving the meal.

BUFFET: FOR EACH PERSON, OFFER:

2 small servings of 2 different salads

2 medium servings of 2 different starches

2 medium servings of 2 different vegetables

8 to 12 ounces of protein (total of all protein offerings)

2 rolls or 2 slices bread

2 small servings or 1 large of dessert (and optional 1 scoop ice cream)

SIT-DOWN MEALS: FOR EACH PERSON, OFFER:

1 large serving of salad

1 medium-large serving of starch

1 medium-large serving of vegetable

8 to 12 ounces of protein

2 rolls or 2 slices of bread

2 small servings or 1 large of dessert (and optional 1 scoop ice cream)

BAR GUIDELINES

We offer guidelines for stocking a full bar with the caveat that these are merely suggestions—preferences and levels of alcohol consumption vary considerably from group to
group. Much will depend on what is on your menu, the season, the time of day, even
where you live (different regions of the country have decidedly different drinking habits).
Follow your intuition in making adjustments to this list.

Note: Our estimates reflect about sixteen drinks to every fifth of liquor; there are approximately five pours to every bottle of wine, so a case of twelve bottles yields about
sixty glasses.

FULL BAR SERVICE FOR 75 PEOPLE

4 to 6 fifths vodka
2 fifths Scotch
2 fifths gin
1 to 2 fifths tequila, optional
1 fifth whiskey
1 fifth bourbon
1 fifth rum
1 small bottle dry vermouth
1 small bottle sweet vermouth
1 fifth cassis, optional
1 case champagne, optional
1½ to 2 cases white wine
8 to 12 bottles red wine
½ case regular beer (domestic or
  imported), optional
½ case light beer, optional

SODAS AND MIXERS FOR 75 ADULTS, 25 KIDS

NOTE: We prefer serving liter bottles; they
are easier to pour and more attractive.

12 liters Coke
8 liters Diet Coke
12 liters sparkling water or seltzer
4 liters ginger ale
4 liters 7-Up or Sprite
2 liters tonic water
2 liters club soda
1 gallon orange juice
2 quarts cranberry juice
8 lemons
8 limes
1 jar prepared horseradish
1 jar Maraschino cherries
1 jar pickled onions
1 jar olives
1 bottle Bloody Mary mix, optional (buy
  3 bottles, if serving brunch)
1 bottle grenadine, optional

GLOSSARY

Adar The twelfth month of the Hebrew calendar, during which Purim is celebrated.

Aliyah; aliyot (plural) To go up to the bimah to say a blessing before and after the Torah is read. Literally means "going up." May also refer to a Jewish person's return or immigration to Israel.

Ashkenazi; Ashkenazim (plural) Jews from central and eastern Europe and their descendants (from the word *Ashkenaz*, "Germany," in Hebrew).

Bimah The area in the synagogue where the Torah is read and from which worship services are conducted. Generally a raised platform, or a pulpit.

Brit milah (usually referred to more simply as brit) The covenant of circumcision performed on the eighth day of a Jewish boy's life.

Candlelighting An optional, relatively recent Jewish American bar/bat mitzvah custom. Typically, thirteen or fourteen people are chosen by the family to light candles on a cake, and perhaps make a special blessing for the child. See chapter 11, "Tradition!" for more information.

Challah A soft, eggy loaf of braided white bread traditionally served on Sabbath and various Jewish holidays.

Dreidel A special four-sided top spun by children during Hanukkah.

***Dvar Torah* (often referred to as the *dvar*)** An interpretation about the meaning and significance of the Torah portion, usually presented as a speech. Literally means "words of Torah, or teaching."

Elijah's cup A special Passover cup that is filled with wine and placed on the table for Elijah, the prophet of hope and faith.

Gabbai The person who administers the Torah service, designating aliyot and other honors.

Haftarah Additional readings from the books of the Prophets and other texts that correspond, by date, to Torah portions and to special holidays.

Hanukkah Known as the Feast of the Dedication or the Festival of Lights, this holiday celebrates the miracle of the Temple flame that burned for eight days, and the victory of the Maccabees over the Syrians, who tried to convert the Jews to Greek polytheism. It usually falls in December.

Havdalah The service that concludes the Sabbath, at sunset on Saturday, with wine, spices, and the lighting of a braided candle.

Kabbalah The highly complex and esoteric main body of Jewish mysticism.

Kaddish The prayer glorifying God's name that is chanted at the close of the worship service. Because this prayer is also recited in memory of the departed, it is often referred to as the Mourner's Prayer.

Kashrut The Jewish dietary laws that determine what is kosher, or ritually fit to eat.

Kiddush Refers to the blessing over the wine recited at the beginning of Shabbat and other special occasions. Also connotes the celebratory collation after the Saturday morning service. Literally means "to make holy."

Kiddush cup The special goblet used for the benediction over wine.

Kippah; kippot (plural) A skullcap or head covering. Also known in Yiddish as a "yarmulke." Symbolizes awareness of God above and humility before God.

Klezmer Eastern European Jewish folk music, generally involving clarinet, flute, trumpet, and string instruments.

Kosher Ritually fit to eat, according to the Jewish dietary laws.

Ladino (also called Judesmo and Judeo-Spanish) The vernacular language spoken by Sephardim. It is based on medieval Castilian Spanish, mixed with Hebrew, Arabic, Turkish, Greek, and medieval French.

Menorah Originally, the seven-branched candelabrum of Temple days; today the word *menorah* most commonly refers to the eight-branched (nine, including the "helper," or shammash, candleholder) candelabrum lit on Hanukkah.

Mezuzah Attached to the doorpost of a synagogue, or a Jewish home or business, this ritual object is a constant reminder of God's presence. Traditional Jews kiss their hand, then touch it to the mezuzah before passing through the doorway.

Miriam's cup This new Passover ritual object originated at feminist seders in the 1970s, but is rapidly becoming more mainstream. It represents the well that accompanied Moses' sister during the years spent wandering in the desert, and provided the Israelites with water.

Miriam's tambourine Decorated with a wide variety of images—reminders of Miriam, who danced, timbrel in hand, after the Israelites crossed the Red Sea—these tambourines are a symbol of women rejoicing in song and dance. They are available at Judaica shops and online.

Misheberach Generally refers to a special prayer recited to heal those who are ill, but may also be a prayer for well-being.

Mitzvah; mitzvot (plural) One or more of the 613 commandments Jews are obligated to perform, but, more commonly, any good deed or kind act.

Motzi The blessing over the bread at the beginning of a meal. See chapter 11, "Tradition!"

Oneg "Enjoyment, delight." Generally, the refreshments served at the synagogue following services.

Parshah The weekly portion read from the Torah.

Passover Also known as the Festival of Freedom and the Festival of Matzot, this joyous spring holiday, occurring in March or April, commemorates the Exodus of the Jews from Egypt.

Purim The exuberant holiday in February or March that celebrates the Persian Jews' triumph over Haman's plot to exterminate them, as told in the Book of Esther.

Rosh Hashanah The first day of the Jewish New Year and the annual Day of Judgment, this solemn but joyous day falls in September or October.

Rosh Hodesh The first day of the new month in the Jewish lunar calendar, which corresponds to the new moon. Literally means "head of the month."

Sabbath (also Shabbat and Shabbos) The Jewish Sabbath begins at sundown on Friday and concludes at sundown on Saturday. For observant Jews, this day of rest is a joyous interlude free not only from work, but certain other tasks, such as cooking and playing music, as well.

Seder The traditional ceremonial meal of Passover.

Sephardi; Sephardim (plural) Jews and their descendants, expelled at the end of the fifteenth century from Spain and Portugal, who settled in Greece, the Middle East, England, Holland, the Americas, and parts of western Europe. The term is often used to refer to all Jews not of Ashkenazi background. (From the word *Sepharad*, "Spain," in Hebrew.)

Seudat mitzvah A festive meal that honors the observance of a mitzvah.

Shavuot Also known as the Festival of Weeks, this holiday commemorates the covenant made between God and Israel on Mount Sinai, when Moses received the Law (Torah). Occurring in May or June, it also celebrates the arrival of the first fruits of the summer season.

Shofar A special ram's horn blown in the synagogue on Rosh Hashanah and Yom Kippur. It is a reminder of Abraham's sacrifice, since the ram was sacrificed in place of his son, Isaac.

Simcha A joyous occasion; a celebration or party.

Simchat Torah A holiday that falls on the day after Sukkot outside of Israel, when the weekly readings in the Torah are completed with the end of Deuteronomy and then recommenced with the beginning of Genesis.

Sukkah; sukkot (plural) A booth of temporary shelter erected out-of-doors for Sukkot. According to Jewish law, the stars must be visible through the roof. The sukkah is typically decorated with fruits, vegetables, flowers, and branches from the early autumn harvest. During Sukkot, the family eats in the sukkah, weather permitting.

Sukkot Originally an autumn harvest festival of thanksgiving, this holiday, known as Feast of the Booths or Festival of the Tabernacles, commemorates the period of wandering in the Sinai Desert, when the Israelites lived in booths (sukkot).

Tallit; tallitot (plural) The Jewish prayer shawl, with fringes (tzitzit) at each of its four corners.

Talmud A massive collection of writings, comprising the Mishnah and the Gemara. It contains not just exegeses on the Hebrew Bible, but reflections on a huge array of more mundane subjects as well, including diet, ethics, philosophy, medicine, jurisprudence, and so on. The Jerusalem Talmud was completed around the fifth century A.D.; the Babylonian Talmud was completed around the sixth century A.D. The influence of the Babylonian Talmud has been far greater and is the one to which most scholars refer.

Tefillin Small ritual leather boxes containing passages from the Torah. They are worn, tied around the head and arm, during weekday morning services.

Tikkun olam "Repair of the world," through good deeds and social action.

Torah The sacred parchment scroll containing the Five Books of Moses, beginning with Creation and ending with the death of Moses. The five Books are Genesis, Exodus, Leviticus, Numbers, and Deuteronomy. A portion of the Torah is read in the synagogue every morning on Sabbaths, Mondays, Thursdays, the New Moon, and festivals. Completing the entire Torah cycle takes one year. Literally means "teaching."

Tu B'Shevat Known as New Year's Day for the Trees, it is celebrated on the fifteenth day of the Hebrew month of Shevat (usually in late January or February). It is often marked by planting trees and eating various special fruits.

Tzedakah The act of giving to charity, one of the Jewish commandments or mitzvot. Literally means "justice."

Tzitzit The fringes on a tallit.

Yahrzeit Commemoration of the anniversary of a person's death.

Yiddish Almost a thousand years old, this vernacular language, spoken by Ashkenazi Jews of eastern and central Europe, mainly comprises Old German, but also includes elements of Hebrew and various Slavic and other European languages, including French and English. It is written in Hebrew characters.

Yom Kippur The day of repentance, this is the holiest day of the Jewish calendar, marked by fasting and solemn prayer. It occurs in September or October.

BIBLIOGRAPHY

Belitsky, Helen Mintz. "One Family's Multicultural Coming-of-Age Celebration." *InterfaithFamily.com,* issue 6, February 1999.

Falk, Marcia. *The Book of Blessings: New Jewish Prayers for Daily Life, the Sabbath, and the New Moon Festival.* Boston: Beacon Press, 1996.

Friedland, Ronnie, and Edmund Case, eds. *The Guide to Jewish Interfaith Family Life.* Woodstock, Vt.: Jewish Lights, 2001.

Ganor, Solly. "Hope in Times of Despair: A Continuation of the Bar Mitzvah Story." *Solly Ganor—Remembrance.* October 26, 2001. Available at www.rongreene.com/jackson/html.

Goldberg, Loeb, Sorel, and Barbara Binder Kadden. *Teaching Torah: A Treasury of Insights and Activities.* Denver: A.R.E. Publishing, 1997.

Gottlieb, Freema. *The Lamp of God: A Jewish Book of Light.* Northvale, N.J.: Jason Aronson, 1989.

Hornstein, Becca. "Jewish Life Cycle Events: Including Children with Developmental Disabilities." *Disability Solutions,* November–December 1996, vol. 1, #4.

Jewish Heritage Online Magazine. Available at www.jhom.com.

Leneman, Helen, ed. *Bar/Bat Mitzvah Basics: A Practical Family Guide to Coming of Age Together.* Woodstock, Vt.: Jewish Lights, 2001.

Plaut, W. Gunther (trans. Chaim Stern). *The Haftarah Commentary.* New York: Union of American Hebrew Congregations, 1996.

Plaut, W. Gunther, ed. *The Torah: A Modern Commentary.* New York: Union of American Hebrew Congregations, 1981.

Prager, Marcia. *The Path of Blessing.* New York: Bell Tower, 1998.

Remsen, Jim. "The 'Tallit' Wraps Wearer in a Spiritual Richness." *Philadelphia Inquirer,* September 10, 2000.

Rosenberg, Shelly Kapnek. *Adoption and the Jewish Family: Contemporary Perspectives.* Philadelphia: Jewish Publication Society, 1998.

Salkin, Jeffrey. *For Kids—Putting God on Your Guest List.* Woodstock: Jewish Lights Publishing, 1998.

Schnur-Fishman, Anna. "God Has Many Messengers: A Wise-for-Her-Years Thirteen-Year-Old Looks Back on Life." *Lilith,* Winter 2000.

Siegel, Danny. *Gym Shoes and Irises: Personalized Tzedakah.* Bks. 1 and 2. Spring Valley, N.Y.: Town House Press, 1982, 1987.

———. *Mitzvahs.* Pittsboro, N.C.: Town House Press, 1990.

Siegel, Richard, Michael Strassfeld, and Sharon Strassfeld, eds. *The First Jewish Catalog.* Philadelphia: Jewish Publication Society, 1973.

Stern, Chaim, ed. *On the Doorposts of Your House.* New York: Central Conference of American Rabbis Press, 1994.

Strassfeld, Michael, and Sharon Strassfeld, eds. *The Second Jewish Catalog: Sources and Resources.* Philadelphia: Jewish Publication Society, 1976.

———. *The Third Jewish Catalog.* Philadelphia: Jewish Publication Society, 1980.

Strassfeld, Michael. *Jewish Holidays.* New York: HarperResource, 1993.

Strom, Yale. *The Book of Klezmer.* Chicago: Chicago Review Press, 2002.

Telushkin, Joseph. *Jewish Literacy: The Most Important Things to Know About the Jewish Religion, Its People, and Its History.* New York: Morrow, 1991.

Trapp, Caroline Broida. "Celebration of Life Amid Sadness and Horror." *Detroit Jewish News,* September 2001, reported at www.rongreene.com/jackson/html.

Waskow, Arthur. *Seasons of Our Joy: A Modern Guide to the Jewish Holidays.* Boston: Beacon Press, 1982.

INDEX